CONAN DOYLE

11 JUN 2023

WITHDRAWN

CONAN DOYLE

WRITING, PROFESSION, AND PRACTICE

DOUGLAS KERR

OXFORD
UNIVERSITY PRESS

OXFORD

UNIVERSITY PRESS

Great Clarendon Street, Oxford, OX2 6DP,
United Kingdom

Oxford University Press is a department of the University of Oxford.
It furthers the University's objective of excellence in research, scholarship,
and education by publishing worldwide. Oxford is a registered trade mark of
Oxford University Press in the UK and in certain other countries

First published 2013
First published in paperback 2015

Published in the United States of America by Oxford University Press
198 Madison Avenue, New York, NY 10016, United States of America

British Library Cataloguing in Publication Data
Data available

Library of Congress Cataloging in Publication Data
Data available

ISBN 978–0–19–967494–7 (Hbk.)
ISBN 978–0–19–872807–8 (Pbk.)

This book is dedicated to the memory of
my grandfather John Kerr, GP

Contents

Acknowledgements

I acknowledge with gratitude a grant HKU 7438/06H from the Hong Kong Research Grants Council which helped me carry out the research for this book.

Warmest thanks to Kelvin Au, Katherine Isobel Baxter, Tammy Ho Lai Ming, and Kitty Zhang Chengping for their help. This book has benefited from generous advice from many people, including Lee Aitken, Geetanjali Chanda, Wendy Gan, Christopher Hutton, Tina Pang, and the anonymous readers at OUP; its remaining faults are, I am afraid, my own.

I am grateful to Elaine Ho for more than I can say, as ever.

An earlier version of part of Chapter 2 was first published in *Victorian Literature and Culture*, 38/1 (March 2010), 187–206, and an earlier version of part of Chapter 4 was first published in *Literature and History*, third series, 19/2 (2010), 36–51. I thank the editors of these journals for permission to publish the revised versions here.

Abbreviations

The following abbreviations are used in the text to indicate frequently cited volumes of work by Arthur Conan Doyle.

Adventures	*The Adventures of Sherlock Holmes* (1892), ed. Richard Lancelyn Green (Oxford: Oxford University Press, 1993)
Case-Book	*The Case-Book of Sherlock Holmes* (1927), ed. W. W. Robson (Oxford: Oxford University Press, 1993)
Coming	*The Coming of the Fairies* (1922) (Lincoln, Nebr.: University of Nebraska Press, 2006)
Crime	*The Crime of the Congo* (London: Hutchinson, 1909)
"Dr. Koch":	"Dr. Koch and his Cure", *Review of Reviews*, 2 (1890), 552–6
GBW	*The Great Boer War* (1900), 2nd edn. (London: Thomas Nelson, 1908)
HLB	*His Last Bow* (1917), ed. Owen Dudley Edwards (Oxford: Oxford University Press, 1993)
Hound	*The Hound of the Baskervilles* (1902), ed. W. W. Robson (Oxford: Oxford University Press, 1993)
LM	*The Land of Mist* (London: Hutchinson, 1926)
LW	*The Lost World* (1912), ed. Ian Duncan (Oxford: Oxford University Press, 1998)
M&A	*Memories and Adventures* (1924, repr. with additions and deletions 1930) (Oxford: Oxford University Press, 1989)
Maracot	*The Maracot Deep and Other Stories* (London: John Murray, 1929)
Memoirs	*The Memoirs of Sherlock Holmes* (1893), ed. Christopher Roden (Oxford: Oxford University Press, 1993)
Pheneas	*Pheneas Speaks* (London: Psychic Press and Bookshop, 1927)
Red Lamp	*Round the Red Lamp*, 2nd edn. (London: Methuen, 1894)
Return	*The Return of Sherlock Holmes* (1905), ed. Richard Lancelyn Green (Oxford: Oxford University Press, 1993)
RS	*Rodney Stone* (London: Smith, Elder & Co, 1896)

Sign   *The Sign of the Four* (1890), ed. Christopher Roden (Oxford: Oxford University Press, 1993)

SM   *The Stark Munro Letters* (London: Longmans, Green, 1895)

Story   *The Story of Mr. George Edalji* (1907), ed. Richard and Molly Whittington-Egan (London: Grey House Books, 1985)

Study   *A Study in Scarlet* (1888), ed. Owen Dudley Edwards (Oxford: Oxford University Press, 1993)

Valley   *The Valley of Fear* (1915), ed. Owen Dudley Edwards (Oxford: Oxford University Press, 1993)

WC   *The White Company*, 3 vols. (London: Smith, Elder, 1891)

I

Introduction

Practice

Arthur Conan Doyle was, arguably, Britain's last national writer. Though he might speak of himself as English, he was a Scotsman of Irish ancestry: his idea of the nation, which I will consider in the following chapter, was an inclusive one. He embodied, in his work and life and person, qualities and values which the British reading public felt to be peculiarly their own. It was a role that Dickens had played before him, and that in retrospect had been conferred on Shakespeare, but I cannot think of any significant author who has taken it up since Conan Doyle's death.[1] Indeed in modern cultural circumstances the role itself is probably defunct. I believe Conan Doyle came to think of himself in these terms too, at least until the last decade of his life when his idea of his role changed radically (madly, some said). It was not just that he had a gift for producing stories that excited, intrigued, and beguiled large numbers of people, in a society more literate than ever before, or since. Nor was it simply because in Sherlock Holmes he had created one of the best-known invented literary characters ever, whose almost mythic function was to guarantee the safety of the national city and its people. Conan Doyle's privileged place in the culture was the result of his whole practice as man of letters, his cultivation of what nowadays we would call his image, his interventions in national affairs and issues, and his espousal of causes, in particular cases of injustice as he saw it, his journalism and history-writing as well as his fiction. He

---

[1] J. B. Priestley in the 1930s and 1940s made some claim to the title of national writer, but it was not a lasting one. George Orwell has proved a stronger candidate, though only posthumously.

was a public figure, a member not just of the profession of letters, but of the establishment. He was trusted; people felt they knew him: he was one of them. And in the end, all this was jeopardized, as he well understood, by his stubborn and tireless advocacy of Spiritualist beliefs and practices most people thought of as sinister or ludicrous.

This is a critical book about Conan Doyle's writings and also an attempt at a cultural biography of the writer. There are plenty of narrative biographies of Conan Doyle: indeed most book-length studies have been in this genre. Some of them are very good, I have drawn on them for this study, and of course I do not exclude narrative from this work. But my focus is elsewhere, not so much on the author's life but on his writing and on his practice as man of letters. Narrative biographies tell the author's story, but a cultural biography is about the life and times of his work. What I want to do is to portray Conan Doyle as a product, historian, and creator of culture. Instead of the usual divisions of chronological biography—student days, medical practice, the move to London, and so on—the story is organized here in terms of a number of domains of the culture of his times. Each domain is an activity, like medicine, or sport, with their associated institutions, ideas, special language, and values—what might be called a discourse. In each chapter, Conan Doyle's own writing provides the most important evidence of how he absorbed, reflected, and generated knowledge about these things. This book is about what Conan Doyle *knew* about his world. But it was not just a matter of the acquisition of knowledge, like stamp-collecting. Writers are also creators of knowledge, and in his writing Conan Doyle brought a world into being and made it knowable to his readers.

My method has been to place this writing in the context of cultural activity, the cultural element in which he and his readers led their lives, but then also to show how the writing never simply offers a picture of his times, but works on its material to produce a cultural knowledge which may disclose contradictions, fears, hopes, and desires that might not be expressible in other ways. This is the kind of claim usually made for serious literature, and arguably it is yet more likely to be relevant to popular writing, like Conan Doyle's, in which there is a large element of fantasy. (His Spiritualist writing, for example, comes to imagine a community with features that compensate for what was lacking or wrong, in his view, in modern England.) He was not much of an original thinker, but he was an unrivalled inventor of tales, characters, and situations in which the ideas of his time were given striking, memorable, and simple human form. One example would be the stories about Professor Challenger, the egomaniacal scientist of *The Lost World*. These stories heroize the modern scientific investigator in the form of the familiar genre of an adventure for boys, satirize the institutions and procedures of the scientific profession, and carry intuitions that the relentless march of scientific modernity may be bearing on to a future more tragic and grotesque than that envisaged in Mary Shelley's *Frankenstein* a century before. They do all these things at the same time. Conan Doyle's own experience of scientists (he was one himself), and scientific ideas and institutions, is adduced to help make sense of this important ambivalence about science, which can certainly be generalized as an ambivalence about modernity itself, and which Conan Doyle shared with and articulated for his readers. For readers and for the writer, a new century was providing reasons to marvel at what scientists could do, and to worry about what they might do. For Conan Doyle, this was an ambivalence with its roots in his own student days in Edinburgh in the late 1870s. He returns it, as it were, to the culture in the somewhat lurid form of the popular genre of the scientific romance of *The Lost World*, and the science fiction of "When the World Screamed"—and, of course, in the tales about a great detective and his science of deduction. And it was to emerge as one of the capital themes of the history of the twentieth century.

The cultural domains I have selected are far from exhaustive, it hardly needs saying. The chapters that follow are essays, and do not pretend to add up to a complete cultural portrait, which would be massive indeed in the case of any subject. But I have chosen those domains that seem to me capable of shedding light on the distinctiveness of Conan Doyle as a maker of culture. Nor are they self-contained. It would have been worrying if they were. Moreover, as these domains, science and the rest, make up the horizontal plane of this study, they are each intersected vertically by another set of recurrent preoccupations: modernity, art, nation, gender, profession. Conan Doyle's lifetime was one in which changes in the culture were pressing on each of these terms, and his writing, which is always curious if not deep, registers and responds to these changes.

In thinking about Conan Doyle's work in and about these matters, as a writer and man of letters, I have found a useful metaphor from his work in another of his professions. The figure is that of practice, which finds its way into the title of this book, and this introduction.

When Dr Arthur Conan Doyle arrived in the Portsmouth suburb of Southsea, on 24 June 1882, it was with the intention of establishing a medical practice of his own. He was 23 years old and had a bachelor's degree in medicine from Edinburgh University. He had held various temporary medical positions, both on land and as a ship's doctor, most recently an informal junior partnership in the Plymouth practice of his Edinburgh fellow student, the alarming George Turnavine Budd, which had not turned out well. Now the young Conan Doyle was impatient to launch an independent career as a general practitioner (GP). He was to work as a physician in Southsea for seven years.

A practice is a place, and a body of work. Conan Doyle's new practice was based at No. 1 Bush Villas, the house he rented in Elm Grove in Southsea, where he set up his surgery—a consulting room and a waiting room—on the ground floor. Bush Villas was the centre of the practice, and, like most GPs, Conan Doyle did most of his work in the neighbourhood. The practice had no fixed boundaries, for it was defined simply by the places where the young doctor could find patients who wanted his services, on whom he could exercise his skills. He had chosen his location very carefully: after all, the practice was also a business. He needed to find a place where there was a realistic chance of attracting enough paying patients to enable him to make a living. At the local post office he had bought a large shilling map of Southsea, and he spent several days tramping the streets, scouting the location, map in hand, marking the empty houses, and the surgeries of other doctors with whom he would be competing for patients. In the end, Bush Villas was well chosen, as Andrew Lycett says, at a point "where the comfortable residences of the local bourgeoisie met the brash shopping streets where they made their money".[2] Portsmouth was a seafaring town with a big naval base and

[2] Andrew Lycett, *Arthur Conan Doyle: The Man who Created Sherlock Holmes* (London: Weidenfeld and Nicolson, 2007), 86. See also Martin Booth, *The Doctor, the Detective and Arthur Conan Doyle* (London: Hodder and Stoughton, 1997), 87–9, and Geoffrey Stavert, *A Study in Southsea: The Unrevealed Life of Doctor Arthur Conan Doyle* (Portsmouth: Milestone, 1987), 9–29. There is a lightly fictionalized account of the setting up of the practice in ACD, *The Stark Munro Letters* (London: Longmans, Green, 1895), 220–43. Hereafter *SM*.

dockyards, but Southsea was more genteel. Elm Grove was a main thoroughfare, constantly busy with pedestrians and vehicles, and the house itself stood between a Pentecostal church and a pub, the Bush Hotel. Unlike some specialists, the general practitioner's patients might be drawn from all classes, occupations, and stations in life within travelling distance of the surgery. Conan Doyle's list came to include plenty of well-heeled Southsea bourgeois and retired professionals, but his work also, and especially in the early days, brought him often into contact with the neighbourhood's poor, malnourished, and deprived.

Once established, Dr Conan Doyle's practice would never be marked on a map. It had no defined space, like a parish or municipality or a police district. It overlapped with the practices of other doctors (in fact there was another Edinburgh graduate, William Pike, in practice in Elm Grove). It expanded and contracted continuously, with new patients coming onto Conan Doyle's list and others transferring their loyalty to another man, drifting away, or dying off. Some were regular, serial visitors to the surgery, others might appear once and never be seen again. So to call the practice a place is not quite accurate. The practice was the practitioner's knowledge of a place, a location brought into being in his mind, and maintained through his attention. The people and institutions, the families and the streets that made up his work, in those seven years, were a cross-section of late-Victorian provincial England, but not an entirely random one. Representative or not, and regardless of how aware they were of each other, they had this in common: they were known to the practitioner. They were his practice.

The practice of medicine was also a profession. Like those other respectable old vocations, the Church and the law, it was something men "went in for", having acquired a body of professional knowledge, a place in the professional hierarchy, and a platform from which to exercise their skills. Conan Doyle had been trained in the medical faculty at Edinburgh University in the years 1876 to 1881, studying the natural sciences and the medical disciplines of anatomy, clinical medicine, pharmacy, surgery, medical jurisprudence, and so on. His professional consecration came with the award of his MB or Bachelor of Medicine in 1881. Without a degree, he would not have been allowed to practise. But he was to signal his medical ambition by going on to study for the higher degree of MD, awarded by Edinburgh in 1885 for a research dissertation on *tabes dorsalis*, syphilis of the spinal cord.[3] Later, very briefly, and half-heartedly, in 1891 he tried his hand at consultant medicine, setting up as an eye specialist in London.

Success in medical practice may have required certain temperamental qualities; it certainly depended on a body of knowledge acquired in the lecture room and laboratory, and then in the treatment of the sick. But doctors needed to know more than was contained in the textbooks and professional journals of an increasingly scientific medicine. A specialist might concentrate only on the narrow particularities of the case referred to him, but a doctor in general practice, besides his technical skills in diagnosis and treatment, needed a humanistic knowledge of the patients under his care—not just their ailments, but their history, family, work circumstances, and character.

Even then, a good clinical knowledge and an empathetic manner did not guarantee a good practice. Besides his knowledge of ailments and treatments, and his familiarity with his individual patients, a doctor had to foster good relations with his profession, and with the public. He needed a network of professional contacts, the consultants to whom he could refer difficult cases for a second opinion, the hospitals and nursing homes in his district, other institutions such as working men's associations or insurance companies or sports clubs that might be a useful source of work, the suppliers of drugs and equipment, neighbouring colleagues with whom he might find himself cooperating, or competing. And of course his work could not be done if he was not known. A doctor was not allowed to advertise, but Conan Doyle— a lifelong compulsive joiner of societies and clubs and teams and committees, in a compulsively associative age (especially for men)[4]—

---

[3] ACD, "An essay upon the vasomotor changes in tabes dorsalis and on the influence which is exerted by the sympathetic nervous system in that disease", Edinburgh University MD thesis, 1885 (Edinburgh Research Archive, <http://hdl.handle.net/1842/418>). For a discussion of Conan Doyle's MD thesis, see *Medical Casebook of Doctor Arthur Conan Doyle*, ed. Alvin E. Rodin and Jack D. Key (Malabar, Fla.: Robert E. Krieger, 1984), 87–98.

[4] A trawl through one of the biographies reveals the following associations of which Conan Doyle was a member—and often an office-holder—though not all at once: the Allah-Akbarries (cricket team); the Amateur Field Sports Association; the Athenaeum; the Authors' Club; the Beckenham Golf Club; the Boys' Empire League; the British College of Psychic Science; the British Medical Association; the Congo Reform Association; the Conservative and Unionist party; the Crowborough Beacon Golf Club; the Divorce Law Reform Association; the Freemasons; the General Jewish Colonizing Organization (London Committee); the Idlers Club; the Incogniti (cricket club); the International

put himself about Southsea and Portsmouth with great vigour, writing to the local papers and speaking at political meetings, participating in all sorts of sporting and cultural and scientific activities. The networking, the constant clubbability, the occasional controversy: these public performances were all part of the practice. The medical practice benefited from the name—the good name—of the doctor being widely recognized in the neighbourhood.

A writer is not a doctor. Conan Doyle, however, was both, and there are interesting and illuminating congruences between the practices of his two professions, in a professional age. The practice of a GP includes his knowledge of a human environment, with its streets and institutions and neighbourhoods and their inhabitants, and his knowledge of what doctors do, derived from study and experience; the application of one on the other was, as it were, the practice of his practice. Writers too deploy knowledge of the world they live in, both actual and imaginary. The "world" of Arthur Conan Doyle the writer, brought into being by the practice of his writing, was an extensive and colourful one, the world he knew and wrote about ranging from Baker Street to Bloemfontein, from a hospital ward in Berlin to the rookery of pterodactyls in the Lost World, and from the Hundred Years War to the end of the world. The professional knowledge the writer brought to bear on this world expressed itself in the work of storytelling, invention, research, polemic, and so on. The work brought the "world" into being, the "world" elicited the work. And from our reading of this work emerges an imaginary picture of the real culture Conan Doyle inhabited and, in his way, helped to shape and define: the late-Victorian years and the early decades of the twentieth century, as seen, imagined, and understood in the practice of an outstanding writer.

Spiritualist Congress; the Liberal Unionist party; the London Spiritualist Alliance; the Marylebone Cricket Club (MCC); the Marylebone Spiritualist Association; the Middlesex Yeomanry (reserve list); the National Sporting Club; the New Vagabonds Club; Our Society (the Crimes Club or Murders Club); the Portsmouth Football Association Club; the Portsmouth Literary and Scientific Society; the Reform Club; the Royal Automobile Club; the Sixth Royal Sussex Volunteer Regiment; the Society of Authors; the Society for Psychical Research; the Society for the Study of Supernormal Pictures; the Undershaw Rifle Club; the Union Jack Club; the Upper Norwood Literary and Scientific Society. As a distinguished man of letters he had countless invitations to chair or speak at meetings of clubs, associations, social gatherings, and pressure groups.

Profession

When he decided, in August 1891, to give up medicine and make his living as a full-time writer, Conan Doyle was exchanging one professional practice for another. As he became quite rapidly a literary celebrity, his former career as a doctor seems to have been one of the things that most readers knew about him, a titbit of knowledge no doubt given extra relish because of Dr Watson, and one element in his reputation for unimpeachable probity, both within the literary world and with the public.[5] Like more formal professions, the profession of letters in the late decades of the nineteenth century was a career and a business which also had some of the characteristics of a club. The gregarious Conan Doyle knew hundreds of writers, publishers and journalists, and formed most of his close friendships within the literary world. He developed an impressive network of connections in literature and journalism, and later in public life. There was no literary equivalent of the British Medical Association or the Law Society, but literature was a community developing its own quasi-professional institutions. In 1884, Walter Besant established the Society of Authors to promote copyright reform and protect writers' interests.[6] (Inexperienced authors were often in a weak position. In 1887 Ward, Lock & Co persuaded Conan Doyle to part with the copyright of the first Sherlock Holmes novel for £25.[7]) Besant later founded the Authors' Club in 1891. Conan Doyle was to become its second president.

But when Besant reviewed the business in an essay on "Literature as a Career" in 1892, the prospect he sketched was not very encouraging. Unlike other professions, the profession of letters was open to anyone, but Besant complained that in Britain writers were unhonoured, if not treated with actual contempt, and most of them were at the mercy of publishers. "No worker in the world, not even the needlewoman, is more helpless, more ignorant, more cruelly sweated than the author."[8]

---

[5] See Philip Waller, *Writers, Readers and Reputations: Literary Life in Britain 1870–1918* (Oxford: Oxford University Press, 2006), 131.

[6] Professional association was very much in the air. The London Booksellers' Society was formed in 1890 and the Publishers' Association in 1896.

[7] This was £5 more than Joseph Conrad was to be offered by T. Fisher Unwin in 1894 for the copyright of his first novel, *Almayer's Folly*. He accepted.

[8] Walter Besant, "Literature as a Career", *Forum*, 13 (March–August 1892), 693–708; at 696.

Besant estimated that there were some 15,000 people in London who followed a literary career. No more than fifty writers in Britain and the United States made £1,000 or more a year by writing novels. Another hundred novelists, a handful of dramatists, and a few writers of educational books were able to make a living by their pen. This excluded journalism, which indeed was a lifeline for some writers, but often at the expense of their literary ambitions. "There are but few who can afford to live by writing novels, plays, poems, essays, or the like."[9] These were the perilous waters into which Conan Doyle had set sail the previous year. As it happened, a revolutionary tide had already begun to transform the publishing world, for both writers and readers. Conan Doyle himself was part of that change, and benefited greatly from it: already in 1891 he was earning about £1,500 from his writing.[10] Still, embarking on the profession of letters at the beginning of the 1890s was a risky business. There was a warning in the dreary fate of Edwin Reardon, the unsuccessful writer in George Gissing's novel *New Grub Street* (published in 1891 by Smith, Elder, who brought out Conan Doyle's *The White Company* in the same year).

The change that was overtaking the publishing business derived ultimately from large developments in the society, economy, and culture of the late-Victorian age. Liberal legislation—the Reform Act of 1867 and the Representation of the People Act of 1884—had increased the voting population to five and a half million men, and the political campaign was already afoot that would eventually see the enfranchisement of women (over 30, with property restrictions) in 1918, and finally equal political rights for all adult men and women in 1928. This revolution, which provided the political basis for a modern mass society, and was attended like all revolutions with profound misgivings and anxieties, was accomplished in Conan Doyle's lifetime (1859–1930). A vital part of the creation of this "new democracy" was an investment in public education. In a series of Education Acts between 1870 and 1891, provision was

---

[9] Besant, "Literature as a Career", 706.

[10] This was already five times more than he had earned as a doctor in Southsea in 1890. See ACD, *The Adventures of Sherlock Holmes* (1892), ed. Richard Lancelyn Green (Oxford: Oxford University Press, 1993), xiii–xiv. Hereafter *Adventures*. It was ten times more than his income for the first year of medical practice—£156 2s. 4d.—which included £30 from his mother and £42 from his writing. See ACD to Mary Doyle, n.d., in *Arthur Conan Doyle: A Life in Letters*, ed. Jon Lellenberg, Daniel Stashower, and Charles Foley (London: Harper, 2007), 204.

made for board schools, run by municipalities, paid for by local taxation, and empowered to require attendance by pupils between the ages of 5 and 10, and up to 14 unless an exemption certificate was granted. By 1891, elementary education was compulsory and free. In 1918, the school leaving age was raised to 14. These changes brought a dramatic increase in literacy, in white-collar jobs, leisure time, and spending power, and now many more people than before wanted things to read.

With this new literacy came the "new journalism"—a phrase associated with the campaigning editor W. T. Stead, whom we will meet in a later chapter, commissioning Conan Doyle to go to Berlin on a reporting assignment in 1890—and a proliferation of periodicals and cheap newspapers in the 1880s and 1890s. The pattern was of a cheaper and more accessible product and a much expanded—indeed the beginnings of a mass—market. A similar change in the mode of literary production and consumption was beginning to happen in fiction. The standard vehicle for the first issue of novels had been the three-volume (three-decker) format, dictated by the demands of the commercial libraries, but relatively expensive for individual book-buyers. At the beginning of the 1890s this form of publishing was being challenged by the appearance of first editions in cheap single-volume format, destined for popular sales and public-library borrowing. It was a change that would usher in the age of bestsellers, but it did not happen overnight. Conan Doyle's historical novel *Micah Clarke* came out in one volume in 1889 but his *The White Company*, though a shorter book, was published in 1891 as a three-decker.[11] Nonetheless, in the 1890s the doom of the three-decker was sealed. Between 1894 and 1897 the publication of three-volume novels fell from 184 to 4.[12] The size of novels quite visibly shrank.[13] But there was a constant demand by periodicals of every kind for serial novels and short fiction. Meanwhile the literature-reading public was bigger than ever, and growing.

It has been argued that these circumstances helped to produce a "great divide", between elite or modernist literary writing on one

[11] See Richard Lancelyn Green and John Michael Gibson (eds.), *A Bibliography of A. Conan Doyle* (Oxford: Clarendon Press, 1984), 15–16, 42–3. Gissing's *New Grub Street*, with its portraits of commercial success and failure in the literary profession, also came out in 1891 as a three-decker.

[12] Waller, *Writers, Readers and Reputations*, 668.

[13] Peter Keating, *The Haunted Study: A Social History of the English Novel 1875–1914* (Athens, Oh.: Ohio University Press, 1986), 342.

hand, and popular stuff on the other.[14] There is evidence for this, for example, in the difficulties experienced through much of their careers by Henry James, by George Gissing, and by Joseph Conrad, in finding a public that would understand or buy their books. Nicholas Daly has shown, however, that the literary culture was still largely homogeneous, at least until the end of the nineteenth century.[15] Serious and popular writers mingled, often belonged to the same clubs, wrote for the same magazines and publishers, and dealt in their books with similar subjects. The cult of aestheticism in the *fin de siècle* might be seen as the assertion of a specialized art domain, distant from people's everyday concerns, but after the downfall of Oscar Wilde in 1895 fewer writers were concerned to claim, out loud at least, a position aloof from the world their readers inhabited, or to talk about pursuing their art for its own sake. The decade of the 1890s, in the words of John Gross, was followed by "a period dominated by writers who were closer to the Early Victorians than to their immediate predecessors in their readiness to enter the public arena as preachers, debaters, entertainers".[16] Commercially successful writers saw themselves as part of the same profession as those who appealed only to a more educated readership soon to be christened "highbrow", were equally ready to speak out on issues of the day with, perhaps, the extra warrant of their wide appeal, and took their work just as seriously. This was the profession, and the market, that Conan Doyle was already familiar with when he abandoned medicine for full-time writing. His professional responsibility was now focused not on a practice of patients, but on the reading public of the new democracy, with its appetite for literary enjoyment and for learning about the world by means of a good story.

George Newnes, the publisher, was both a beneficiary and an enabler of this new democracy of culture.[17] He was 30 years old when he founded the penny weekly *Tit-Bits* in October 1881. Appealing to the mass readership created by educational reform, *Tit-Bits* was a miscellany

<hr/>

[14] See Andreas Huyssen, *After the Great Divide: Modernism, Mass Culture, Postmodernism* (Bloomington, Ind.: Indiana University Press, 1986).

[15] Nicholas Daly, *Modernism, Romance and the Fin de Siècle* (Cambridge: Cambridge University Press, 1999), 4.

[16] John Gross, *The Rise and Fall of the Man of Letters* (London: Weidenfeld and Nicolson, 1969), 210.

[17] See Jonathan Rose and Patricia J. Anderson (eds.), *British Literary Publishing Houses 1881–1965* (Detroit: Gale Research, 1991), 266–71.

of jokes, short articles, snippets from elsewhere in the press, statistics, scandal, fiction, and answers to correspondents; it came with an insurance policy against railway accidents and included competitions offering prizes. It had a huge and sustained success—the first printing of 5,000 sold out in two hours and in 1897 the magazine was selling 671,000 copies a week. Newnes moved his offices to the Strand in 1886, and George Newnes Ltd was incorporated in 1891 (Conan Doyle became a shareholder in the company). By the mid-1890s it had a book list, including a Penny Library of Famous Books. In 1890, Newnes had formed a partnership with W. T. Stead, until recently editor of the *Pall Mall Gazette*, to launch the combative sixpenny monthly *Review of Reviews*. It was an uneasy alliance. After a few months Stead bought out his partner, and Newnes used his now surplus production facilities to found the *Strand Magazine*, a middle-class stable-mate for *Tit-Bits*, modelled on the American *Harper's* and *Scribner's* magazines.[18] By 1896 the *Strand* was selling 392,000 copies a month, with 60,000 of them going to America. Its literary editor for forty years was Herbert Greenhough Smith and his contributors included Rudyard Kipling, H. G. Wells, Edith Nesbit, Winston Churchill, W. W. Jacobs, P. G. Wodehouse, Sapper, W. Somerset Maugham, Agatha Christie, Dorothy L. Sayers, and Arnold Bennett (whose literary career had begun when he won a competition in *Tit-Bits* in 1890). But the *Strand's* star contributor was Conan Doyle, whose first Sherlock Holmes short story, "A Scandal in Bohemia", appeared in the magazine in July 1891. Holmes stories immediately became a part of what we would now call the magazine's brand, and remained the staple of the *Strand* until the final one, "The Adventure of Shoscombe Old Place", was published in 1927.

The partnership between the *Strand* and Sherlock Holmes was an extraordinary success, for Conan Doyle had assessed the market just as shrewdly as George Newnes. "Considering these various [monthly] journals with their disconnected stories it had struck me that a single character running through a series, if it only engaged the attention of the reader, would bind that reader to that particular magazine," he was to remember, and he had gone on to reason that a serial could be offputting to a reader who happened to miss an episode, but that

---

[18] Stead, whose path crossed Conan Doyle's in a number of ways, continued to edit the *Review of Reviews* and in 1893 launched *Borderland*, a quarterly review of psychic phenomena. The two were to quarrel over the Boer War, a conflict Stead vehemently opposed. Stead went down with the *Titanic* in 1912.

self-contained stories about a favourite recurring character would be a way of making sure the purchaser "could relish the whole contents of the magazine".[19] So the Holmes tales, on which Conan Doyle's fortune and reputation rested, evolved from a business plan that took into account publication outlets and the market they fostered and served. As in his earlier career as a doctor, practice for Conan Doyle the writer meant not only the exercise of a set of professional skills, but also a sympathetic knowledge of the people to whom those skills were offered.

Authors of fiction derived income from both magazine and book publication. Joseph Conrad, for example, got by through publishing novels in instalments in periodicals—*Blackwood's Magazine* being his most stalwart partner during a critical period of five years—before issuing them in book form, and an American edition (the American market had recently been regulated) would often yield a third stream of income. Conan Doyle calculated that with serialization he could earn four times as much as from a single-volume publication.[20] Fiction writers also sold individual stories to magazines, and would aim to collect and republish them in book form. The Edinburgh-based *Blackwood's* seems to have been the first outlet to which Conan Doyle sent a story, in 1879, though the magazine did not accept any of his work for publication until 1890; when one of his stories was accepted by another old warhorse, the *Cornhill Magazine*, in 1884, publication in this prestigious outlet had been a significant breakthrough for the young writer.[21] When Sherlock Holmes became famous, the early *A Study in Scarlet* and *The Sign of the Four* made the reverse journey, from book to periodical publication, and were re-serialized in *Tit-Bits* in 1893. But Holmes was best known through magazine publication, and although Conan Doyle was universally famous (to his chagrin) as the creator of the great detective, his Sherlock Holmes books were outsold by his historical novels, such as *The White Company*, which went through fifty editions before 1914.

[19] ACD, *Memories and Adventures* (1924, repr. with additions and deletions 1930) (Oxford: Oxford University Press, 1989), 95–6. Hereafter *M&A*. See also Peter D. McDonald, "The Adventures of the Literary Agent: Conan Doyle, A. P. Watt, Holmes and *The Strand* in 1891", *ACD: Journal of the Arthur Conan Doyle Society*, 8 (1998), 17–27.

[20] Booth, *The Doctor, the Detective and Arthur Conan Doyle*, 255. From the mid-1890s onwards, *The Strand* never paid Conan Doyle less than £100 per thousand words. See Christopher Roden, "Conan Doyle and *The Strand Magazine*", *ACD: Journal of the Arthur Conan Doyle Society*, 2/2 (1991), 135–40.

[21] Lycett, *Conan Doyle*, 100–1, 61–2.

As he had done when a physician at Southsea, but now on a national rather than a local scale, Conan Doyle kept his name before the public by writing to newspapers, and he was now also the willing subject of new journalistic genres like the interview (pioneered by Stead), and the photographic portrait.[22] For the struggling writer, publicity boosted sales. But for the celebrity author, fame could be a platform from which to speak out on all sorts of matters, and when he became a national figure Conan Doyle took his standing with the public seriously as an obligation, and an opportunity to make a difference, sometimes, to opinion and even policy.[23] But it was also a living. Once a writer had become well established, income from periodical and book publication, on both sides of the Atlantic, could be usefully supplemented by translations, by Tauchnitz continental rights, by writing or having work adapted for the theatre and later the cinema, and by lecture tours, especially in America, a lucrative option for celebrity authors from Elinor Glyn to Winston Churchill.[24] Publishers might deal directly with an author, like the American Joseph Marshall Stoddart of *Lippincott's Magazine* who commissioned the stories that became *The Sign of the Four* and *The Picture of Dorian Gray* over dinner with Conan Doyle and Oscar Wilde at the Langham Hotel in 1889. But literature was becoming a complex business, and many writers turned to agents to help them market their work and protect their interests. In 1890, on the advice of the ubiquitous Walter Besant, Conan Doyle became a client of A. P. Watt, London's leading literary agent.

Conan Doyle was a writer of unique character, history, passions, and skills. But he was also, as a writer, formed by his practice—the profession of authorship, and the expanding, increasingly literate late-Victorian reading public, and later their twentieth-century children, for whom he wrote. In the last quarter of the nineteenth century there was lively debate in the profession as it adapted to changing circumstances and new readers. The prestige of the novel form had risen steadily, and

---

[22] See Waller, *Writers, Readers and Reputations*, 409–17 (for interviews) and 357–63 (portraits).

[23] His hard work for divorce law reform is a good example. In lending his name to this cause, which had nothing directly to do with the literary profession, he was doing what he could "to rescue thousands and tens of thousands from hopeless lifelong misery, from the embraces of drunkards, from the bondage to cruel men, from the iron which fetterlocks them to the felon or the hopeless maniac". ACD, "Preface" to Christina Sinclair Bremner, *Divorce and Morality* (London: Frank Palmer, 1912), 7–15; at 7.

[24] See Waller, *Writers, Readers and Reputations*, 575–614. Conan Doyle lectured on four continents.

there was a recognition that fiction could perform an educative role: but should a novel be judged for its artistic worth, its moral lessons, or its entertainment value? How should it relate to its readers' lives? Novelists canvassed different kinds of practice, with shifting terms: realism and idealism, realism and romance, the fiction of character, and the fiction of incident. (I will return to this in a later chapter.) Henry James felt it was the novelist's job to represent experience with an "air of reality", so that the novel might compete with life.[25] Robert Louis Stevenson, on the other hand, took issue with this aesthetic, and argued that the novel of domestic realism and psychological investigation, of the sort Henry James recommended, was likely to lack excitement and fail to nourish the imagination. "English people of the present day are apt, I know not why, to look somewhat down on incident, and reserve their admiration for the clink of teaspoons and the accents of the curate. It is thought clever to write a novel with no story at all, or at least with a very dull one."[26] Against this model, Stevenson was ready to recommend a different kind of fiction, a fiction of incident. Sometimes he called it romance and at other times, the novel of adventure. It was a formula well suited also to shorter novels and to the newly fashionable form of the "short story"—a term first coined in 1884.[27]

Conan Doyle's temperament and tastes, his own extraordinary gift for narrative, and his commercial instincts all inclined him to find a more inspiring model in Stevenson than in James. His mimetic style in all his work is straightforward and undecorated, and always delivers precise and vivid detail: to this extent he is a realist. But the tradition of domestic realism in the novel, with its emphasis on the manners of class and family, the slow changes of time, and the patient exposition of the psychology of characters and their intimate relationships, had little appeal for him.[28] Whether it has a historical or a contemporary setting, his fiction is marked above all by strong narrative, punctuated

---

[25] Henry James, "The Art of Fiction", in *Partial Portraits* (London: Macmillan, 1884), 375–408; at 390.

[26] Robert Louis Stevenson, "A Gossip on Romance" (1882), in *R. L. Stevenson on Fiction*, ed. Glenda Norquay (Edinburgh: Edinburgh University Press, 1999), 51–64; at 57.

[27] Keating, *The Haunted Study*, 39.

[28] He did sometimes write domestic fiction, for example in *Beyond the City: The Idyll of a Suburb* (1892) and *A Duet with an Occasional Chorus* (1899). The latter, the story of a young married couple, was withheld from serial publication because its author thought it "a work depending…for its effect upon feeling and atmosphere rather than on incident". See Green and Gibson (eds.), *A Bibliography of A. Conan Doyle*, 113.

by striking incident. When the meticulously furnished scene of realism is to be found in a Conan Doyle story—like the drawing-room at Baker Street—it is an anteroom to the unexpected and unsettling. The prosaic everyday world does feature in his stories, but it is there to be interrupted and transfigured by the extraordinary, by mystery and crime and adventure, by the exotic, the eccentric, or the supernatural.

There is no doubt of the public appetite for this kind of genre fiction in its various forms. "In the late nineteenth century there were certain genres that the mass reading public favoured. Among them, adventure, romance, horror, crime, and sport clearly led."[29] The list pretty well covers Conan Doyle's fictional output, if we class his historical novels as an important subspecies of the adventure tale, and if we exclude "romance" in the sense of narratives about love, which is never the primary focus of his stories. "In British fiction", he complained in *Through the Magic Door*, "nine books out of ten have held up love and marriage as the be-all and end-all of life. Yet we know, in actual practice, that this may not be so."[30] If we take the word in a less restrictive sense, it will be convenient, following Stevenson himself, to give the general name "romance" to this popular non-domestic fiction of incident, for which Nicholas Daly makes the claim that, towards the end of the nineteenth century, "this fiction in effect takes over from the domestic realist novel as the narrative flagship of middle-class Britain".[31] In the hands of Conan Doyle (and others like Rider Haggard and Stevenson), it is a manly, action-oriented kind of writing. Indeed there is a pervasive assumption in contemporary critical accounts that the late-Victorian romance was a more healthily masculine form than the realist novel, and an antidote to "the feminizing—and thus morbid—effects of the virus of French realism".[32] (It is notable that the cerebral Sherlock Holmes, who is subject to periods of lassitude and *ennui* and has a taste for the *paradis artificiel* of drugs, is always able to shake off these deplorable tendencies and emerge as a decisive and sporting hero when action is required.)

While this was a popular kind of writing with a broad appeal, it also performed a social function, in the dissemination of knowledge to the

---

[29] Waller, *Writers, Readers, and Reputations*, 635.
[30] ACD, *Through the Magic Door* (London: Smith, Elder, 1907), 264.
[31] Daly, *Modernism, Romance and the Fin de Siècle*, 4.
[32] Daly, *Modernism, Romance and the Fin de Siècle*, 18.

expanded reading public of the new democracy. Conan Doyle's books were rarely didactic, but they were educative. Tellingly, when he first settled down to write a full-length novel, he neglected to provide it with a story, but he relished the opportunity to parade, by means of his narrator, a large catalogue of his views.[33] He would not make the same mistake again in fiction. The knowledge his work transmitted came not in the form of data or dogma, but in stories. By telling adventurous stories about the past, the historical novelist—and the historian— educated his readers about the traditions and values of the nation, and encouraged that spirit of valour and service that was needed, he believed, to preserve both nation and empire. In narratives with more contemporary settings, a popular writer could provide characters and stories that could help readers imaginatively understand the modern world, in which the pace of change accelerated throughout the decades of Conan Doyle's writing life. The opening pages of a Sherlock Holmes tale, for example, might encode in the form of narrative a wealth of knowledge about professionalism, masculinity, friendship, class, domesticity, the geography of London, the family, leisure, duty— all ideas whose meaning was not static, but evolving with the evolutions of modernity, as well as being subject to the particular circumstances in the story, and the beliefs and practice of Conan Doyle and of his characters.

Writing is produced out of knowledge, but is not a mere reflection of society's knowledge of itself; writers create and disseminate knowledge in their turn. Knowledge of what? The titles of the following chapters give an answer—hardly an exhaustive one—to this question in the case of Arthur Conan Doyle: sport, medicine, empire, and the rest. A different kind of organization might have produced a different set of categories—gender, profession, race, and Church, for example. A writer's interpretation of the world gives a shape to cultural knowledge; when that knowledge is shared, it becomes a part of the culture, to be interpreted and reshaped in its turn by others.

[33] ACD, *The Narrative of John Smith*, ed. John Lellenberg, Daniel Stashower, and Rachel Foss (London: The British Library, 2011). In this book, unfinished and unpublished in Conan Doyle's lifetime, the narrator is immobilized by gout and never leaves the house.

2

Sport

Sport and the nation

In the last years of the nineteenth century, Arthur Conan Doyle, a prolific writer with a global reputation and readership, was settled with his family at Hindhead in Surrey, and in his *Memories and Adventures* he was to recall this period as an interlude of peace. "The country was lovely. My life was filled with alternate work and sport. As with me so with the nation" (*M&A*, 151). That last sentence refers chiefly to the apparent placidity of the time, soon to be rudely spoilt by the outbreak of the South African war, which was to prove a critical and formative testing-ground for Great Britain and for Conan Doyle personally. But the sentence can also refer to the plenitude of a life divided between work and sport, and he had some right to claim his own experience as in some sense representative in this respect too. At the end of the century which invented modern sport besides so much else, Conan Doyle's enthusiastic participation in sports, his writing about the subject, and his understanding of it have a great deal to tell us about the Britain of his time. As with him, so with the nation. Sport was an important part of what he did and who he was, and what he knew about sport was one of the ways he knew about the world.

Conan Doyle is unusual among writers in the importance he accorded to sports in his life and the pleasure he derived from them. He may have been a professional writer living entirely by his pen, but he was pleased when, after they had become the first men to travel on skis between Davos and Arosa in Switzerland, his companion Tobias Branger entered Conan Doyle's profession in the Arosa hotel registry as "Sportesmann" (*M&A*, 293). It is crucial to this question that Conan Doyle professed sport as an amateur, but his sportsmanship does not make him less important than more indoor authors, or less interesting, either as a literary writer or as a man of letters. To raise the question of sport is to activate the most vital issues of late-Victorian and early twentieth-century culture, not only the stalwart trinity of gender, race, and class, but also physical and moral health, empire and war, modernity and tradition, freedom and community, pleasure and money. Especially, sport was involved in an ideal of nation and of manhood.

In Conan Doyle's lifetime the idea of the nation was undergoing an important metamorphosis in England, which Richard Holt has described in this way:

The formation of a distinctive English national culture in the late-Victorian and Edwardian era is undeniable but still not widely understood. The new consciousness of English culture that arose at this time ranged from an interest in the purity of the English language and its literature to music, folklore, landscape, and the idea of games as an embodiment of English spirit.... Sports were not just the source of high-minded ideals, they were inseparably associated with the more down-to-earth, assertive, and patriotic Englishness.[1]

There has been a good deal of work on this late nineteenth-century development. Philip Dodd's essay "Englishness and the National Culture" was one of the important instigations.[2] Stefan Collini has shown how "the 'nationalization' of English culture" was expressed in the creation or extension of national cultural institutions, and notably in the arrangement and celebration of a particular tradition of English literature as a curriculum subject and a national heritage.[3] Krishan Kumar more recently, in *The Making of English National Identity*, writes of a "moment of Englishness" at the end of the nineteenth century. The English had been senior partners in social structures and political systems—Great Britain, the British Empire—that directed their attention away from their own ethnic identities and somewhat inoculated them against the nationalism that was transforming Europe. "Ruling

---

[1] Richard Holt, *Sport and the British: A Modern History* (Oxford: Clarendon, 1989), 264.

[2] Philip Dodd, "Englishness and the National Culture", in Robert Colls and Philip Dodd (eds.), *Englishness: Politics and Culture 1880–1920* (London: Croom Helm, 1986), 1–28. José Harris identified in the late-Victorian period "a subterranean shift in the balance of social life away from the locality to the metropolis and the nation". José Harris, *Private Lives, Public Spirit: Britain 1870–1914* (Harmondsworth: Penguin, 1994), 19.

[3] Stefan Collini, *Public Moralists: Political Thought and Intellectual Life in Britain 1850–1930* (Oxford: Clarendon, 1991), 347.

the roost, they felt it impolitic to crow."[4] Imperialism was felt to trump nationalism, Kumar argues. "In the Crystal Palace that housed the Exhibition [of 1851], the British half was divided into raw materials and industrial applications; the other half, devoted to the exhibits of other nations, followed no such order, and exhibits were classified by nation. The British contribution, in other words, was 'universal', that of other nations merely 'national'."[5] But later in the century when new commercial and imperial rivals threatened Britain's supremacy, and other domestic nationalisms (most especially the Irish)[6] grew more insistent, there appears an English cultural nationalism, a preoccupation with the "English spirit" and what Kumar calls "a wide-ranging discovery of England",[7] and the production or refurbishment of an English national character in which sport plays a crucial part. Conan Doyle is among the most important participants in this ideological discourse. His own Irish-Scottish (and Catholic) provenance—he has been described as "at most a convert to Englishness"[8]—made him always alert to and appreciative of differences, sometimes down to a quite local level, but the importance of the empire in his idea of the nation makes him above all British in identity: it was the British and not the English Empire, even though Conan Doyle, like other empire enthusiasts including Kipling and Churchill, often used "English" and "British" interchangeably. At its widest, this was a community which in his view included (or should include) Ireland, and—as we shall see— the English-speaking people of the dominions, and even the United States. He relished the inclusiveness of his nation, bound together, as he believed, by the common values that added up to a national character. It was a favourite theme of his contemporaries.[9]

[4] Krishan Kumar, *The Making of English National Identity* (Cambridge: Cambridge University Press, 2003), 187.

[5] Kumar, *The Making of English National Identity*, 193.

[6] For one Irish reaction to English cultural nationalism, see Andrew Gibson, *Joyce's Revenge: History, Politics and Aesthetics in* Ulysses (Oxford: Oxford University Press, 2002), especially 8–20.

[7] Kumar, *The Making of English National Identity*, 218.

[8] Owen Dudley Edwards, "Introduction", in ACD, *The Complete Brigadier Gerard* (Edinburgh: Canongate Classics, 1995), xiv.

[9] In the course of the nineteenth century, "England" became "no longer attached to a particular place, but rather to imaginative identifications such as the countryside, Shakespeare or sport", and "a synonym that could be used equally to describe the country England, Great Britain and Greater Britain". Robert J. C. Young, *The Idea of English Ethnicity* (Oxford: Blackwell, 2008), 231.

This new and belated cultural nationalism, with its palaver of national identity and character, manifested itself in high culture—in historiography, in literary studies and teaching, in the founding of institutions like the National Trust (1895), the National Portrait Gallery (1896), and the *Dictionary of National Biography* (1885–1900)—and also in popular culture, from an appreciation of the countryside and pageantry to music-hall songs to sport itself. Out of this self-consciousness emerged a generally satisfying sense of the national spirit, with its individuality, sincerity, moderation, liberalism, love of freedom and justice, and incapacity for abstraction and system.[10] And Conan Doyle played a very important role in this discourse of the nation, in theoretical and mythographic ways in his journalistic, historical, and fictional writing, but also as a cultural sign himself. At the height of his celebrity, at least until his Spiritualistic campaigns forfeited much of his credibility, Conan Doyle was nationally known and respected—a national writer not only because of his extraordinary popularity and standing, but also because his personal celebrity was constituted of qualities that seemed to coincide with the nation's image of itself, rather as an ego-ideal.

It was, to be sure, a gendered ideal, one in which Britishness was not to be easily separated from masculinity. "His version of authorship was socially engaged and combative, his task as much the social performance of masculinity as the production of texts," Diana Barsham has argued; Conan Doyle's reputation "has been fixed in time as a museum piece of British manhood".[11] His contemporaries, who read his magazine stories and books, articles about and interviews with him, and his torrent of letters to the press, knew him as adventurous and responsible, manly and honourable: he was everything the English meant when they used the phrase "a good sport".[12] Victorian ideas of both sport and nation are themselves thoroughly imbricated with Victorian ideas of masculinity, and the history of the sportsman in the nineteenth century is an episode in the history of the man in this period.

[10] See especially Collini, *Public Moralists*, 342–73, and Kumar, *The Making of English National Identity*, 175–225.

[11] Diana Barsham, *Arthur Conan Doyle and the Meaning of Masculinity* (Aldershot: Ashgate, 2000), 11, 12.

[12] "Sport" in the sense of a likeable person who participates in a generous and sportsmanlike spirit, is a late nineteenth-century usage. The *OED*'s first citation in this sense is 1881.

Feminist historians have paid attention to hegemonic modes of masculinity in the nineteenth century, ideas and images of the male which were seen as sustaining the relations of power of men over women in the patriarchy, based on the cultural predominance of normative masculinities. Gender studies has cautioned against what has been called "the monolithic view of men as uncomplicated agents of oppression", and there is now something of a consensus that Victorian manhood was neither monolithic nor stable, but on the contrary was often riven with internal contradiction and fraught with anxieties.[13]

Certainly a cult of manliness was practised in the Victorian patriarchy, and sustained by stories of masculine heroism and adventure in the domains of sport, war, empire, and exploration. Sometimes there was a connection between this cult and the culture of Evangelical and Broad Church forms of Protestantism, above all in muscular Christianity.[14] Such manliness was given a national stamp by the example of soldier-saints like Henry Havelock, hero of the Indian Mutiny, or General Gordon (whose portrait was on the wall in the rooms shared by Holmes and Watson at 221B Baker Street). But its particularly Protestant modality must have resonated in rather different ways for someone like Conan Doyle, brought up in the Roman Catholic faith which in Victorian times was popularly stereotyped, according to Carol Marie Engelhardt, "as an irrational, emotional and highly decorative religion, which particularly appealed to women and unmanly men".[15] Conan Doyle soon drifted away from the Catholic Church, to be sure, but not into forms of religion recognized as more masculine.

Herbert Sussman, in an influential study, has argued that for the Victorians "manhood is not an essence but a plot, a condition whose achievement and whose maintenance forms a narrative over time".[16] To see the matter in these social-constructionist terms is to get away from an essentialist discourse of gender (though it was precisely on such an essence that the Victorians erected their sense of male identity).

---

[13] See Andrew Dowling, *Manliness and the Male Novelist in Victorian Literature* (Aldershot: Ashgate, 2001), 117.

[14] See J. R. Watson, "Soldiers and Saints: The Fighting Man and the Christian Life", in Andrew Bradstock, Sean Gill, Anne Hogan, and Sue Morgan (eds.), *Masculinity and Spirituality in Victorian Culture* (Basingstoke: Macmillan, 2000), 10–26; at 18.

[15] Carol Marie Engelhardt, "Victorian Masculinity and the Virgin Mary", in Bradstock et al. (eds.), *Masculinity and Spirituality in Victorian Culture*, 44–57; at 47.

[16] Herbert Sussman, *Victorian Masculinities: Manhood and Masculine Poetics in Early Victorian Literature and Art* (Cambridge: Cambridge University Press, 1995), 11, 13.

Sussman sees masculinity itself as an inner force, a strong libidinal current that constantly threatened to sweep men away towards madness and disorder; manliness, then, was the difficult and ongoing process by which Victorian masculinity was managed, controlled, and channelled into acceptable and useful forms of activity. One way this struggle is expressed is in a recurring plot, in which the manly hero rejects both the perilous love of women, and male-to-male intimacy too unless it is thoroughly desexualized; the monkish male in a community of men "becomes the central figure through which the contradictions and anxieties about manhood are registered".[17] We might find a social form of this literary trope in the all-male British public schools, where a healthily exhausting day on the football field was a prophylactic against impurity as well as an education in male teamwork. Another example of the celibate hero is Sherlock Holmes, famously immune to Cupid's darts. But James Eli Adams, in his *Dandies and Desert Saints*, has traced a paradox in the way that a display or performance of ascetic manhood (notably in Carlyle's self-dramatization as a prophet) itself produces a kind of dandyism;[18] and in this too, Sherlock Holmes, that incorrigible show-off and self-admirer, is a later case in point.

Various virile exploits in Conan Doyle's adventure fiction also partake of this paradigm of ascetic manhood—though Conan Doyle's expeditionary heroes are often explicitly fighting for the reward of the love of a woman, whether the chivalrous eponym of *Sir Nigel*, or Edward Malone in *The Lost World*, who joins the all-male Challenger expedition in obedience to his fiancée's injunction to go away and do something heroic. Sporting activity itself appears in Conan Doyle as almost always a ritual of male companionship: it gets men out of the house and is something they do together.[19] It may be a healthy outlet for the boisterous drives of masculinity, but it is also importantly, as I will show, both a test and a guarantee of successful manhood.

In Conan Doyle we see not only the man of letters as sportsman, but the sportsman as man of letters. The age which made a hero of the unworldly creative artist, and also validated the woman writer, was one in

---

[17] Sussman, *Victorian Masculinities*, 16.

[18] See James Eli Adams, *Dandies and Desert Saints: Styles of Victorian Manhood* (Ithaca, NY: Cornell University Press, 1995).

[19] The exception would be sports such as tennis and croquet, in which women participated. These "lawn" sports were both ideologically and literally closer to the home with its mixed company and feminine domestic space.

which social concerns about gender were implicated in the figure of the author. In English Romanticism the artist was somewhat feminized, the exceptional but vulnerable genius of sensitivity removed from the sphere of action. But the Victorian age also saw the birth of the artist as professional.[20] The novel, it was true, might have an agenda tuned to social realities and the world of action, yet the readership of Victorian novels was mostly female.[21] Here it seems was another site for gender anxieties to express themselves. Male writers were commonly assessed not only in terms of writing but also in terms of manliness.[22] Conan Doyle, with his overwhelmingly masculine themes and his robust and plain style, embodied the manly model of the writing career, as much as his contemporary Oscar Wilde represented a scandalous deviation from this straight path. If this contrast appears to cast Conan Doyle as the rather boring pillar of normative Victorian masculinity, it is a picture that can be complicated by the undoubted fact of his warm admiration for Wilde, and his later championship of the even more scandalous and demonized homosexual Roger Casement. These are attractive instances of Conan Doyle's loyalty and courage, the more so since, as we have begun to see, he took seriously his status as a man of letters who was a public figure. That status was one that came with responsibility, as can be seen in a letter to his mother in which he had explained his decision to volunteer for military service at the time of the South African war. "What I feel is that I have perhaps the strongest influence over young men, especially young athletic sporting men, of anyone in England (bar Kipling)."[23] It is a statement in which masculinity, writing, sport, and the nation come together. It is now time to return to the question of just what the nation was.

He himself was an Irish Scots Englishman, a lapsed Catholic, educated first by the Jesuits and then by the heirs to the Scottish Enlightenment in the medical establishment at Edinburgh. This interesting provenance, and no doubt his early experience of a broken family life too, played a part in forming in him an emotional and intellectual

---

[20] See the discussion of the career of Millais in Sussman, *Victorian Masculinities*, 140–58, and his argument that "the social formation of professional man resolved specific contradictions of nineteenth-century manhood by reconciling the demand to follow a morally valued calling with the imperative of achieving the financial success that defined bourgeois manliness" (153).

[21] See Kate Flint, *The Woman Reader 1837–1914* (Oxford: Clarendon Press, 1993).

[22] See Dowling, *Manliness and the Male Novelist*.

[23] ACD to Mary Doyle, n.d. [25 or 26 December 1899], in *Arthur Conan Doyle: A Life in Letters*, 434.

drive towards reconciliation and synthesis that seems to be a key to much of his life and work. He wrote to please, and he wrote for a living, but he also had a mission (though he would not have put it so pompously, before his Spiritualist campaigns made the word apt), and this expressed itself in a programme of nation writing as self-conscious and populist as Shakespeare's history plays—though a more direct genealogy can be traced through Walter Scott. This project was partly a didactic one; he saw it as his function as a writer not just to interpret his nation but also to change it, or rather give it a clearer sense of itself, both its history and its potentiality; so his letters to the press about divorce law reform are as much a part of the programme as *Sir Nigel*. Sport is only one of the domains in which this project expresses itself, but it is a fascinating one, and it can give us a startling insight into its ambitions and problems. A number of sports had a particular national significance for Conan Doyle, but none more so than what he called "the noble old English sport of boxing" (*M&A*, 272).

The straight left

Boxing is the sport that Conan Doyle wrote about most, but it was essential to his idea of sportsmanship that he himself was not a specialist, and participated in a bewildering number of sports and games. The map of his writing practice too is full of spaces dedicated to sporting activities. The few sports he claimed to be uninterested in can tell us something important about him. He was not excited by horse-racing, being of the opinion that sport is what a human being does, not what a horse does: besides, he wrote, horseracing was so corrupted by gambling that "I cannot avoid the conclusion that the harm greatly outweighs the good from a broadly national point of view" (*M&A*, 270). Target shooting fostered a vital national skill, shooting for the pot was justified but not a sport; but game shooting, with innocent birds or animals as the quarry, he considered cruel, and his explanation gives an insight into what he believed sport meant or should mean. "But there is another side of the question as to the effect of the sport upon ourselves—whether it does not blunt our own better feelings, harden our sympathies, brutalize our natures. A coward can do it as well as a brave man; a weakling can do it as well as a strong man. There is no ultimate good from it" (*M&A*, 271). Here sport emerges as frankly ideological, its value measured in terms of its effect on health, moral even more than bodily. How much "good" was to be derived from it, as measured in somatic, psychic, constitutional, and spiritual health?[24] A sport should be good, and it should be true. A technology-dependent sport like shooting could not be relied on to tell the truth about the sportsman, and reveal the coward as cowardly or the weakling as weak. As with so many of the things he disapproved of, Conan Doyle expressed the touching hope that game shooting would wither away with the progress of human civilization, and "in a more advanced age it will no longer be possible" (*M&A*, 271). This disapproval did not extend to the sport of angling, whose victim was "a cold-blooded creature of low organization" (*M&A*, 272).

Having cleared the field of those sports he was not keen on, Conan Doyle still had plenty left to enjoy and be knowledgeable about. One or two, such as field athletics and baseball, he savoured only as a spectator, but there is an impressive list of sports in which he participated. Apart from boxing, these include Rugby football and Association football (soccer), cricket, golf, hunting, ski-ing, fencing, shooting (marksmanship), fishing, archery, cycling, ballooning, motoring and motorbicycling, bowling, and billiards. He also claimed to have experienced a sporting pleasure in risky activities including war and whaling. He took a course of muscular development with his friend Eugene Sandow, the strong man who was said to be able to lift an elephant. Among what might be called the negative highlights of his sporting career, he failed to teach golf to Rudyard Kipling on a visit to Vermont in 1894; he was reported (inaccurately) to be one of those spectators who helped the exhausted Italian marathon runner Dorando across the finishing line in the 1908 London Olympics, causing him to be disqualified; he declined an invitation to referee the world heavyweight boxing championship bout between Jim Jeffries and Jack Johnson in 1909;[25] he was chosen, after a campaign in the

---

[24] "The physiological model of the healthy body was, in the nineteenth century, a common means of conceptualizing psychological health, as well as the health of the whole person, mind and body together." Bruce Haley, *The Healthy Body and Victorian Culture* (Cambridge, Mass.: Harvard University Press, 1978), 19. Haley notes that in English, the words health, wholeness, and holiness are related.

[25] Jeffries was white and Johnson was black. Conan Doyle was apparently the only person the two managers could agree on to referee the match impartially. He declined, in the end, on the grounds that his hands were full with work for the Congo Reform Association. See Booth, *The Doctor, the Detective and Arthur Conan Doyle*, 274–5.

press, to coordinate British preparations for the Olympic Games scheduled to be held in 1916 in Berlin, and which never took place.

"I have never specialized," he wrote, "and have therefore been a second-rater in all things. I have made up for it by being an all-rounder, and have had, I dare say, as much fun out of sport as many an adept" (*M&A*, 269). He continued playing football till the age of 44, and cricket for ten years more: on the whole cricket had, he said, given him more pleasure than any other branch of sport (*M&A*, 281). Rugby was the finest team sport, in his opinion, billiards the best indoor game. Golf was "the coquette of games" (*M&A*, 278), never quite to be mastered. And yet while all these and other sports occupied his time and gave him pleasure, it is above all boxing that captured his imagination, and that features more than any other in his writing, and this is because it is an activity which for him was invested with profound personal, national, and even metaphysical significance. When he remembered a dangerous bout of fever he suffered as a young man on the coast of West Africa, it seems to have come naturally to him to cast the experience in a boxing idiom: "I lay for several days fighting it out with Death in a very small ring and without a second" (*M&A*, 52).

Sport is both a cultural and a competitive activity. It brings people together in order to set them in opposition. In a moment I will look at some of Conan Doyle's purely fictional stories about boxing, but first I will say something about the occurrence of man-to-man fist-fighting in his autobiographical writing, to point out that, in the account he gave of his own experience in different narratives, bouts of pugilism are associated with what might be called liminal or threshold moments in his career. In choosing three of these and indicating their structural similarities, I do not mean to allege that Conan Doyle was an unreliable historian of his own life—which would rank high, or low, among futile critical activities—but to claim that these stories, whatever their basis in experience, show that boxing was implicated in his conception of himself, and of the trajectory of his manhood. If, as we have seen, shooting could not be relied upon to tell the truth about a man, boxing was prized because that is just what it did.

In 1880, while still a medical student, Conan Doyle spent seven months at sea as ship's surgeon in the whaling vessel *Hope*. Seeing that the young doctor had brought two pairs of boxing gloves in his luggage, the steward Jack Lamb proposed a bout there and then. The steward was the smaller man and knew nothing of sparring; Conan

Doyle describes how he "kept propping him off as he rushed at me", and eventually "had to hit him out with some severity". Comically, his prowess as a boxer earned him the steward's respect as a doctor—"the best surr-geon we've had!"—and seems to have guaranteed good relations thereafter between the medical student and the working-class crew.[26]

The second incident is in *The Stark Munro Letters*, the autobiographical novel published in 1895 which Conan Doyle acknowledged to follow pretty accurately (with the exception of the Lord Saltire episode) his own experiences when setting out in life as a young adult. Here we see Stark Munro paying a visit to Cullingworth, a friend from student days, with whom he will soon go into partnership in a medical practice. At Cullingworth's suggestion, they spar in the drawing room in the evening. "I led off, and then in he came hitting with both hands, and grunting like a pig at every blow. From what I could see of him he was no boxer at all, but just a formidable rough and tumble fighter" (*SM*, 32).[27] Stark Munro, a trained amateur boxer, gets the better of Cullingworth, who loses his temper, and demands that they fight without gloves, Mrs Cullingworth fortunately intervening in time to prevent this. Again, though this time against an antagonist of his own class, the protagonist proves his skill and character, particularly in containing the wildness of his opponent—manliness, in Sussman's terms, defeating masculinity. But the bout also reveals the volatility and vindictiveness of Cullingworth, which will eventually bring the partnership to an acrimonious end. (Cullingworth soon proves to be not above unethical or unprofessional behaviour in his medical practice.)

Stark Munro will then set up on his own in a new town, where on his first evening he undergoes another testing ordeal. Seeing a drunken man beating his wife in the street, he intervenes, and discovers once again that his opponent is dangerous but unskilled. "The fellow was a round hand hitter, but so strong that he needed watching. A round blow is, as you know, more dangerous than a straight one if it gets home; for the angle of the jaw, the ear, and the temple, are the three weakest

---

[26] ACD, "Life on a Greenland Whaler", *Strand Magazine*, 13 (January 1897), 16–25. Conan Doyle seems to have boxed quite regularly aboard the *Hope*. See ACD, *Dangerous Work: Diary of an Arctic Adventure*, ed. Jon Lellenberg and Daniel Stashower (London: The British Library, 2012).

[27] Cullingworth is the fictional portrait of George Turnavine Budd, Doyle's medical partner in Plymouth.

points which you present" (*SM*, 215–16). Once again, Stark Munro acquits himself well against this unorthodox opponent, and this augurs well for his professional and personal fortunes in the new place, where he will set up a successful practice, and eventually marry. In his non-fictional account of the incident, Conan Doyle reports that his antagonist that night unwittingly became one of his first patients (*M&A*, 63).

There are other instances in the writing, besides these three, of what we could call the challenge of the round hand hitter. The story recurs as part of what Conan Doyle knew about the world, this knowledge derived from the experience of sport. Whether or not these incidents actually took place as he described them, they are instances of a trope in Conan Doyle's life narrative which we may call a proof—in the double sense of test and demonstration, experiment and conclusion. Like the biblical Jacob wrestling with his angel on the bank of a river, the Doyle protagonist finds himself on the threshold of a new and challenging experience, and undergoes a test of character and manhood which will tell if he is fit for it. The association of sport, and above all boxing, with goodness and truth makes it a symbolically appropriate vehicle for the physical and moral ordeal which anticipates and in some sense guarantees an adventure on a very much grander scale. This is a pattern which will be reproduced as a national drama in Conan Doyle's 1896 novel of pugilism, *Rodney Stone*.

Rodney Stone narrates the story, looking back from 1851 to the time of his youth before the battle of Trafalgar. At the dramatic centre of the novel is the sport of prizefighting, with its bare-knuckle champions and the aristocratic "fancy", the Regency bucks who sponsor and bet on them. This theme is embedded in a fairly preposterous melodrama, with a supposedly haunted house, a man falsely accused of murder, a blacksmith's nephew who is revealed to be the son of a lord, and an aristocratic rotter. And all this takes place against the wider backdrop of the Napoleonic wars, and ends with Rodney Stone and his father preparing to join the fleet that would eventually triumph under Nelson at Trafalgar. As with all his historical novels, *Rodney Stone* is carefully researched and Conan Doyle took pains to make the historical detail, and especially the prizefighting, as accurate as he could. Several actual Regency fighters make their appearance, as well as figures like the Prince himself, Beau Brummel, and Lord Nelson.

Boxing was peculiarly British, as had been patriotically claimed in the anonymous *Fistiana; or, The Oracle of the Ring*. "Among the sports and games for which this country is distinguished, perhaps there is not one so purely national, or so decidedly indigenous to our soil as that of boxing; and whether viewed as a sport, or as a means of settling those differences which are constantly arising among men, however peaceably disposed, it is equally deserving encouragement."[28] Rodney Stone himself sets prizefighting in the Regency carefully in the context of a national history and character.

Public opinion was then largely in its favour, and there were good reasons why it should be so. It was a time of war, when England with an army and navy composed only of those who volunteered to fight because they had fighting blood in them, had to encounter, as they would now have to encounter, a power which could by despotic law turn every citizen into a soldier. If the people had not been full of this lust for combat, it is certain that England must have been overborne. And it was thought, and is, on the face of it, reasonable, that a struggle between two indomitable men, with thirty thousand to view it and three million to discuss it, did help to set a standard of hardihood and endurance. Brutal it was, no doubt, and its brutality is the end of it; but it is not so brutal as war, which will survive it.[29]

This is what boxing meant to the nation. England (actually Britain, whatever Nelson expected), being a free country, had no official conscription and relied on volunteers to defend it, and the country's fighting spirit was demonstrated and fostered by the spectacle of bare-knuckle fighting. Conan Doyle in his *Memories and Adventures* expressed very similar sentiments. "I have never concealed my opinion that the old prize-ring was an excellent thing from a national point of view—exactly as glove-fighting is now. Better that our sports should be a little too rough than that we should run a risk of effeminacy" (*M&A*, 274). Especially in times of peril, boxing was "good" for the nation.[30]

---

[28] *Fistiana; or, The Oracle of the Ring. Comprising a Defence of British Boxing; a Brief History of Pugilism, from the Earliest Ages to the Present Period; Practical Instructions for Training; Together with Chronological Tables of Prize Battles, from 1780 to 1840 Inclusive, Alphabetically Arranged with the Issue of Each Event. Scientific Hints on Sparring &c. &c. &c. By the Editor of Bell's Life in London* (London: Wm. Clement, 1841), 19.

[29] ACD, *Rodney Stone* (London: Smith, Elder, 1896), 12. Hereafter *RS*. It seems reasonable to call this a Regency story though Prince George was not actually appointed Regent until the Regency Act of 1811.

[30] A physician like Conan Doyle would be used to a patient asking "What's good for it?"—in other words, what is the effective treatment for a particular condition. In Conrad's *Lord Jim*, this is the question Marlow asks after Stein has diagnosed Jim's problem as romanticism.

And this explains the relation between the prizefighting fore-ground and the geopolitical background of *Rodney Stone*: in a narra-tive trope of the kind we have encountered before, the crisis of 1805 is a liminal moment in England's fortunes, and the boxing ring is the proof of Trafalgar, a kind of ritual prefiguring of the victory to come. The national ethos, exemplified and fostered in competitive fair play, is the base upon which the superstructure of national success is erected: this is the theory.[31] The sport, and its narrative climax in the meticulously described match between Crab Wilson and Champion Harrison, is the arena for the testing and display of the qualities of indigenous heroism that will defeat Napoleon and underwrite future imperial triumphs. These qualities include natural ability, endurance, the skills which contemporary handbooks insisted constituted a "sci-ence" of boxing, and what Conan Doyle called "the traditions of British fair play" (*M&A*, 274). Importantly, both Wilson and Harrison, loser and winner, exemplify these values, which are shared by the other working-class professional fighters in the story.[32] Boxing was a display of character as well as of skills. "The best men were always the best behaved," William Hazlitt noted with admiration in his essay "The Fight" in 1822.[33] And just as importantly, sterling qualities are also embodied in *Rodney Stone* in the Corinthians, that class of sport-ing dandies exemplified by Rodney's uncle, Sir Charles Tregellis. Sir Charles, at first sight ludicrously foppish and affected (not unlike Sir Nigel Loring in Conan Doyle's medieval adventure stories), turns out to be both fearless and honourable, and the institution of prize-fighting is shown to be a collaborative venture, bringing together the working-class professionals who did the fighting and the aristocratic patrons who sponsored them. Boxing is in an absolute sense an indi-vidual sport. This is why for Conan Doyle it was so true. But boxing was also a shared experience, a ritual and an institution in which

---

[31] The theory also holds in the medieval adventure *The White Company* (1891), where English military triumphs are prefigured by success in the jousting lists.

[32] It is the same story in Conan Doyle's "The Lord of Falconbridge", *Strand Magazine*, 38 (August 1909), 139–51, where a professional boxer is hired by a mysterious lady to fight a man who turns out to be her cheating husband, but refuses her command to beat him when he is down.

[33] William Hazlitt, "The Fight", *Selected Writings*, ed. Ronald Blythe (Harmondsworth: Penguin, 1985), 78–97; at 88. Hazlitt was a spectator at a bout between Bill Neate and Tom Hickman ("the Gas-man") which went to eighteen rounds.

fighters *represented* others, and they and their supporters were interdependent.[34]

In fact this pugilistic utopia is yet more inclusive. There is a scene at the heart of the novel in which Sir Charles gives a supper to the fancy at the Waggon and Horses, a well-known sporting public house, inviting both the chief fighting men of the day and the gentlemen of fashion most interested in the ring. This is where the wager is made that will lead to the great match between Harrison and Wilson. Guests at the supper range from Prince George himself (incognito as the Earl of Chester) to Joe Berks, a drunken Whitechapel bruiser. The narrative emphasizes the inclusiveness of this scene, naming famous pugilists from all over England, and others present who were Irish, Jewish, or black American.[35] But above all it is a scene of national manhood, the manners and powerful physique of the boxers reminding the narrator of their Norse or German ancestors, while here and there "the pale, aquiline features of a sporting Corinthian recalled rather the Norman type" (*RS*, 163). It is boxing that brings together classes and ethnicities and demonstrates what they have in common, and the Waggon and Horses is a fantasy of the nation as union, indeed a "version of pastoral" in William Empson's sense, with the boxer as swain (or arguably with the Corinthian as swain and the boxer as sheep).[36]

The scene, so like one of those broad didactic social canvases the Victorians were fond of, epitomizes the national fighting spirit.[37] Sir

---

[34] For a remarkable examination of the personal and cultural meanings of boxing, in a different time and place, see essays in Gerald Early, *The Culture of Bruising: Essays on Prize-fighting, Literature and Modern American Culture* (Hopewell, NJ: Ecco Press, 1994), 1–109.

[35] The admiring portrait of the black pugilist here is in marked contrast to the portrayal of Steve Dixie the bruiser, in the late story "The Adventure of the Three Gables" (1926), where Sherlock Holmes's insulting mockery of the boxer is a rare instance of overt racism in Conan Doyle. ACD, *The Case-Book of Sherlock Holmes* (1927), ed. W.W. Robson (Oxford: Oxford University Press, 1993), 133–50. Hereafter *Case-Book*.

[36] William Empson, *Some Versions of Pastoral* (London: Chatto, 1950). For sport and national identity during the Napoleonic wars, see Derek Birley, *Sport and the Making of Britain* (Manchester: Manchester University Press, 1993), 151–71.

[37] This is a ubiquitous argument in the literature of pugilism, making its way even into the title of the anonymous *Pancratia, or a History of Pugilism. Containing a full account of every battle of note from the time of Broughton and Slack, down to the present day. Interspersed with anecdotes of all the celebrated pugilists of this country; With an argumentative Proof, that Pugilism, considered as a Gymnic Exercise, demands the Admiration, and Patronage of every free State, being calculated to inspire manly Courage, and a Spirit of Independence—enabling us to resist Slavery at Home and Enemies from Abroad* (London: W. Oxberry, 1812).

Charles, the host, makes a speech in which he claims that in the crisis of war "we should be forced to fall back upon native valour trained into hardihood by the practice and contemplation of manly sports" (*RS*, 174), and the story of *Rodney Stone* goes on to prove this, the exhibition of English manhood in competitive sport guaranteeing the success to come in the struggle against Napoleon, promised on the last page. The battle of Waterloo may or may not have been won on the playing fields of Eton, but the battle of Trafalgar, the novel argues, was won in the prize ring. Conan Doyle himself, writing in the 1920s, felt that the revival of boxing in modern England, for which he took some credit, was vindicated in "the supreme test of all time", the Great War, when "the combative spirit and aggressive quickness gave us the attacking fire and helped especially in bayonet work".[38] France, now an ally, also benefited. "It was a great day for France when English sports, boxing, Rugby football and others came across to them, and when a young man's ideal ceased to be amatory adventure with an occasional duel. England has taught Europe much, but nothing of more value than this" (*M&A*, 275). Further, Conan Doyle was an enthusiast for international competitive sport, but he understood it as a competition between sportsmen representing their nations: memories of the rancour of the America's Cup yacht races in 1893 and the rivalries of the Olympic Games of 1908 left him "by no means assured that sport has that international effect for good which some people have claimed for it", and he guessed that in ancient Greece the awards at Olympia had probably started more wars than they stopped (*M&A*, 231).

The fight between Jim Harrison and Crab Wilson is the narrative climax of *Rodney Stone*. It takes place on Crawley Downs in the rain, before a crowd of 30,000 people, for as Rodney explains, "the love of the ring was confined to no class, but was a national peculiarity, deeply seated in the English nature".

The ale-drinking, the rude good-fellowship, the heartiness, the laughter at discomforts, the craving to see the fight—all these may be set down as vulgar and trivial by those to whom they are distasteful; but to me, listening to the far-off and uncertain echoes of our distant past, they seem to have been the

---

[38] Kipling, on the other hand, did not think much of sport as a training for war, to judge by "The Islanders" (1902), his poem about his country's unpreparedness for the South African war. "Then ye returned to your trinkets; then ye contented your souls | With the flannelled fools at the wicket or the muddied oafs at the goals." *The Definitive Edition of Rudyard Kipling's Verse* (London: Hodder and Stoughton, 1940), 302.

very bones upon which much that is most solid and virile in this ancient race was moulded. (*RS*, 251)

But this paradisal vision of essential Englishness contains a snake, and it is here that the relentless simplicities of *Rodney Stone* have to admit a problem. The sporting crowd may be another image of utopian England, but it gets out of hand, and so does the fight itself. The very success and popularity of the prize ring guarantees its corruption, by betting, match-fixing, and cheating; at the same time, Conan Doyle's melodrama requires a dastardly villain bent on ensuring the best man should not win. The excitement of the plot is dependent on the agency of the wicked who is a bad sport. The villainous Sir Lothian Hume tries to nobble Sir Charles's fighter so as to win the huge wager by default. When the fight goes ahead, and as it becomes clear Crab Wilson is going to lose, Sir Lothian's armed thugs break the ring in an organized pitch invasion, steal the time-keepers' watches, and threaten Harrison: a draw has to be declared.

So even this supreme demonstration of English goodness, truth, and commonality is borne down by villainy, money, and the mob. Rodney Stone from his mid-century vantage had already entered into the narrative record the corruption that overtook prizefighting: "[f]or this reason the Ring is dying in England" (*RS*, 12). Conan Doyle in *Memories and Adventures* made the same point about this most English of sports. "It was ruined by the villainous mobs who cared nothing for the chivalry of sport or the traditions of British fair play as compared with the money gain which the contest might bring. Their blackguardism drove out the good men—the men who really did uphold the ancient standards, and so the whole institution passed into rottenness and decay" (*M&A*, 274). If sport tells the truth about England, then a spoilsport greed, cheating, and thuggery are part of that truth. The sporting ideal has proved unable to defend itself from rampant materialism. Here is the poignancy of nostalgia, that to narrate what you feel nostalgia for is sooner or later to tell the story of how it disappeared. To adapt Proust, the only true story about paradise is paradise lost.

A nation of amateurs

How could the sport, and the nation, counter the defilement that money and competitive greed seemed inevitably to spread like pitch on its sturdy traditions? The redeeming agent was, of course, the cult of the amateur as the embodiment of fair play and sport for its own sake.[39] The still current sporting meaning of this word, to designate someone who does sport as a pastime and not for money, is a Victorian invention, and the breeding ground for the ideology of the amateur was the great public schools, with their emphasis on sport as the cultivation of the moral qualities that distinguished a gentleman, particularly in public and imperial service.[40] We may be inclined to think of the professional sportsman as a phenomenon of modernity, but this is only true inasmuch as the professional is constituted by difference from the amateur, and it is the amateur that is the formation of an emergent cluster of nineteenth-century ethics, including muscular Christianity, team spirit, and "the white man's burden".[41] Now, *Rodney Stone* had celebrated pugilism, but in doing so had also shown how the fight game in England had been inevitably corrupted and discredited. A few years later, in 1899, Conan Doyle wrote another prizefighting story, "The Croxley Master", as if to purge the skulduggery of the earlier tale and restore boxing to its proper meaning as a ritual of the true national ethos.

How to reconcile the representative or popular notion of the sporting champion with the more disinterested and high-minded values of the gentlemanly amateur? In "The Croxley Master" this problem is solved with the almost metaphysical trope of the amateur professional. The young hero of the story is Montgomery, a sporting but poor medical student who accepts an invitation to box against an old professional, Silas Craggs, the champion of the iron-workers at the Croxley smelting works, in Yorkshire.[42] This is not a bare-knuckle

---

[39] See Holt, *Sport and the British*, 74–134.

[40] See J. A. Mangan, *Athleticism in the Victorian and Edwardian Public School* (Cambridge: Cambridge University Press, 1981) and *The Games Ethic and Imperialism: Aspects of the Diffusion of an Ideal* (Harmondsworth: Viking, 1986). See also Holt, *Sport and the British*, Haley, *The Healthy Body*, Dennis Brailsford, *British Sport: A Social History* (Cambridge: Lutterworth Press, 1992), and Birley, *Sport and the Making of Britain*.

[41] See Birley, who adds that legislators of sport "felt obliged to spend a great deal of time trying to reconcile old notions of gentlemanly privilege with the emergent idea of amateurism". Birley, *Sport and the Making of Britain*, 6.

[42] There appears to be a particularly close association between sport (especially boxing) and medical students, who were inclined to be boisterous and disreputable when released from long hours of study. "These aspects of student life were as conspicuous as its brutalizing character was notorious. Even when sport provided an alternative outlet for youthful energy, a focus on work remained unfashionable." Anne Digby, *The Evolution of British General Practice 1850–1948* (Oxford: Oxford University Press, 1999), 55.

contest but a modern boxing match fought with gloves over twenty rounds and according to Queensberry rules, with a celebrity referee brought up from London. In this bout Montgomery will represent the workers of the Wilson coal-pits. For the student, winning the money prize will enable him to complete his medical studies at university and qualify as a doctor. Though fighting the Master for money means he will forever forfeit his amateur status, this is no problem for Montgomery, who is quite content to show his mettle in this bout and never box again. Though he is an outsider, his manifest pluck soon makes him a local hero for the Yorkshire miners and, in a familiar way, a strangely idyllic image of the nation crystallizes around the fight.

Sometimes brutal, sometimes grotesque, the love of sport is still one of the great agencies which make for the happiness of our people. It lies very deeply in the springs of our nature, and when it has been educated out, a higher, more refined nature may be left, but it will not be of that robust British type which has left its mark so deeply on the world. Every one of these ruddled workers, slouching with his dog at his heels to see something of the fight, was a true unit of his race.[43]

As with *Rodney Stone*, the fight is at the centre of the tale and is narrated at length and with much technical detail. Montgomery wins a fierce and fair bout that reflects credit on both him and his working-class opponent. He claims the prize, but resists his backers' urging to make a career as a sportsman, for he has turned professional for a day only in order to get the means to gain entry into his true profession, of medicine. As with the young Conan Doyle on the whaler, Montgomery's prowess with the boxing gloves seems to guarantee his qualities as a physician with the locals, and earns him a demotic endorsement: "we've plenty of doctors, but you're the only man in the Riding that could smack the Croxley Master off his legs".[44] Montgomery is neither an aristocrat of the sporting class, nor a horny-handed son of toil. Sport for Conan Doyle was an image of the nation, and one signal difference between the Regency fight and the Victorian one is the arrival on the scene of a new national hegemon, the professional-administrative middle class.

---

[43] ACD, *The Green Flag and Other Stories of War and Sport* (London: Smith, Elder, 1900), 134–5.
[44] ACD, *The Green Flag*, 168.

An amateur was not just someone for whom sport was not a trade. He was, crucially, not bound to a single specialism. You can see this most interestingly in the physique of the opponents. The Master, a professional fighter, has huge shoulders and great arms, out of proportion to his lower body. His single trade has made him ungainly and ugly, with a hint of Mr Hyde-like recession to the simian. "Montgomery, on the other hand, was as symmetrical as a Greek statue. It would be an encounter between a man who was specially fitted for one sport, and one who was equally capable of any."[45] Amateurism has made Montgomery, the all-rounder, a well-rounded man, and has given him the special gift of versatility which his class brought to administration and leadership at home and abroad. Government, and Government House, was not a place for narrow specialists: in this sense, Britain and the British Empire really were run by amateurs. A gentleman could exercise leadership quite literally anywhere, and so colonial governors might be posted from one continent to another and expected to get on with the job, and ministers (like Churchill), subject to cabinet reshufflings, were counted on to be equally capable of running the Colonial Office or the navy or the Exchequer. It was also an important part of the ethos of British leadership that a man in authority, like any amateur, should not appear to be trying too hard. Conan Doyle was delighted to find this sporting *sprezzatura* in Lord Cromer, *de facto* ruler of Egypt for a quarter of a century, who was in the habit of bringing critical diplomatic interviews to an abrupt conclusion "with the explanation that the time had come for his daily lawn-tennis engagement" (*M&A*, 128).

And it would be hard to find a better embodiment of the amateur ethos than Conan Doyle himself, that enthusiastic practitioner of so many sports. He was an accomplished cricketer, playing on occasion for the MCC, his best performance at Lords being seven wickets for fifty-one against Cambridgeshire in 1904; and on one memorable occasion he bowled out the legendary W. G. Grace. But he was just as happy to turn out for several years for the ramshackle team put together by his friend J. M. Barrie, and named the Allah-Akbarries in token of their inability to win without divine intervention.[46] This

---

[45] ACD, *The Green Flag*, 157.
[46] See Kevin Telfer, *Peter Pan's First Eleven: The Extraordinary Story of J. M. Barrie's Cricket Team* (London: Sceptre, 2010).

was what might be called jocular amateurism. At the further end of
the amateur scale were the great champions such as Grace himself,
the cricketing "gentlemen" who competed alongside professional
"players" who were paid and belonged to a lower social order. In
cricket these two kinds of sportsman sustained a double narrative
about sport and the nation, with one taken to speak of the sturdy
native qualities of the English folk that Conan Doyle had attributed
to the prizefighters of old, and the other held to exemplify the unself-
ish accomplishments of superior men born and trained to lead and
serve country and empire.[47]

It looked like a serviceable allegory of the nation, but it never really
worked. The more skilful and dedicated (and successful) the amateur,
the more amateurism was burdened with contradictions. W. G. Grace
himself was an example. As Derek Birley puts it, "many instances of his
excessive keenness to win and the reluctance of umpires to give him
out were recorded".[48] Grace charged large fees for exhibition matches
and for raising teams to tour overseas. In 1879 there were several testi-
monial matches for the great amateur and at a ceremony at Lords he
was presented with a cheque for £1,400, towards the purchase of a
medical practice. Less than a year earlier the Gloucestershire County
Cricket Club had called a special meeting to investigate various charges
of irregularity involving the Grace family (W. G.'s brother E. M. was
club secretary and kept the accounts). Keeping amateurism unsullied
by money was not easy, as Conan Doyle himself was to discover when
he was involved in the committee charged with ensuring that Britain
put up a better show in the 1916 Olympics than they had done in
Stockholm in 1912, where British athletes' performance was considered a national humiliation. His committee launched an appeal for a
fund of £100,000 for athletic training and facilities—and were
promptly accused on all sides of "developing professionalism" (M&A,
235–7).

Amateurism then proved in practice not quite the simplification of
sport that it had seemed to promise. But there was another dimension
to sport, and justification for it, that was of prime importance. It was

---

[47] For a useful profile of the latter, see the memoir by the long-serving Colonial
Service director of recruitment, Ralph Furse, *Aucuparius: Recollections of a Recruiting
Officer* (London: Oxford University Press, 1962), 219–22.

[48] Birley, *Sport and the Making of Britain*, 332. For the glories and contradictions of Grace's
career, see also David Kynaston, *WG's Birthday Party* (London: Bloomsbury, 2010).

acknowledged in the amateur creed that sport, as Richard Holt puts it, "had not only to be played in good spirit, it had to be played with style".[49] Sport might be healthy, educative, morally uplifting, socially adhesive, but it was also beautiful—as is repeatedly demonstrated in Conan Doyle's mildly homoerotic descriptions of boxers' bodies. The gifted sportsman was an example of style, just as much as the gifted musician or orator. There was a beauty in what he did. Among Conan Doyle's sportsmen, the great exemplar of style is Lord John Roxton, who joins the expedition to the Amazon in *The Lost World*, and is described as "one of the great all-round sportsmen and athletes of his day".[50] An intrepid soldier, hunter and crack shot, Lord John moves through the story with an apparently effortless grace which is as much aesthetic as athletic and moral—for example, when the others scramble and crawl across a sixty-foot tree trunk over a precipice in the jungle, Lord John will simply walk across. His bachelor apartment in the Albany is decorated with sketches of boxers, ballet girls, and racehorses, alongside paintings by Fragonard, Girardet, and Turner. The coolness and integrity of the true sportsman express themselves in ethical terms too, for only three years earlier Lord John had carried out a single-handed and freelance war against Peruvian slave-drivers on the Putamayo River. This is not an international war but an amateur one. "Declared it myself, waged it myself, ended it myself," he tells the narrator Malone (*LW*, 52). This is the disinterestedness of the amateur, the determination of the competitor, and the panache of the stylist. For the true sportsman, style is ethical and goodness is beautiful; the straight bat, and the straight left, could not be wielded by a crooked heart.[51] All Conan Doyle's practice is a proof of this simple ethical principle, learned in the domain of sport.

Those liminal encounters, in the whaling memoir and in *The Stark Munro Letters*, which pitched the trained sparring man against an undisciplined fighter, the straight left against the round hand hitter, were ethical as well as physical tests. Style underwrote goodness—or it

---

[49] Holt, *Sport and the British*, 99. He quotes the words of the Harrow School song, "Strife without anger, art without malice."

[50] ACD, *The Lost World* (1912), ed. Ian Duncan (Oxford: Oxford University Press, 1998), 48. Hereafter *LW*.

[51] For a wonderful example of the ethical meaning of sporting straightness, see J. S. N. Sewell, *The Straight Left: being nine talks to boys who are about to leave their preparatory schools* (London: SPCK, 1928).

should. His faith in this precept of straightness helps explain why Conan Doyle could not entirely approve his brother-in-law E. W. Hornung's character A. J. Raffles, the "amateur cracksman" who played cricket for England but was secretly a thief: Conan Doyle thought these stories "rather dangerous in their suggestion" (*M&A*, 259). Straightness in sport was the mark of the stylist, and was also a bulwark against crooks like Sir Lothian Hume, the unstable and unethical like Cullingworth, or ruffians like the wife-beating drunk in *The Stark Munro Letters*. One final instance concerns a gentleman, in a story of 1903, who claims to have "some proficiency in the good old British sport of boxing", and returns from a visit to the country with a black eye, to tell his friend about his enquiries in a local pub about a nefarious character called Woodley.

We had got as far as this, when who should walk in but the gentleman himself, who had been drinking his beer in the tap-room and had heard the whole conversation. Who was I? What did I want? What did I mean by asking questions? He had a fine flow of language, and his adjectives were very vigorous. He ended a string of abuse by a vicious back-hander, which I failed to entirely avoid. The next few minutes were delicious. It was a straight left against a slogging ruffian. I emerged as you see me. Mr Woodley went home in a cart.[52]

In the next chapter, we will see this stylish amateur at his professional work.

---

[52] ACD, "The Solitary Cyclist", in *The Return of Sherlock Holmes* (1905), ed. Richard Lancelyn Green (Oxford: Oxford University Press, 1993), 62–3. Hereafter *Return*. Watson records that the adventure took place in 1895. The story was serialized in *Collier's* (1903) and the *Strand* (1904) and both had an illustration, by Frederick Dorr Steele and Sidney Paget respectively, of the incident of the "straight left against a slogging ruffian". See also Kasia Boddy, " 'A Straight Left against a Slogging Ruffian': National Boxing Styles in the Years Preceding the First World War", *Journal of Historical Sociology*, 24/4, Special Issue on Sports and History, ed. Alan Tomlinson and Christopher Young (December 2011), 428–50.

3

Medicine

The statement of the case

"I crave for mental exaltation. That is why I have chosen my own particular profession, or rather created it, for I am the only one in the world."

"The only unofficial detective?" I said, raising my eyebrows.

"The only unofficial consulting detective," he answered.[1]

This exchange of words, between Sherlock Holmes and his friend and colleague Dr John Watson, falls into a shape which happens to be typical, indeed paradigmatic, of the relationship and the dialogue between them. Some data are presented. Watson offers a tentative epitome. Holmes supplements and corrects Watson's account with a definitive statement of the case. There is an epistemological hierarchy here. Watson knows something, but Holmes knows more, as he always does. In both its form and its content, the topic of this exchange is expertise, a practice of knowledge. Expertise is an invention of the Victorians, and arises at a particular moment in the history of the professions in the Victorian age. Sherlock Holmes is a fictional character who embodies more than a fair share of paradoxes, and one of these lies in the fact that he is both an amateur detective and a professional one. Here, however, he identifies himself as a professional, and of a particular kind. He is a consultant, that is, a professional expert. The entry of the voice of the consultant into Victorian talk (and writing) is a significant moment

---

[1] ACD, *The Sign of the Four* (1890), ed. Christopher Roden (Oxford: Oxford University Press, 1993), 4. Hereafter *Sign*. The story first appeared under this name in *Lippincott's Magazine* in February 1890, but the first British edition of the book was published as *The Sign of Four* by Spencer Blackett in October 1890.

in the unfolding of modernity, which could well be defined as the age of the consultant.[2] Conan Doyle was, for perfectly intelligible reasons, especially alert to this development. This voice, and its interlocutors, can be studied in the Sherlock Holmes stories.

Before looking at the history of professional expertise and the rise of the consultant, we may pause to note how Sherlock Holmes exhibits several of the unmistakable signs of expert status here in the opening pages of *The Sign of the Four*, which is the second Holmes novel and was published in 1890. For a start, he is treated with great deference by Dr Watson, who testifies to his friend's "great powers" in the second paragraph of his narrative and uses the same phrase when speaking to Holmes (*Sign*, 3, 4). Holmes does not demur. These powers, however, are not being exercised, for it is a condition of his profession that the consultant is powerless unless consulted; like the vampire, he can do nothing unless invited across the threshold of someone's affairs, and Holmes has had nothing to do for many months, it appears, but sit around at home and inject himself with morphine or cocaine, much to Watson's disapproval. He does give a brisk description of his work, however. When lower-grade practitioners find themselves out of their depths with a problem, the matter is laid before Holmes. "I examine the data, as an expert, and pronounce a specialist's opinion" (*Sign*, 4). Detection, he maintains, is a science. The scope of his activities is very broad, and commensurate with his reputation. He tells Watson that his practice has extended recently to the Continent, for he has been consulted by an eminent figure in the French detective service over a case involving a will. In this matter his expertise expressed itself not in analysis or deduction, but in his knowledge of the relevant literature, and he was able to refer his French counterpart to two parallel cases, one at Riga in 1857, the other at St Louis in 1871, which suggested to him the true solution. Here Holmes's expertise is cybernetic, having to do with the management of knowledge, and in other stories we hear of his prodigious memory and his extensive filing system.

Holmes then lays out for Watson's instruction "the three qualities necessary for the ideal detective" (*Sign*, 6)—the powers of observation and deduction, and knowledge. As a further proof of his expertise, he con-

---

[2] "The twentieth [century] is not, *pace* Franklin D. Roosevelt, the century of the common man but of the uncommon and increasingly professional expert." Harold Perkin, *The Rise of Professional Society: England since 1880* (London: Routledge, 1990), 2.

fesses that he has written several monographs, all upon technical subjects, which include the enumeration of 140 forms of tobacco ash, the uses of plaster of Paris as a preserver of the impress of footprints, and a study of the influence of a trade upon the form of the hand. That is, they are specialist research outputs, publications of no interest or use to the general public, a constituency from whom the consultant is professionally aloof and insulated. (In this respect the consultant of consultants is the paranoiacally isolated Mycroft Holmes, Sherlock's brother—"All other men are specialists, but his specialism is omniscience"—who never goes anywhere or has any human contact outside his Pall Mall lodgings, the Diogenes Club, and Whitehall.[3])

To emphasize that his skills are technical and analytical, Holmes expatiates on the importance of minutiae, and then gives a practical demonstration when challenged by Watson to deduce what he can about the former owner of a pocket watch. Though this is a game (since Watson already knows all about the previous owner of the watch, his own brother, now deceased), what follows is an exchange which has the classic configuration of the scene of consultancy. The case is proposed to the consultant and accepted by him. "I should be delighted to look into any problem which you might submit to me," Holmes says (*Sign*, 8). The data are then referred to the expert—"I handed him over the watch"—in a gesture which confirms the superiority of the referee while also putting him to the test, and at the same time places the referrer in the position of suppliant while also absolving him of responsibility for the problem. In this moment of what we might call manumission, the case is handed over, consigned to the consultant; it becomes for the time being, his. Holmes now handles the watch and proceeds famously to read the complete history of Watson's deceased brother from it, including the embarrassing fact that he was an improvident drunkard, and then apologizes for this frankness. "Viewing the matter as an abstract problem, I had forgotten how personal and painful a thing it might be to you" (*Sign*, 9). The consultant's abstraction from the personal, and his exoneration, to a degree, from the human consequences of the opinions solicited from him, will later be restaged under the limelight of the romance Holmes so despises, when the main plot of *The Sign of the Four* gets going with the visit of Miss Mary

[3] ACD, "The Bruce-Partington Plans", in *His Last Bow* (1917), ed. Owen Dudley Edwards (Oxford: Oxford University Press, 1993), 39. Hereafter *HLB*.

Morstan to consult him. When she has left, Watson declares her a very attractive woman. "Is she?" says Holmes languidly; "I did not observe" (*Sign*, 15). So much for observation, "one of the three qualities necessary for the ideal detective", and yet this is much to the point: Holmes's powers of observation are themselves so specialized as to filter out and render invisible to him obvious but irrelevant phenomena, such as that Miss Morstan is pretty, and this leads Watson to accuse him of being an automaton or calculating machine. Holmes merely smiles at this. " 'It is of the first importance,' he said, 'not to allow your judgement to be biased by personal qualities. A client is to me a mere unit, a factor in a problem' " (*Sign*, 15).

In *The Sign of the Four* we find the figure of the consultant, and the drama of consultancy, already fully developed, mature enough to be immediately recognizable, at least to the tale's middle-class Anglo-American reading public, and with that public's ambiguous feelings about consultants inscribed in the ways Holmes is both heroized (for his "great powers") and satirized (an inhuman calculating machine). Conan Doyle had almost certainly never met a consulting detective and Holmes may have been right when he claimed to be the only one in existence. If we ask where Conan Doyle had had experience of the specialist professional expert, the answer is obvious enough: in his own training and career in the science—or was it an art?—of medicine, which he was still practising at the time of writing the first two Holmes books, *A Study in Scarlet* (1888) and *The Sign of the Four* (1890).[4]

Traditionally there had been three orders of the embryonic medical profession—a small body of physicians who were trained in the classics, a larger number of surgeons who were regarded as craftsmen and were particularly in demand in times of war, and apothecaries, originally tradesmen who belonged to the Company of Grocers and retailed groceries and spices as well as potions and herbal remedies. But doctoring was unregulated and there was a vast number of people in the business. As late as the beginning of the nineteenth century, a survey done in Lincolnshire found that there were nine "quacks" to every one doctor belonging to a recognized body.[5] Most of the Medical Acts

---

[4] There is a wealth of data on Conan Doyle's medical career and writings in *Medical Casebook of Doctor Arthur Conan Doyle*, ed. Rodin and Key.

[5] D. U. Bloor, "The Rise of the General Practitioner in the Nineteenth Century", *Journal of the Royal College of General Practitioners*, 28 (May 1978), 288–91; at 289.

passed by Parliament, going back to the first one in 1540, had been concerned with distinguishing between orthodox and unorthodox practitioners, and the growing number of untrained people dispensing and prescribing treatment led to the first modern reform with the Apothecaries Act of 1815, which instituted improvements in medical education and required all apothecaries to be licensed (though it did nothing to outlaw or regulate unqualified druggists).[6] It is at this time that the term "general practitioner" first came to be used. For the practice of medicine it was the beginning of the acquisition of respectability, and the nineteenth century was to see a radical change in the social status and role of the doctor. Between the mid-nineteenth century and the First World War (or, roughly, in the lifetime of Arthur Conan Doyle who lived from 1855 to 1930), according to José Harris, "Doctors moved from the margin to the mainstream of social life; and, although there were many gradations within the medical profession, by 1914 both specialists and general practitioners were well on the way to acquiring the exalted prestige and high public profile that their profession was to enjoy later in the twentieth century."[7]

The watershed moment for medicine in Britain was the passing into law of the Medical Act of 1858, the first and most important of three pieces of legislation that formed the modern profession of medicine, and the one that set the conditions for a widespread medicalization of society later in the nineteenth century.[8] Before the Medical Act, there was no regulated medical profession in Britain, there was simply practice, and anybody could set up in the business if they could persuade others to pay for the treatment they offered. The Act of 1858 regulated (though it did not modernize) medical education, established the General Medical Council as the organ of the profession, and instituted state registration of qualified practitioners; once on its register, physicians and surgeons had a legal right to practise as "doctors" and

---

[6] In a House of Lords decision in 1704, apothecaries had won the right to prescribe as well as to dispense drugs, over protests from the Royal College of Physicians. See Bloor, "The Rise of the GP", 288. For the Apothecaries Act, see also Roy Porter, *Disease, Medicine and Society in England 1550–1860*, 2nd edn. (Basingstoke: Macmillan, 1993), 49–50.

[7] Harris, *Private Lives, Public Spirit*, 56.

[8] The later two were to be the National Health Insurance Act of 1911, which introduced a state panel doctor for poorer patients, and the creation of the National Health Service in 1946, with capitation payment rather than payment per treatment, and medical care free at the point of use.

unregistered practitioners, of course, did not.[9] For the Act provided the means of consecrating certain people as *bona fide* professionals, but also of banishing others, in larger numbers, to the unprofessional outer darkness where druggists, homeopaths, purveyors of folk remedies, and most quacks and mountebanks continued to flourish beyond the pale of professional respectability, peddling their wares to patients who were too poor to afford a proper doctor or too ignorant to know the difference.[10] It was now a legal offence for people not on the Medical Register to represent themselves as medical practitioners. Undoubtedly a major advance in public health, the Medical Act of 1858 was at the same time, says Irvine Loudon, "a prime example of professional consolidation and monopolization based on motives of self-interest".[11] "Parliament had achieved what the doctors never could," as Roy Porter puts it; "it had, symbolically at least, united the much-divided medical profession, by defining them over and against a common Other, not to say enemy."[12]

The Act drew more than one line. It excluded many traditional practitioners—and all women, incidentally—from the profession.[13] But it also entrenched an important distinction, among qualified and registered doctors, between the consultant (almost always a specialist, whose status was recognized by the medical corporations) and the general practitioner. The old hierarchy of physician, surgeon, and apothecary disappeared, but only to be replaced by a new one, of consultant and general practice. The institution of medical consultant

---

[9] Not until 1912, however, was a byelaw of the Royal College of Physicians amended so that general practitioners could be called "doctors" and not plain "Mr". See Bloor, "The Rise of the GP", 291. But Dr Watson and Dr Conan Doyle were correctly so titled as they both held the degree of MD.

[10] "Yet many fields of irregular medicine were actually growing in tandem with the expansion of regular physic, surgery and the apothecaries's trade." Porter, *Disease, Medicine and Society*, 44.

[11] Irvine Loudon, *Medical Care and the General Practitioner 1750–1850* (Oxford: Clarendon Press, 1986), 298.

[12] Porter, *Disease, Medicine and Society*, 51.

[13] The profession's restrictive practices utterly debarred women from medicine until the 1870s. Though an opponent of women's suffrage, Conan Doyle was a supporter of women's rights in professional life. See R. Dixon Smith, "Feminism and the Role of Women in Conan Doyle's Domestic Fiction", *ACD: Journal of the Arthur Conan Doyle Society*, 5 (1994), 50–60. His comic story "The Doctors of Hoyland" is about the alarm among men doctors caused by the arrival of a woman in general practice. She goes on to become a specialist. ACD, *Round the Red Lamp: Being Facts and Fancies of Medical Life*, 2nd edn. (London: Methuen, 1894), 295–315. Hereafter *Red Lamp*.

was an important instantiation of Victorian expertise, and the profession brought it formally into being through making a radical and (in career terms) permanent distinction between consultancy and general practice, thereby acknowledging a difference between two orders of knowledge, and the two career paths along which these knowledges were deployed in practice. For while the Act conferred on the GP an important professional standing and respectability, it also confined him, and later her, to the lower of the two rungs in the new hierarchy of clinical practitioners. "For an outsider, the prospects of rising up the profession to become a top consultant were negligible: such eminences still largely came from a self-selecting and -perpetuating elite."[14] The conservative Royal College of Physicians issued its licence only to consulting physicians, and still refused to supervise the training and examination of general practitioners.[15]

To be sure, this was not just a hierarchy, but a system. For while there was a growing tendency among physicians and surgeons to practise as consultants, usually centred on hospitals, this depended on a solid base of general practitioner in the community, and "the gradual acceptance of the peculiarly British principle of referral" ensured a symbiotic relationship between the two: it became accepted practice that a patient could (with a few exceptions) obtain access to a physician or surgeon only by first consulting a general practitioner.[16] Still, Loudon is of the view that while the Medical Act of 1858 benefited everyone who found themselves inside the profession, it did more for the specialists than for the generalists, whose professional standing, and self-esteem, was to be haunted thereafter by the stigmatic phrase "subordinate grade". "The authentication of the corporations and medical qualifications [by the Act] had the effect of fossilizing the prospects of the general practitioner and ensuring that he remained as a subordinate grade. To this extent the general practitioners were disappointed people who had challenged the medical corporations and lost."[17]

---

[14] Porter, *Disease, Medicine and Society*, 54.
[15] Bloor, "The Rise of the GP", 290.
[16] Loudon, *Medical Care and the GP*, 301.
[17] Loudon, *Medical Care and the GP*, 300. Efforts made as early as in the 1840s to found a Royal College of General Practitioners were thwarted by the established medical corporations and the College did not see the light until 1952.

I will have more to say later about the history and culture of medical specialists and generalists, but I want to keep as backdrop to this discussion our primal scene of consultancy, in the rooms at 221B Baker Street, at the start of *The Sign of the Four*, for there is a larger argument here which bears on the importance of Conan Doyle as a historian and critic of expertise and practice, and therefore of modern knowledge. Though I shall try to show this drama playing out in the field of medical discourse and its institutions, and to read Conan Doyle's fiction as a reflection on these developments in the culture, I ought to enter the caution that the relationship we are watching in the second Sherlock Holmes novel is not, of course, one between a medical consultant and a general medical practitioner. In fact, an example of neither is present in the room. Holmes is a consultant but he is not a doctor but a detective. Further, if we were looking for a properly symmetrical consultant–generalist dialogue, we ought to look not at Holmes's exchanges with Watson but those with Athelney Jones, the comic Scotland Yard man who makes his appearance in chapter 6 (immediately arresting the wrong man) and embodies the sort of clod-hopping qualities that many specialists would no doubt have been quite ready to impute to the average GP.[18] And as for Watson himself, at the time of the adventure he relates in *The Sign of the Four* he is not practising medicine at all, but is a half-pay army surgeon, still recovering from the wound he received at the battle of Maiwand in Afghanistan in 1880.[19] When Mary Morstan accepts his proposal of marriage late in the story, he will move out of the bachelor establishment in the Baker Street rooms. A later story tells of his setting up in general practice in the Paddington district of London, and we may feel sure he has chosen a career suitable to his talents.[20] But at the beginning of the story he is still a general medical practitioner only *in potentia*.

[18] But even here the analogy is inexact, for the Scotland Yard men were themselves consultants within the profession of the police, detective experts with no "beat" of their own who were called in to take command of particularly difficult or important cases likely to be beyond the criminological competency of the local police.

[19] Watson is still keeping up with the medical literature, however. He has a book on pathology on his desk.

[20] ACD, "The Stockbroker's Clerk", in *The Memoirs of Sherlock Holmes* (1893), ed. Christopher Roden (Oxford: Oxford University Press, 1993), 73. Hereafter *Memoirs*. But later still he sells the practice (which has migrated to Kensington) for a handsome price which, unbeknown to Watson, has actually been put up by Holmes as a way of ensuring Watson's return to share the rooms at Baker Street (*Return*, 26).

The consultants

Before the middle of the nineteenth century, the number of doctors in Britain in consultant practice was very small indeed, and they scarcely existed outside London and a few large centres of population. Most physicians, "pure" surgeons, and general practitioners were largely or wholly engaged in what is now called primary care, their consultations initiated directly by patients rather than by other doctors seeking a second opinion. Remarkably, the number of general practitioners in England and Wales in 1971 was virtually unaltered from 1841, at about 20,000, but the most obvious difference in the period is in the greatly increased number and proportion of consultants and specialists.[21] The rise of the consultant is the great evolutionary success story of modern medicine. The practice of consultancy may be defined in several ways. In Britain the consultant is usually understood to be a doctor whose occupation is dependent on the referral of patients by general practitioners requiring an expert opinion. Also, a post may be prefixed by the term consulting, as in a consulting physician or a consulting surgeon, a title which is a mark of "both the esteem in which the individual is held (usually towards the end of a very distinguished career), and of the part-time or occasional nature of the services to be expected from the position".[22] Again, the term may also simply be used for a specialist in a particular branch of medicine. Some of the friction between consultants and GPs probably arose from the fact that their distinctive respective roles were not as well demarcated as, for example, those of modern solicitors and barristers—and when we return to Sherlock Holmes we shall see him, in the domain of detection, sometimes wandering across the border between consultancy and something like general practice. Anne Digby warns of the difficulty of making generalizations about GPs and consultants when she adduces the example of "no less a person than the Editor of the *BMJ*, who stated in 1878 that he did not wish to make a hard and fast line between the two, because essentially there was only a difference in the ability to command levels of fees".[23]

---

[21] In 1971 there were 23,806 hospital medical staff in England and Wales and 8,655 consultants. For data in this paragraph see Loudon, *Medical Care and the GP*, 208–27.

[22] Digby, *The Evolution of British General Practice*, 289.

[23] Digby, *The Evolution of British General Practice*, 294.

But by all of these definitions—including by implication by the
last—the consultant was recognized to be an expert, perhaps in a specialized field, with a level of knowledge greater than was at the disposal
of the ordinary practitioner. While his knowledge had a theoretical
base and was acquired by study, not simply practice, it differed from the
knowledge of (say) the expert in classical archaeology in that it could
be applied to intervene in people's lives: the expert in this sense is a
specialist purveyor of *practical* knowledge, or knowledge put into practice. "Medicine," writes Nikolas Rose, "was perhaps the first positive
knowledge to take the form of *expertise*, in which the human being
was not only to be known but to be the subject of calculated regimes
of reform and transformation, legitimated by codes of reason and in
relation to secular objectives."[24] The consultant emerges as an instrument in the "medicalization" of existence, studied by Michel Foucault
and others, a process in which individuals came to describe themselves
in the languages of health and illness, the body under the clinical gaze
became legible as an object that might harbour an analysable lesion—
to be seen, in other words, as a "case" for treatment—and a powerful
medical discourse flooded into what had previously been viewed as
"common sense" areas of human life, such as child care, sexuality, physical fitness, diet, and crime.[25] Many branches of the institution of modern medicine played a part in this transformation, but the consultant
was in the vanguard, at what we might legitimately call the cutting
edge. He was an emergent formation and an agent of change because
he was by professional definition more scientific than other doctors,
and therefore, self-evidently, more modern.

The second expository chapter of *A Study in Scarlet*, and the first
chapter of *The Sign of the Four*, bear the same title, "The Science of
Deduction". Sherlock Holmes's claim to pre-eminence in his field—the
point is repeatedly made—rests on his profession of detection as a science. His application of observation, deduction, and knowledge is sys-
tematic, materialist, and secular, and this makes him equally impatient
with the blundering of the Scotland Yard hacks and with the distracting
romanticism, as he sees it, of Watson's narratives, such as the story Watson
had written up and published about how Sherlock Holmes solved the

[24] Nikolas Rose, "Medicine, History and the Present", in Colin Jones and Roy Porter
(eds.), *Reassessing Foucault: Power, Medicine and the Body* (London: Routledge, 1994), 48–72;
at 49.
[25] Harris, *Private Lives, Public Spirit*, 56–7.

Jefferson Hope case. Holmes does not object to Watson's publishing the story—far from it, since fame is a great asset to a consultant—but, as we have seen, he dislikes the way he wrote it. "Detection is, or ought to be, an exact science, and should be treated in the same cold and unemotional manner.... The only point in the case which deserved mention was the curious analytical reasoning from effects to causes, by which I succeeded in unravelling it" (*Sign*, 5). Watson had given his narrative of the Jefferson Hope case an up-to-date art-for-art's-sake title, *A Study in Scarlet*, which sounds like the sort of name the artist and aesthete Whistler gave to his paintings.[26] But Holmes's criticism of Watson's narrative is that it is the opposite of modern, a reactionary narrative, a hopelessly old-fashioned, sentimentalized, and sensationalized account of what was an entirely cerebral and abstract event, as if, he says, Watson had "worked a love-story or an elopement into the fifth proposition of Euclid" (*Sign*, 5)—and here we might take note of the gender implications of this reproach, for another quality of Holmes's brand of modernity is that it is exclusively a masculine domain.

There is a sense in which Holmes is quite right to complain about Watson's narrative methods, for Watson—who was later brazenly to entitle a collection of these stories *The Case-Book of Sherlock Holmes*—has violated the generic conventions of the professional case report. "Whatever their purpose," according to Brian Hurwitz, "case reports involve discursive performances that reorganize clinical data using a variety of narrativizing techniques."[27] This is a complicated matter, as Hurwitz's studies have shown, but a simple way to put it would be that the formation of a medical "case" is a process in which the highly personal presentation of a human being, as a body with certain symptoms and a "history" elicited and noted by the doctor, is transformed into a medical abstraction through the assemblage of evidence and an

[26] Such as "Symphony in Blue and Silver", "Harmony in Grey and Green", and "Arrangement in Grey and Black no. 1" ("Whistler's Mother"). As for *A Study in Scarlet*, Holmes seems to have forgotten he himself came up with this title for the case. See ACD, *A Study in Scarlet* (1888), ed. Owen Dudley Edwards (Oxford: Oxford University Press, 1993), 127. Hereafter *Study*.

[27] Brian Hurwitz, "Form and Representation in Clinical Case Reports", *Literature and Medicine*, 25/2 (Fall 2006), 216–40; at 217. Owen Dudley Edwards has argued that in the Holmes tales Conan Doyle was following the blueprint of Edinburgh medical case studies, "with their enunciation, erroneous diagnosis, accurate diagnosis, course of treatment, final resolution with statement from protagonist as well as medical consultant". See "Introduction" to ACD, *The Complete Brigadier Gerard*, xxi.

impersonal and sober argument made in narrative terms for the information or instruction of others (and something similar happens in a
legal case narrative). Holmes's complaint is that Watson's literary methods have allowed back those elements of the personal, interpersonal,
and contingent which would normally be purged from the record as
the "history" is turned into a "case". Holmes thinks a case report
should be cool and unemotional and he is irritated that Watson has
raised the temperature of the genre in an unwarranted way.

This is a quarrel between two different possible ways of telling a
story—that is to say, it is a quarrel about history.[28] We can follow up the
contention between modern science and unmodern romance, and
further examine its relation to gender, in a lesser-known Conan Doyle
story about a scientific specialist, called "A Physiologist's Wife".[29] This
was published in his collection of medical tales *Round the Red Lamp:
Being Facts and Fancies of Medical Life* (1894), whose title recapitulates
the war between Holmesian facts and Watsonian romance. "A Physiologist's Wife" tells the story of the neurologist Professor Ainslie Grey,
a man of great reputation as a scientist, and of fastidious and unbroken
habits. "He had been referred to by one of the greatest living authorities as being the very type and embodiment of all that was best in
modern science" (*Red Lamp*, 122). He lives with his maiden sister. This
is the sort of conversation they have over breakfast.

> "You have no faith," she said.
> "I have faith in those great evolutionary forces which are lead-
> ing the human race to some unknown but elevated goal."
> "You believe in nothing."
> "On the contrary, my dear Ada, I believe in the differentiation
> of protoplasm." (*Red Lamp*, 126)

And well he might, for it was scientists who were the prime agents and
ideologues of the material progress every day apparent to Victorians,
which it was easy to understand in terms of Darwinian evolution. It was
scientists whose discoveries seemed to underwrite what Jean-François

---

[28] In this case, between a historiography based on traditional humanism including the
observation of mental states, and an objective scientific positivism. Though modern medical narratives tend to be characterized by clinical literalism, Hurwitz shows that in the
driest of case reports, the subjectivity of the narrator and the personhood of the patient
cannot always be entirely eclipsed from the story.

[29] The story first appeared in 1890 in *Blackwood's Magazine*, that most masculine of
contemporary periodicals.

Lyotard calls the *grand récit* or grand narrative of emancipation from nature, a theory of history as an inexorable if uneven advance in human knowledge and control of the world, deriving from the Enlightenment.[30]

But the early pages of "A Physiologist's Wife" make it clear there is another kind of story, at which the hapless specialist will prove less adept. He has decided to marry the widow Mrs O'James, and proposes to her in his own way. "I am not an emotional man, but I am conscious in your presence of the great evolutionary instinct which makes either sex the complement of the other" (*Red Lamp*, 132). Rather surprisingly Mrs O'James succumbs to this effort at sweet talk, though she finds his manner a little unromantic, to which reproach her suitor replies, as Holmes might have replied to Watson: "Romance is the offspring of imagination and of ignorance. Where science throws her calm, clear light there is happily no room for romance" (*Red Lamp*, 135). Professor Grey marries the widow, but predictably enough the scientist soon finds himself entangled in a romantic melodrama, as it is revealed that his new bride is in fact still the wife of his colleague O'Brien, who had believed her drowned in Australia. Though his wife has knowingly entered on a bigamous marriage with him, and now proposes to desert him and go back to O'Brien, Ainslie Grey consents to let them leave together without reproach or scandal. If this refusal to be agitated seems admirably forgiving, it also shows him to be an irredeemably cold fish. "How far the individual monad is to be held responsible for hereditary and engrained tendencies, is a question upon which science has not yet said her last word," is what he says (*Red Lamp*, 150). He returns to his bachelor existence and his physiological researches, but soon dies apparently of a broken heart, a condition unadmitted in modern physiological science.

There is an ethnic as well as a gender architecture to this story, for the prosaic Ainslie Grey's forename indicates that he is Scottish, and his downfall comes when he strays unwisely into the world of the passions and imagination, embodied by the Irish and disconcertingly emotional Mrs O'James, and the equally Irish Mr O'Brien, who, though himself a scientist, speaks of his feelings "with a sudden little

---

[30] This material progress, which included advances in clinical medicine, came at a severe cost in public health, with the increase of slum housing, industrial pollution, and occupational disease caused by urban overcrowding (England's population doubling in the reign of George III) and rapid industrialization.

spurt of Celtic enthusiasm" and is, furthermore, apparently a lapsed
Catholic (*Red Lamp*, 139). There are clues in this to Conan Doyle's
ideas of the racial constitution of his own family and nation. In effect,
"The Physiologist's Wife" is a pretty commonplace example of the
case of the cold consultant. Much is made of Ainslie Grey's expertise
in matters such as the Mesoblastic Origin of Excitomotor Nerve
Roots, and the Nature of Bathybius, with some remarks upon Litho-
cocci, but he is not a person you would approach to ask the way to
the post office. After all, Darwin and Huxley had propounded a theory of biological evolution as essentially a story of ever-increasing
complexity and specialism in the organism, and Herbert Spencer had
found the same pattern in the evolution of human societies and
human knowledge.[31] Ainslie Grey's successes as a specialist mark him
as modern indeed, and highly evolved, but they have been achieved at
the expense of a more general competence in the ordinary business of
living. His narrow expert insights concomitate a broad general blind-
ness, or at least myopia. Here we can recall Sherlock Holmes's professional appraisal of Mary Morstan as a factor in a problem (which he
will brilliantly solve), and his failure—or unwillingness—to observe
that she was a good-looking woman.

The coldness of the specialist may be temperamental, but it is certainly a function of his job. As a consultant he is called in, but always
remains aloof, his detachment being a professional asset, indeed a condition of consultancy. He is, or ought to be, a solver of problems, and
the people and situations he encounters present themselves to his necessarily reductive gaze as cases (such as might be recorded in a case-
book). To see a person as a "case" may be a way of not seeing them as
a person. So at least it was to appear to the 19-year-old poet Wilfred
Owen, working as unofficial curate in a parish near Reading in 1912
and visiting the impoverished family of a 5-year-old girl dying of
tuberculosis.

Isn't it pitiable? She is going to a hospital (weeks hence *of course*), and may be
beyond the reach of doctors by that time.... This, I suppose, is only a typical

---

[31] The advance from military to industrial societies was achieved, Spencer explained,
through the increasing division of labour, and in science "there is an advance from a few,
simple, incoherent truths, to a number of specialized sciences forming a body of truths
that are multitudinous, varied, exact, coherent". Herbert Spencer, "The Factors of Social
Evolution", in *On Social Evolution: Selected Writings*, ed. J. D. Y. Peel (Chicago: Chicago
University Press, 1972), 121–33; at 132.

case; one of many *Cases*! O hard word! How it savours of rigid, frigid professionalism![32]

The young poet's hostility to professionalism comes with the familiar charge of coldness, even morbidity. But even when warmed up, as it were, there might seem something inadequately human about the specialist's enthusiasm. "The Crooked Man" is one of the most heartbreaking of the Sherlock Holmes stories, but pursuing the case kindles in the consulting detective "a state of suppressed excitement" and a "half-sporting, half-intellectual pleasure" which communicates itself to Watson, though they are on their way to interrogate a sick and friendless cripple who has been destitute for thirty years (*Memoirs*, 168).

There is an interesting example of the syndrome in another of Conan Doyle's medical tales, "The Third Generation". Dr Horace Selby, a successful specialist with a European reputation, is conducting an examination of a young patient, Sir Francis Norton, in his consulting room. First he scrutinizes a rash on Sir Francis's shin, then his teeth.

"Now the eye." He lit a lamp at the patient's elbow, and holding a small crystal lens to concentrate the light, he threw it obliquely upon the patient's eye. As he did so a glow of pleasure came over his large, expressive face, a flush of such enthusiasm as the botanist feels when he packs the rare plant into his tin knapsack, or the astronomer when the long-sought comet first swims into the field of his telescope. (*Red Lamp*, 53)

The last phrase is probably a half-memory of John Keats's poem about the pleasure of intellectual discovery, "On First Looking into Chapman's Homer", with its lines "Then felt I like some watcher of the skies | When a new planet swims into his ken".This is a thoroughgoingly Foucauldian scene, with its objectification and disarticulation of the patient, the concentrated gaze of the physician through the body to uncover the lesion within, his deployment of expert knowledge ("This is very typical") and his appropriation of the patient as if he were a specimen for his collection and professional advancement. "Curiously enough, I am writing a monograph upon the subject. It is singular that you should have been able to furnish so

[32] Wilfred Owen to Susan Owen (27 March 1912), in Wilfred Owen, *Collected Letters*, ed. Harold Owen and John Bell (London: Oxford University Press, 1967), 126.

well-marked a case" (*Red Lamp*, 53–4). What has Dr Selby seen in his young patient's eye, to give him this warm glow of pleasure? It is the decisive clue that enables him to resolve this case, if not without a necessary circumlocution. He is able to diagnose in Sir Francis what he calls "a constitutional and hereditary taint" (*Red Lamp*, 54). For Dr Selby is a consultant venereologist, and Sir Francis has inherited from his dissolute grandfather a congenital, incurable, and deadly syphilis, which has now begun to present in skin, teeth, and eyes. Further, he is to be married in a few days. This appalling tragedy is the well-marked "case" which imparts a momentary warm glow to the great consultant. In the end he prescribes some powders and ointment, and advises Sir Francis to cancel the wedding and emigrate to Australia, but he will never see his patient again; the next morning Dr Selby reads in the newspaper of Sir Francis Norton's suicide, and the case is closed.

It may seem a reckless leap to go from something as insubstantial as the warm glow experienced by a fictional specialist to a generalization about the history of knowledge in the nineteenth century. But what better place to look for that history than in the work of a figure like Conan Doyle, who was both a scientific professional and a popular author? Written in the age of the triumph of the professions, and of the consulting specialists at their apex (particularly in the clinical domain), his work is everywhere inscribed with both excitement and misgivings about the management of knowledge, a structure of feeling which amounts to nothing less than excitement and misgivings about the direction of modernity itself. It had been a long while since knowledge had escaped the monopolizing grasp of the Church, and almost as long since a time when a single polymath might claim possession of all that was worth knowing. The information revolution had accelerated enormously in the nineteenth century, but we do well to remember that for most people this meant there was more and more to be ignorant about. In many domains, knowledge had proliferated far beyond the comprehension of the "layman".[33] Increasingly it had to be entrusted to a class of specialists, consecrated by professional and academic institutions, enjoying high prestige, confidence, and commensurate rewards, and

---

[33] In the modern sense of "A man who is an 'outsider' or a non-expert in relation to some particular profession, art, or branch of knowledge (esp. with reference to law and medicine)" (*OED*).

consulted for their expert advice. But there was disquiet too about this clerisy into whose hands so much was manumitted, to whose beady gaze—once solicited—no less than everything had to be submitted, whose expertise removed them to a chill distance from the people whose needs they served, and seemed to require a complete trust beyond disagreement or question (for nobody could challenge an expert but another expert). The second opinion was usually the last word. But who could be consulted about the consultants? The most highly evolved, most sapient of *homo sapiens*, was there not something about their very knowledge that made them, or some of them, less human than the rest?

The reason for this disquiet is to be found in the nature of the knowledge revolution, spearheaded by professional expertise. "Knowledge comes, but wisdom lingers," in the words of Tennyson, a poet whose abiding theme is misgiving about the direction of modernity;[34] and a sentimentalist like Dr Watson might observe that proliferating knowledge of the material world was not at all matched by an increase in human understanding. Science dealt with measurable material facts, scientific investigation was analytical, and analysing and magnifying material facts could lead the practitioner into an inability to see that there was anything else. In "A Medical Document" (in *Round the Red Lamp*), Conan Doyle has an alienist—a mental pathologist or "mad-doctor"—put it in this way, in conversation with other doctors.

"... Is it not a shocking thing—a thing to drive a reasoning man into absolute Materialism—to think that you may have a fine, noble fellow with every divine instinct and that some little vascular change, the dropping, we will say, of a minute spicule of bone from the inner table of his skull on to the surface of his brain, may have the effect of changing him to a filthy and pitiable creature with every low and debasing tendency?"

"Faith and hope," murmurs the general practitioner.

"I have no faith, not much hope, and all the charity I can afford," says the surgeon. "When theology squares itself with the facts of life I'll read it up." (*Red Lamp*, 209)

Still, it is time to pay attention to the quiet voice intercalated, in that exchange, between the voices of the two specialists.

[34] "Knowledge comes, but wisdom lingers, and I linger on the shore, | And the individual withers, and the world is more and more." "Locksley Hall", ll. 143–4, *Tennyson: A Selected Edition*, ed. Christopher Ricks (London: Longman, 1969), 190.

In general practice

Exactly as much as the consultant was associated with science and modernity, so the general practitioner by contrast was a traditional figure, representing a continuity with the clinical practices of the past, and with the art of healing. The ambitious young doctor, Elizabeth Gaskell's Harrison or George Eliot's Lydgate, bringing modern clinical skills and techniques into a provincial practice where these things were likely to be viewed with distrust, is a familiar figure in Victorian fiction. But it is a theme that reinforces the idea that scientific methods and instruments were associated with the metropolis and often seemed dangerously newfangled to patients (and doctors) used to the older ways of country practice.[35] "[T]he gap between science and medical practice—more particularly general practice—remained wide until well into the twentieth century," according to Anne Digby. "There were important scientific developments, notably in hospital-based surgery and in the development of germ theory, but therapeutics (i.e. the treatment of disease) changed much less dramatically than epistemology (i.e. the theory of the grounds of knowledge), so that the customary skills of bedside medicine remained important."[36] Conan Doyle gives a satirical portrait of an old-fashioned country doctor in "Behind the Times", a story in *Round the Red Lamp* about a reactionary old GP who is scornful of vaccination, chloroform, the stethoscope, and the germ theory of disease. The tale measures how far medicine has come in the nineteenth century, but also celebrates the virtues of a less instrument-and-drug dominated profession; the old doctor's modern young colleagues laugh at him behind his back but, falling ill themselves, they would call him in rather than each other.

For the general practitioner, clinical experience tended to take precedence over diagnostic aids. The American Daniel W. Cathell, in a popular conduct-book for aspiring doctors first published in 1881 and often reprinted, listed the equipment a new doctor was expected to have: microscope, stethoscope, laryngoscope, ophthalmoscope, spirit-lamp,

---

[35] See Mary Fitzwilliam, "'Mr Harrison's Confessions': A Study of the General Practitioner's Social and Professional Dis-ease in Mid-Nineteenth Century England", *Gaskell Society Journal*, 12 (1998), 28–36.

[36] Anne Digby, *Making a Medical Living: Doctors and Patients in the English Market for Medicine 1720–1911* (Cambridge: Cambridge University Press, 1994), 69.

test-tubes, reagents for testing specimens, and other modern aids to precision in diagnosis.[37] But this seems rather optimistic, and meanwhile there is a record of an English branch practice in Derbyshire in the 1920s whose battery of instruments consisted of a stethoscope and a thermometer.[38] Attention to external indicators—tongue, eyes, urine, and stools—gave way only gradually to a more scientific examination of patients, with measurement of pulse, temperature, and blood pressure. Traditional diagnosis was based on a whole-person, symptomatic approach rather than on the disease-centred, impersonal clinical practice of the new medicine. It was empirically rather than theoretically based, and in the nineteenth century, diagnosis for the GP "remained an inexact art rather than a precise science".[39]

One way to put this would be to say that traditional GPs had a pretty limited understanding of disease, and sometimes had little more to offer their patients than a comforting manner and an air of authority, and the certainty that the patient would sooner or later either die or recover. In the eyes of the consultants, the general practitioners who solicited their expert help must often have seemed bumbling, ignorant, provincial, and second-rate. But they probably did not seem so to their patients. Their skills in diagnosis and knowledge of procedures may not have been very impressive, but in many cases patient expectations cannot have been high either. So, in domiciliary practice the social personality of the doctor, and a good bedside manner, were always a factor. "By adopting a holistic approach to the whole person of their patients, GPs were attuned to an art of healing in which the personality of the doctor, and the faith of patients in their family doctor, were used as important weapons in a therapeutic armoury which in other respects remained restricted in scope."[40]

With this we approach a very important distinction between the GP and the consultant. The consultant, as we have seen, was brought in as an outsider, introduced to the patient only when the latter's condition was established and problematic, aloof by virtue of the scene of consultancy and no doubt also by the aura of his expertise, and in

---

[37] See Lilian R. Furst (ed.), *Medical Progress and Social Reality: A Reader in Nineteenth-Century Medicine and Literature* (Albany, NY: State University of New York Press, 2000), 291. Oddly, the list does not include a thermometer.

[38] Digby, *The Evolution of British General Practice*, 188.

[39] Digby, *Making a Medical Living*, 99.

[40] Digby, *The Evolution of British General Practice*, 17.

many cases answerable in his diagnosis not to the patient but to the referring physician, and therefore very likely to speak, sometimes literally, over the head of the patient. All this no doubt contributed to a persistent feeling that the consultant was cold, while militating against much interpersonal contact between consultant and sufferer. By contrast, the commerce between general practitioner and patient may have consisted of little else. General practice was the most personal, dialogical, and therefore the most ethical branch of medicine. The GP dealt with his interlocutor not only as a case but also as a human being, frequently a neighbour. The consultant came and went, or a visit was arranged to his consulting rooms, usually in a big city. But the GP was a local. This goes some way to explaining "the striking feature of practitioners in nineteenth-century fiction" noticed by Irvine Loudon, to wit "the contrast between the adulation of the general practitioner as family doctor and the unsympathetic view of the physician, especially the celebrated London physician".[41]

Establishing themselves in general practice was tough going for many young doctors in an overcrowded profession, and not many could hope to secure a competent living before they were approaching 40.[42] Some young men following in their father's footsteps might hope to inherit his practice. Others, if wealthy enough, might put up the money for a partnership, or buy a viable business from a retiring GP. For most, it was a matter of scouting out a promising location, without too strong competition from other doctors, and then building up a reputation there. "Developing a viable practice usually involved an individual doctor's ability to discern a practice niche,... the possession of social connection and/or social networking skills to develop it, and some managerial competencies in the allocation of resources to organize it."[43] Like clergymen, doctors in their neighbourhood were never really off duty, always on show, and their livelihood depended, more than the clergyman's, on local goodwill and standing. "Before you have practiced long," Daniel Cathell advised young doctors, "you will find that there are three classes of patients: the prompt-paying, the slow-paying, and the never-paying."[44] GPs were not entirely at the mercy of individual patients. Most of them also secured a number of medically related appointments, with nearby

[41] Loudon, *Medical Care and the GP*, 271.
[42] See Porter, *Disease, Medicine and Society*, 53.
[43] Digby, *The Evolution of British General Practice*, 13.
[44] In Furst (ed.), *Medical Progress and Social Reality*, 303.

hospitals or dispensaries, or as medical officer for the local Volunteer (later Territorial) regiment, factories, mines, railway or canal companies, clubs, schools, insurance companies, poor law unions, charities, and voluntary organizations. Such appointments brought in extra income and helped to solidify a doctor's reputation: they also networked the practitioner more firmly into his community.

As it happens, one of the best documented examples of this process, touched upon in my introductory chapter, is the career of Conan Doyle himself. He went into brief partnership with George Turnavine Budd—fictionalized as Cullingworth in *The Stark Munro Letters* and *Memories and Adventures*—who was notorious for his eccentric behaviour and policy of free consultation (he reasoned this would bring in so many patients that he could make a profit on dispensing). Budd's business plan was to attract patients in very large numbers by deliberately becoming a local celebrity. Though he wrote about it at length, this episode in Conan Doyle's medical career was short-lived. He was embarrassed by Budd's professional style, troubled by his dubious ethics, and in the end unable to cope with Budd's apparently paranoiac instability. Deciding to set up on his own, he surveyed Southsea ("Birchespool" in *The Stark Munro Letters*) like a seasoned campaigner, before settling on a solid-looking house in a promising area. Next it was a question of deciding matters such as where to place an announcement of the address of the practice, how much to charge for consultations and drugs, whom to approach and cultivate for potential patients and partners, individual or institutional. The point about all this is that it was *research*, the creation of a kind of knowledge which was just as vital to the GP as his knowledge of anatomy and clinical technique. He was, or aspired to be, the local man.

The consultant was professionally detached from community, a clinical nomad migrating from one case of his specialism to another, regardless of where they came from. Sherlock Holmes, the consulting detective, loathes every form of society, does not encourage social visitors, and has no friends at all apart from Watson.[45] But the foundation of a GP's practice was what Raymond Williams called the "knowable community".[46] Williams contended that the conditions

---

[45] He gives this bleak information to Watson in "The Five Orange Pips" in *Adventures*, 103.
[46] See Raymond Williams, *The Country and the City* (1973) (London: Hogarth Press, 1993), 165–81.

of modernity—the breaking up of rural ways of life, developments in
education, shifting patterns of work and relationship in family and
parish and neighbourhood—were making communities less knowable as the nineteenth century went on, a phenomenon traceable in
the work of the novelists. But if modernity is the destroyer of the
knowable community, this is another way in which the GP continued
to embody residual cultural practices, at least when contrasted with the
professionally alienated specialist. For the local doctor had to know his
community, and the community had to know him. This reciprocity of
knowledge was the necessary condition of successful practice.

Doctors could not advertise. (Stark Munro had a brass nameplate at
the front of the house and says he used to go out and polish it himself
under cover of darkness (*SM*, 248).[47]) But the GP whose practice
depended largely on word-of-mouth reputation had to put himself
about. One way to do this was by writing. The new doctor in Southsea
was soon busy writing letters for publication in the Portsmouth *Evening
News* and *Evening Mail*, the *Hampshire Post*, and the *Hampshire County
Times*.[48] Some are on medical subjects and these are signed A. Conan
Doyle M.D., C.M. But others are on literary or political subjects, or
local matters. They announce and practise the young man's membership of the community. They are affirmations of neighbourhood. The
same motive lies behind the extraordinarily energetic way in which he
plunged into the social, cultural, and sporting life of Southsea and
Portsmouth.[49] His early psychic researches grew out of friendships
with a local architect and a retired general who was his patient. He
addressed political meetings in the Liberal Unionist interest. He joined
the Freemasons, a shrewd move for a young professional on the lookout for useful local contacts and goodwill.[50] He was a member of the
local bowls and cricket clubs, and became a founder of the Portsmouth
Football Association Club (he played in goal). Even in his self-
characterization as a sportsman he sounds like a general practitioner,

[47] Conan Doyle says he himself performed this office every morning. *M&A*, 63.
[48] ACD, *Letters to the Press*, ed. John Michael Gibson and Richard Lancelyn Green
(Iowa City: University of Iowa Press, 1986), 16–37.
[49] See Stavert, *A Study in Southsea*.
[50] Between 4% and 12% of general practitioners were known to be Freemasons. Digby,
The Evolution of British General Practice, 80. Conan Doyle resigned from the Masons after
two years, though he rejoined fifteen years later. See Stavert, *A Study in Southsea*, 94–5.

for he never specialized, but was an "all-rounder" (*M&A*, 269).[51] Perhaps above all there was the Portsmouth Literary and Scientific Society. He was a stalwart of this highly Victorian institution, addressing them on the subject of his own Arctic travels—a lecture enlivened, if that is the word, by a selection of twenty stuffed birds borrowed from a local taxidermist. He also lectured to the Society on his literary hero Thomas Carlyle, and attended lectures by other members. He may have first become interested in Spiritualism as a result of conversations with Major-General Alfred Drayson, the president of the Literary and Scientific Society who also became one of the first members of the Society for Psychical Research.[52]

I earlier described general practice as a dialogical practice of medicine. This is part of what I meant, the accumulation and fostering of reputation and trust among local people through continuous face-to-face contact in a range of activities. This social profile, secured by his knowledge of the community and the community's knowledge of him, is the exterior dimension of the famous "bedside manner", that balance of authority and familiarity that was the most valuable skill deployed in the GP's dealings with patients, often over a long time and often too as physician not only to the "whole person", but also to whole families: the family doctor frequently became a valued arbitrator and authority in domestic difficulties.[53] The specialist was called in only in the crisis of serious illness, but the general practitioner saw many of his patients in their everyday lives, in sickness and in health.

There appears to be, in Conan Doyle, an intuition that such mundane human interactions with his patients were inclined to keep the GP on an even keel, whereas the consultant, perhaps working at the outer edge of knowledge and habitually on critical cases, was subject to particular ethical temptations. An example is the brilliant and arrogant society surgeon Douglas Stone, in the story "The Case of Lady Sannox". "Again and again his knife cut away death, but grazed the very springs of life in doing it, until his assistants were as white as the patient" (*Red Lamp*, 157). But his own powers and daring are the downfall of this surgical Übermensch, who begins an adulterous affair, and is then

---

[51] The general practitioner was thought of as "the all-rounder of medical practice". Digby, *The Evolution of British General Practice*, 287.

[52] Not to be confused with Conan Doyle's other Spiritualist friend from the Southsea days, Lieutenant-General Thomas Harward.

[53] See Porter, *Disease, Medicine and Society*, 64.

tricked by the wronged husband, in a bizarre and revolting plot, into performing a disfiguring surgical operation without anaesthetic on the woman he loves, taking his knife to her mouth; the shock destroys him, leaving "his great brain about as valuable as a cap full of porridge" (*Red Lamp*, 156–7). Such is the fate of the phallic specialist, led into temptation by his selfishness, pride, and greed.[54] It is hard to imagine anything of this kind happening to a general practitioner, at least in the pages of Conan Doyle, and one explanation is given at the end of "The Surgeon Talks", the final story in *Round the Red Lamp*, where the following ethical theory of domiciliary medical practice is advanced.

It is such a pleasure to do a little good that a man should pay for the privilege instead of being paid for it. Still, of course, he has his home to keep up and his wife and children to support. But his patients are his friends—or they should be so. He goes from house to house, and his step and his voice are loved and welcomed in each. What could a man ask for more than that? And besides, he is forced to be a good man. It is impossible for him to be anything else. How can a man spend his whole life in seeing suffering bravely borne and yet remain a hard or a vicious man? (*Red Lamp*, 327–8)

But these are the comfortable sentiments of the after-dinner speech.[55] There was indeed an organic relation between the practitioner and the community he served, but it would not do to idealize it. Conan Doyle was himself a moderately successful doctor.[56] Everything we know about the culture he participated in at Southsea suggests it was thoroughly provincial, intellectually mediocre, and bourgeois. Medical training was expensive, which meant that doctors were middle class, though Anne Digby notes that recruitment to the Victorian medical profession seems generally to have been from people of modest social backgrounds in comparison with the two other traditional professions of the law and the Church.[57] The local doctor's life was not equally

[54] Lady Sannox meanwhile, who does not have a speaking part in the story, suffers torture and loses her lover, her husband, and her beauty.

[55] They are not sentiments shared by Sherlock Holmes, as he tells Watson in "The Speckled Band": "When a doctor does go wrong, he is the first of criminals. He has nerve and he has knowledge" (*Adventures*, 192).

[56] This is not an opinion universally shared. "In the field of medicine he was much less than mediocre, and literature's gain probably saved many lives." Pasquale Accardo, *Diagnosis and Detection: The Medical Iconography of Sherlock Holmes* (London: Associated University Press, 1987), 14. No evidence is advanced in support of this view.

[57] Digby, *The Evolution of British General Practice*, 40. She adds that Daisy Countess of Warwick ruled that doctors and solicitors might be invited to garden parties though never, of course, to lunch or dinner.

integrated into all the community's social groups: his step and his voice were not necessarily "loved and welcomed" in every house. Conan Doyle was a Victorian gentleman and so were almost all his friends. But his work in general practice did bring him into intimate and continuing contact with all social ranks, in a way probably not matched by any other job at that time, even the clergy. A general practice in medicine, especially in a town, brought an accumulation of knowledge of a broad spectrum of people, both in their everyday lives and sometimes *in extremis*, that proved an invaluable asset to the writer. It was a kind of knowledge not available to the consultant, whose patients were usually expected to come to him, in his consulting rooms or clinic. Though his fees were higher, it is conceivable that a specialist would have seen patients from among the poor, but their relation would not have been long term. It would have been a "case". But—leaving aside the question of his clinical competence—the GP's practice was socially ecumenical, his bedside manner was for everyone, and it was warm. With less scientific expertise at their disposal, general practitioners were obliged to draw more heavily on their instinct and emotion in their work.

While (to repeat) we are dealing with two different kinds of clinical practices, two different kinds of knowledge, and two different career paths, it can also be said in general terms that general practice had more of the characteristics of the traditional art of healing, while consultants were considered, and thought of themselves, as exemplars of a modern science of medicine. "During the century between 1850 and 1948 a transition was perceived to have occurred from the social skills of the bedside manner to more scientific accomplishment," says Anne Digby, who sums up the contrast: "Traditional medicine was centred in symptomatic diagnosis and a humane interaction with the patient, whilst modern medicine relied to a much greater extent on precise and mechanistic measurements achieved with instruments, together with powerful pharmaceuticals that cured rather than palliated the disease."[58] The traditional ways were not strong in therapeutic power, and often the more old-fashioned doctor had little to offer but intuition based on experience, and the humane and caring quality of his personality, conveyed through speech with the patient. Meanwhile the

---

[58] Digby, *The Evolution of British General Practice*, 304, 187.

thoroughly modern medical specialist operating as consultant could draw on the very impressive record of scientific advances in medical knowledge, instruments, and drugs, but often seems to have been subject to the interpersonal shortcomings that expertise is heir to: impatience, rudeness, snobbery, narrow-mindedness. There was a conservatism in the Victorian medical profession which hampered the ordinary practitioner's ability to make accurate diagnoses (with a resistance to new scientific methods developed in Germany, for example), thus perpetuating a traditional form of bedside medicine.[59] And the grandees of the profession perpetuated this divide in their own interest, with the medical schools staffed by a professoriate of specialists who neglected the key skills and attributes valuable for general practice, and very few general practitioners involved in teaching.[60]

So on one side we have the knowledge and practice embodied in the consultant, the science of medicine, modern, materialistic, specialist, rational, impersonal, alienated, and cold; and on the other side the knowledge and practice of the GP, with his art of healing, traditional, humanistic, generalist (the "all-rounder"), compassionate, interpersonal, local, and warm. Real life is rarely as neat as the structural models we can build to describe it, and modernity never proceeds at an even pace or in a straight line; furthermore, the point has already been made that these two modalities of medicine coexisted interdependently: neither could have operated without the other. But having said all that, it is still possible to say that in Conan Doyle's lifetime the former can be described as the emergent, the latter as a residual form of medical and other professional practice: if anyone was set fair to take over the world, it was going to be the expert. And there is another parameter to add.

The general practitioner was more intuitive than cerebral, his realm was largely domiciliary with its home visits and bedside medicine and care for families, and he sometimes offered little more than comfort and compassion. Compared to the consultant, his was a subordinate grade, with no prospects of outstanding worldly success. He was associated with domestic ministrations (he was not above nursing) rather than with the advanced impersonal treatments and scientific instruments of the hospital and clinical laboratory. What I am suggesting is

---

[59] Digby, *Making a Medical Living*, 102.
[60] The world's first professorial chair in general practice was established at Conan Doyle's university, Edinburgh—in 1963.

that the opposition I have described had a gender dimension. The consultant was not only the figure of modernity, but also of masculinity, while the GP had many of the qualities and functions the Victorians associated with femininity.[61] Before taking these ideas back to the scene in Baker Street, I will call in evidence Francis Galton, explorer and statistician and anthropometrist and—as everyone remembers—a cousin of Charles Darwin.[62] In 1874 Galton conducted a survey of the leading Victorian scientists, many of whom he knew personally, and published his conclusions, including the following.

The female mind has special excellencies of a high order, and the value of its influence in various ways is one that I can never consent to underrate; but that influence is towards enthusiasm and love (as distinguished from philanthropy), not towards calm judgement, nor, inclusively, towards science. In many respects the character of scientific men is strongly anti-feminine; their mind is directed to facts and abstract theories, and not to persons or human interests. The man of science is deficient in the purely emotional element, and in the desire to influence the beliefs of others.... In many respects they [scientists] have little sympathy with female ways of thought.[63]

This brings us back to Sherlock Holmes, John Watson, and Mary Morstan.

The cold detective

Sherlock Holmes is not a doctor. In fact, at the beginning of *A Study in Scarlet*, there is some uncertainty among his friends as to just what he is. He has been working at the chemical laboratory up at the hospital, so Watson assumes he is a medical student, but is corrected by his friend Stamford. Holmes is "an enthusiast in some branches of science" but it is not known "what he intends to go in for" (*Study*, 7). Nevertheless, when Watson first meets Holmes it is an encounter that takes place literally in

---

[61] This gender marking belonged also to the profession of the clergy, and for similar reasons.

[62] Conan Doyle probably knew Galton's work on heredity (see Lycett, *Arthur Conan Doyle*, 112, 122), and Sherlock Holmes certainly knew Galton's contributions to criminology. See Ronald R. Thomas, *Detective Fiction and the Rise of Forensic Science* (Cambridge: Cambridge University Press, 1999).

[63] Francis Galton, *English Men of Science: Their Nature and Nurture* (1874), 2nd edn. (London: Frank Cass, 1970), 206–7.

the odour of medical science. They meet in the hospital laboratory. Holmes flourishes a test-tube, and greets Watson—"You have been in Afghanistan, I perceive"—with the kind of virtuoso appraisal Conan Doyle acknowledged having borrowed from his favourite teacher Dr Joseph Bell of Edinburgh, the best known of the models for the great detective. Watson has already been told of another of Holmes's habits, beating the corpses in the dissecting-rooms with a stick to verify how far bruises may be produced after death. This also has its origin in the lore of the Edinburgh medical establishment, in forensic experiments carried out by Professor Robert Christison, nicknamed "Dignity Bob" and known for his cold and imperious manner, and "the great legendary figure of the University" in Conan Doyle's day.[64] Of course, these Edinburgh echoes lie below the surface of the initial portrait of Holmes, but they may be partly responsible for imparting its temperature. Owen Dudley Edwards has discussed "the inhumane attitudes towards patients" that Conan Doyle observed at Edinburgh, arguing that his "indictment of the Edinburgh University faculty for its lovelessness" did not except Joseph Bell, and helps to explain "the less pleasant aspects of Holmes".[65] For Watson's friend Stamford, in any case, the flogging of the corpses is enough: he complains that it is "a little too scientific for my tastes—it approaches to cold-bloodedness" (*Study*, 8).

Watson is not put off by this, and soon the two have settled in to the rooms they share in Baker Street, and Watson begins to satisfy his curiosity about his new companion. What emerges is the portrait of a consultant. There are government detectives (here Lestrade's name is mentioned for the first time) and private ones, Holmes explains, and when they are at a loss they come to him. The strange assortment of visitors who come to Baker Street are clients, he continues, describing the classic process of referral.

They are mostly sent on by private inquiry agencies. They are all people who are in trouble about something and want a little enlightening. I listen to their story, they listen to my comments, and then I pocket my fee. (*Study*, 20)

---

[64] Owen Dudley Edwards, *The Quest for Sherlock Holmes: A Biographical Study of Arthur Conan Doyle* (Harmondsworth: Penguin, 1984), 193. Edwards finds traces of Christison in Holmes, Moriarty, and Challenger. His whole chapter on Edinburgh, "Athens or Sparta" (177–220), is of great interest. It ends with the statement that Conan Doyle was "the greatest celebrant" of the Edinburgh medical faculty, then adds: "But for their coldness, which so closely reminded him of Sparta, he substituted that artistic warmth which elicited that somewhere concealed by Sparta, Athens survived" (220).

[65] Edwards, *The Quest for Sherlock Holmes*, 200, 201.

He sounds patronizing, if not cynical, about the people who come to him for help, but Holmes is not conspicuously generous about anyone. He disparages his referrers including Lestrade ("got himself into a fog recently"), the famous fictional detectives Dupin ("a very inferior fellow") and Lecoq ("a miserable bungler"), and even the crimes and criminals brought to his attention, which are unworthy of his pre-eminent powers (*Study*, 20–2). He is a bully too. The expert who despises his inferiors is an authority on the way to becoming an authoritarian.

The Sherlock Holmes of *A Study in Scarlet*, the Ur-Sherlock, is more satirized, more of a consultant, and more cold, than in his next appearance in *The Sign of the Four*. Mary Morstan in the later story is not referred to him, but consults him on a recommendation by her employer Mrs Cecil Forrester; this is how a new patient might come to a GP. But in *A Study in Scarlet*, Holmes is brought in to the Jefferson Hope case by Gregson, the Scotland Yard man, in recognition of his own inability to deal with a baffling case. The consultancy is initiated by a manumission in the classic professional form, a letter from Gregson setting out in full the details of the case, and soliciting Holmes's help with an invitation to come round and inspect the body, or, if he is unable to come, to give an expert opinion. Holmes feels this is an appropriate *démarche* from the subordinate grade—"He knows that I am his superior, and acknowledges it to me" (*Study*, 25)—and agrees to go.

At Lauriston Gardens he finds both policemen, the professional rivals Gregson and Lestrade (they call him "sir"), and while making his own examination of the scene he speaks patronizingly and sarcastically to them, and laughs at Lestrade's own deductions. Lestrade blusters, as might any stick-in-the-mud GP out of his depth: "You may be very smart and clever, but the old hound is the best, when all is said and done" (*Study*, 32).[66] But the consultant has already decided to bypass his referrers in the case; he does not want their help or interference. "If I fail," he tells Gregson and Lestrade later, "I shall, of course, incur all the blame due to this omission; but that I am prepared for" (*Study*, 64). This too is as it should be. When the case is referred to the specialist it becomes his case, and he assumes clinical responsibility for it.

---

[66] The consultant is advanced in equipment as well as in knowledge. Holmes uses the latest brand of automatically locking handcuffs and recommends them patronizingly to Lestrade, but the policeman prefers the old pattern (*Study*, 65).

Holmes's own rapid and expert observations on the scene at Lauriston Gardens are enough, and when they leave the house Holmes tells Watson, astonishingly, that his mind is already entirely made up on the case, though some details remain to be learned. But he has neglected to share all of what he has discovered with the police—"You are doing so well now that it would be a pity for anyone to interfere," he tells them cruelly (*Study*, 33)—apparently because he enjoys the sight of their bungling ignorance, and perhaps to enhance the mystique and authority of his expertise. Nor does he share his conclusions with Watson at this stage. This refusal to disclose what has come to his knowledge till it can be revealed in an impressive *coup de théâtre* will be, of course, habitual, and Holmes will often take what looks like a sadistic pleasure in leaving others, principally Watson and of course the reader, floundering in his wake. But he is not the first or last expert to hide what he knows in a cloud of flamboyant obscurity.[67]

All this is, of course, enjoyable, and impressive in its way, though Holmes is hardly being portrayed here, in his debut, as a particularly humane character. We have no reason to care much about the way Lestrade and Gregson are humiliated in the scene of consultancy (and they are too doltish to register much of Holmes's mockery). They have in any case consulted Holmes to relieve themselves of responsibility for the case, and they will in the end get the credit for his work. But there is the presence of Watson on the scene to consider, and he is neither consultant, referrer, nor patient, but witness.

Holmes is undoubtedly masterful; and we never doubt that he is right. But Conan Doyle also piles onto his character, for the purposes of his comedy, many of the qualities—arrogance, snobbery, lack of feeling, and the rest—which, Owen Dudley Edwards avers, he had encountered in the medical panjandrums at Edinburgh. And these were also qualities which inclined lay people to be resentful and even fearful of the growing army of expertise, including medical consultants, even while acknowledging a need for their help. When Watson—a war veteran, let us recall—enters the death room at Lauriston Gardens,

---

[67] Holmes is not above scholarly one-upmanship—"It reminds me of the circumstances attendant on the death of Van Jansen, in Utrecht, in the year '34. Do you remember the case, Gregson?" (*Study*, 29)—but at least he has not the consultant's fondness for obfuscating and depressing specialist jargon. The association of professionalism—in all sorts of fields—with a culture of distance and abstraction is discussed in Bruce Robbins, *Secular Vocations: Intellectuals, Professionalism, Culture* (London: Verso, 1993), 57–83.

he does so, he says, "with that subdued feeling at my heart which the presence of death inspires"; he describes the corpse in meticulous detail, but adds that never had death appeared to him in a more fearsome aspect (*Study*, 27, 28). But Holmes, as far as we can see, is completely unmoved by what he has come to inspect. Here is how he handles the case.

As he spoke, his nimble fingers were flying here, there, and everywhere, feeling, pressing, unbuttoning, examining, while his eyes wore the same faraway expression which I have already remarked upon. So swiftly was the examination made, that one would hardly have guessed the minuteness with which it was conducted. Finally, he sniffed the dead man's lips, and then glanced at the soles of his patent leather boots.

"He has not been moved at all?" he asked.

"No more than was necessary for the purposes of our examination."

"You can take him to the mortuary now," he said. "There is nothing more to be learned." (*Study*, 29)

Enoch Drebber is a dead man, of course, not a living patient. But there is something chilling about the way Holmes ransacks his body for information, in a manner which is both highly intimate and completely without affect. This is the cold consultant at his work, his abstraction and human distance signalled in that faraway look with which Watson is familiar, and so are we.[68]

The expert is an expert through specialization. His knowledge is profound, but uneven. Conan Doyle, or perhaps we should say Watson, has already satirized the ruthless narrow-mindedness of the specialist in the simplest way, drawing up a chart of his friend's limits in humanistic knowledge ("Knowledge of Literature—Nil. Knowledge of Philosophy—Nil", and so on). Holmes seems to have succeeded in bypassing General Education entirely in his drive to acquire the specialist knowledge which is his profession. Watson describes the case in a famous passage.

His ignorance was as remarkable as his knowledge. Of contemporary literature, philosophy and politics he appeared to know next to nothing. Upon my quoting Thomas Carlyle, he inquired in the naïvest way who he might be and

---

[68] Holmes is not exactly performing an autopsy, but again the scene has a distinctly medical character. His methods certainly seem to participate in what David Armstrong has called the emergence around the turn of the nineteenth century of "new techniques to make the body legible". David Armstrong, "Bodies of Knowledge/Knowledge of Bodies", in Jones and Porter (eds.), *Reassessing Foucault*, 17–27; at 25.

what he had done. My surprise reached a climax, however, when I found incidentally that he was ignorant of the Copernican Theory and of the composition of the Solar System. That any civilized human being in this nineteenth century should not be aware that the earth travelled round the sun appeared to me to be such an extraordinary fact that I could hardly realize it. (*Study*, 15)

This little paragraph is so interesting, on the topics of knowledge and modernity, that I will risk anatomizing its comedy. Watson "could hardly realize" Holmes's ignorance about cosmology; it is so extraordinary as to be virtually unthinkable by him. Why? It is anachronistic. In "this nineteenth century", everybody knows the earth goes round the sun. It is general knowledge. And of all knowledge, this item is the most definitive of the modern world. Modern people know the earth goes round the sun. How? Science told us, in the form of the calculations and theorizing of Copernicus (and something about Galileo and his telescope): the Copernican theory, which was right, replaced the geocentric Ptolemaic theory, which was wrong. So how to explain, or even realize, the scientific Holmes's amazing primitivism?

The shift from the Ptolemaic to the Copernican theory is the prime example, in Thomas Kuhn's 1962 book *The Structure of Scientific Revolutions*, of what Kuhn calls a paradigm shift.[69] Kuhn argued that the history of science is not to be understood as a process of learning more and more facts about the universe, but in terms of changes in the credibility of concepts. There was nothing wrong with the Ptolemaic theory that the sun goes round the earth, which is a perfectly serviceable way of thinking about things, and there was nothing inevitable about its displacement by the Copernican theory. When the revolutionary science of Copernicus and Kepler produced a new concept, it struggled with the established belief about the universe until it gained acceptance and the paradigm shift became scientific orthodoxy; but initially a change in the paradigm seemed to most people not only unnecessary, but ridiculous, if not actually unthinkable. It could hardly be realized.

What Sherlock Holmes has unwittingly accomplished, to the horror of Watson, is a paradigm shift *back*, from a modern to a pre-modern model of the cosmos, and the common-sense Watson is appalled by

---

[69] See Thomas S. Kuhn, *The Structure of Scientific Revolutions* (Chicago: University of Chicago Press, 1962).

this because it goes against what he has been taught to recognize as scientific progress and its superiority to earlier ways of understanding. But as a matter of fact it is Holmes who is the more modern—actually, postmodern—of the two, for he is a Kuhnian *avant la lettre* in his attitude to knowledge. It would make no difference to him in practice, he says, if the earth went round the moon; it is not that he thinks Copernicus was wrong, but rather that he does not care whether he was right. As far as he is concerned, such questions pertain not to knowledge, but to belief, and they are beside the point. Watson thinks he— and every "civilized human being in this nineteenth century"—knows certain truths about the world, including that it goes round the sun. This is part of the shared fund of knowledge on which civilized modernity is built. Common knowledge is the basis of common sense. But Holmes is ready to deconstruct common knowledge, and common sense, as merely phenomena of shared belief, belonging (as he does not put it) to ideology and not to the real. This is not of course because he is a poststructuralist, but because he is a utilitarian materialist. He says he will not clutter his mind with useless lumber; he wants to save all his mental storage space for useful facts. After all, what good has it ever done Watson to know that the earth goes round the sun (if it does)? What difference does it make? Watson would no doubt reply that general knowledge is good in itself—and we are back to the division between the specialist and the generalist, because Holmes is devoted not to general but to special knowledge, and has no humanistic concept of knowledge as a whole. Knowledge for him is atomized, or anatomized, chopped up into functional bits, over some of which he stakes a monopoly claim. "He said that he would acquire no knowledge which did not bear upon his subject" (*Study*, 16). Expert knowledge gives him mastery, because it is convertible into practice, profession, and power. In a modern knowledge economy increasingly favouring the specialist holding expertise as a commodity, general knowledge—such as what goes round what—is the epistemological small change which can be left to people like Watson. As expert knowledge moves further beyond the reach of lay people (and itself increasingly has to be taken on trust), common knowledge is increasingly discounted. It is about as valuable as "culture", the faculty of knowing things like who Thomas Carlyle was and what he had done.

Thus the Ur-Holmes, the Holmes of *A Study in Scarlet* where he has most of the qualities of the medical specialist, is also the least humane manifestation of the character, narrow-minded, uncultured, vain, arrogant, and cold-blooded for all his brilliance.[70] In the decades of his subsequent career in the novels and stories that followed, in the unfolding of the age of expertise which he embodied, Sherlock Holmes did not lose the alienating qualities that so often adhere to those who are bearers of a knowledge beyond our own powers, which we think we need, and are obliged to trust. Yet the character does change, a change that is already afoot in his next outing in *The Sign of the Four*. Holmes gets a little warmer as he gets closer, in more than one sense, to the general practitioner.

The Sign of the Four contains, in Thaddeus Sholto, a portrait of the useless decadent aesthete which was just as pointed as the portrait of the heartless utilitarian scientist in the person of Holmes in the earlier book. But Holmes, the man whose knowledge of philosophy and literature was nil, according to Watson in *A Study in Scarlet*, now starts to show some unexpected cultural resources. We already knew that he was musical, though Watson suspected his violin-playing was largely an aid to excogitation (*Study*, 17). Now it appears Holmes is given to quoting La Rochefoucauld in French, and Goethe in German. His cultural rehabilitation extends to a knowledge of Richter, and of Carlyle, whom he had never heard of in the earlier book. Though he has not lost the habits of the specialist, he now treats Watson in conversation to a torrent of his general knowledge, as if eager to correct the first impression he gave of narrow-mindedness.

I have never known him so brilliant. He spoke on a quick succession of subjects—on miracle plays, on medieval pottery, on Stradivarius violins, on the Buddhism of Ceylon, and on the warships of the future—handling each as though he had made a special study of it. (*Sign*, 79)

This sort of thing is at odds with the ruthless philistinism of old. But if Holmes has acquired signs of a humanistic cultural knowledge, he appears to have made advances in ethics too. We might recall that the job description he gave of his consultancy, early in *A Study in Scarlet*, was couched in terms of problem-solving, in the service of clients "who are in trouble about something and want a little enlightening" (*Study*, 20).

---

[70] It is entirely appropriate that Holmes should more than meet his match in professional cold-bloodedness in the baleful person of Professor Moriarty, whom the great consulting detective describes as "this great consultant in crime". ACD, *The Valley of Fear* (1915), ed. Owen Dudley Edwards (Oxford: Oxford University Press, 1993), 169. Hereafter *Valley*.

The process he describes is cybernetic, a transaction of information. Justice is not mentioned—indeed it is a word Holmes never utters in the book. At the conclusion of the novel, when the murderer Jefferson Hope dies before being brought before the magistrate, Watson comments piously that a higher Judge has taken the matter in hand, "and Jefferson Hope had been summoned before a tribunal where strict justice would be meted out to him" (*Study*, 122). Holmes's only reaction to the death is to remark that Lestrade and Gregson will be annoyed; he spends the concluding chapter on an exposition of his analytical methodology, and ends by observing that he himself has been given no credit for solving the case. Nor does justice have any part to play in the second account of his consultancy that he gives, early in *The Sign of the Four*. As we saw the excitement of the consulting venereologist in "The Third Generation" when he came upon such a well-marked case of syphilis, so Holmes seems to relish the problems laid before him like a collector—the policeman Athelney Jones is right to call him "a connoisseur of crime" (*Sign*, 118). Again, he will never lose this habit of savouring difficult problems, and his own skill in solving them, for their own sake. But he also has to take into account questions of justice, and the story of *The Sign of the Four* is indeed a case in point.

For in that story, Jonathan Small is a murderer, but he is also a victim, and has exacted his revenge on behalf of other victims, his Indian associates. His crime has been detected by the consultant detective using his analytical, instrumental, and cybernetic resources (his scene-of-crime skills, Toby the tracker dog, and the London-wide intelligence web of the Baker Street Irregulars). But though the detection of the crime has been successfully completed, and the baffling problem about which Holmes was consulted by Mary Morstan has been elucidated, Holmes acknowledges that there is still a deficit of *ethical* knowledge without which the crime cannot be understood, and for this he solicits the criminal's own narrative.

"You forget that we know nothing of all this," said Holmes quietly. "We have not heard your story, and we cannot tell how far justice may originally have been on your side." (*Sign*, 96)[71]

---

[71] Jonathan Small's crime is humanized by his own first-personal story, told to Holmes and the others. Interestingly, this is a formal problem which *A Study in Scarlet* failed to solve, with the unmotivated and unexplained protrusion of the five third-person-narrated American chapters from within Watson's narrative (*Study*, 69–110).

Small then tells the story of the Four, the three Indians and the work-ing-class British soldier, tricked out of a fortune by their officers. Their fate, and their loyalty to one another, surely represents a challenge to Jon Thompson's view that Conan Doyle's fiction "pushes to the mar-gins almost every potentially disruptive subject imaginable—racism, imperialism, class conflict, even women".[72]

Moments of this kind are a response to Conan Doyle's concern that knowledge as it becomes more specialized should not lose its human face, or its ethical responsibilities, as was the danger if knowledge was pursued for its own sake. I do not mean to suggest that a cultured, humane, and ethical Holmes replaces and redeems the narrow-minded materialistic egotist that Conan Doyle first conceived in the character. But it is the case that some of that dialogue between scientist and humanist is now enacted *within* Holmes himself, and a warmer, more compassionate current can now sometimes be found flowing in the veins of the cold consultant detective. Its source, it seems obvious, is the proximity and example of the simple-minded, intellectually dim Watson, whose establishment in general practice in Paddington (or Kensington) has not brought his friendship with Holmes to an end. Holmes never stops taunting and teasing and mystifying Watson, with all the consultant's sense of superiority to the subordinate grade. But he is sometimes capable of recognizing in Watson qualities that he does not himself possess, the virtues of the ordinary which the specialist has left behind, virtues Conan Doyle associated with the traditions and institutions of the nation's culture. This recognition plays out dramati-cally at the end of "The Abbey Grange", another ethically compli-cated case in which Holmes has to decide what to do with a man he knows to be guilty of murder but is reluctant to hand over to the police. He decides to take on "a great responsibility".

"See here, Captain Croker, we'll do this in due form of law. You are the pris-oner. Watson, you are a British jury, and I never met a man who was more eminently fitted to represent one. I am the judge. Now, gentlemen of the jury, you have heard the evidence. Do you find the prisoner guilty or not guilty?"

"Not guilty, my lord," said I. (*Return*, 290)

It is not often, even so, that the consultant consults the general prac-titioner.

[72] Jon Thompson, *Fiction, Crime and Empire: Clues to Modernity and Postmodernism* (Urbana, Ill.: University of Illinois Press, 1993), 68.

MEDICINE 77

There is an odd coda to this story of the cold consultant. I have suggested that Sherlock Holmes is most completely a consultant in his first tale, *A Study in Scarlet*, and that later the features of consultancy—professional, philosophical, and temperamental—were sometimes tempered by humanistic qualities more associated with the figure of the general practitioner and Watson in particular. But *The Hound of the Baskervilles* seems to be an exception to this pattern. In *The Hound*, serialized in the *Strand* in 1901–2, Conan Doyle returned to the detective in an adventure set before his great struggle with Moriarty, and in doing so he reprised the character as the uncompromising consultant we first met in *A Study in Scarlet*.

In many of the tales, as we have seen, Holmes's clients (such as Mary Morstan) come to him by word-of-mouth recommendation, as new patients might come to a general practitioner. But *The Hound* begins by reverting to a classic scene of consultancy, in which a provincial general practitioner, Dr Mortimer, manumits to the London specialist a dangerous case, confessing himself baffled, but also offering his own ludicrously old-fashioned and unscientific gloss (the Baskerville legend), which the specialist immediately and rudely dismisses as fit for "a collection of fairy tales".[73] Holmes accepts the case, gathers information, and secures a promise from Sir Henry Baskerville that he will obey his instructions. But he declines to accompany Sir Henry to Dartmoor, preferring to consign him to the day-to-day care of Dr Watson, who is to send regular reports to Holmes in London. Watson and Sir Henry become friends, sharing the domestic life of Baskerville Hall. As a matter of fact, and without telling Watson, Holmes does travel to Dartmoor, pretending to be a tourist and squatting in an old stone hut on the moor with a commanding view of the cardinal points of the case, Baskerville Hall, Grimpen Moor, and the Stapleton house. This bizarre move ("my presence would have warned our very formidable opponents to be on their guard" (*Hound*, 124), he explains weakly to Watson afterwards) makes little sense in terms of realistic motivation, but is entirely consistent with the consultant's aloofness, self-mystification, and taste for scopic superiority.[74]

[73] ACD, *The Hound of the Baskervilles* (1902), ed. W. W. Robson (Oxford: Oxford University Press, 1993), 14. Hereafter *Hound*.

[74] The aloof viewpoint of superior vantage and superior knowledge recurs in the returned Holmes's narrative, in "The Empty House", of how after his encounter with Moriarty at Reichenbach he looked down on a distraught Watson investigating "in the most sympathetic and inefficient manner" his apparent death (*Return*, 10).

This strange and reckless aloofness is unfair to Watson, and probably
endangers Sir Henry Baskerville, but Holmes is once again intent on
the case rather than on the welfare of the man whose life has been
entrusted to him. "Our case becomes rounded off," he tells Watson.
"I shall soon be in the position of being able to put into a single connected narrative one of the most singular and sensational crimes of
modern times" (*Hound*, 145). But the human consequences of his fastidious delay are nearly fatal, for a sudden fog rises (the weather on
Dartmoor being an elementary piece of local knowledge neglected by
the London specialist), disarranging Holmes's plans, and Sir Henry is
attacked by the hound, and suffers a nervous breakdown in consequence.[75] The last chapter finds Sir Henry, his nerves shattered, embarking on a long cure in the care of Mortimer the GP, and Holmes "in
excellent spirits" over his success in this and other cases (*Hound*, 158).
It has been a very good case for the cold consultant. The most striking
visual image of the story, though, remains the sight Watson had seen on
the moor in the moonlight, as he lifted his eyes and saw a mysterious
man above him, heroic, forbidding, and set apart.

There, outlined as black as an ebony statue on that shining background, I saw
the figure of a man upon the tor. . . . He stood with his legs a little separated,
his arms folded, his head bowed, as if he were brooding over that enormous
wilderness of peat and granite which lay behind him. He might have been the
very spirit of that terrible place. (*Hound*, 98)

Though at the time Watson does not realize it, this distant man of
stone is the Napoleon of consultants, Sherlock Holmes.

---

[75] "You have saved my life," Sir Henry tells Holmes. "Having first endangered it,"
Holmes admits (*Hound*, 152).

4

Science

The curious adventure in Berlin

A large number of the important themes of Arthur Conan Doyle's life, his intellectual character, and the emergence of his vocation cluster in the story of a trip he made to Berlin in 1890, with the purpose of attending a scientific lecture. He tells the story in a chapter of *Memories and Adventures* entitled "Pulling Up the Anchor" in token of his own reading of late 1890 as a turning point in his career and life (*M&A*, 82–92). The Berlin episode constituted a decisive turn in his relation to the professions and discourses of writing and medicine, to science and art, and to the provincial, metropolitan, and continental scene. It dramatized the issue of the professional's responsibility to society. It foregrounded questions of nationality and ethnicity. It provided him with a model of the heroic investigator combating dangerous antagonists, to be developed in the serial figures of Sherlock Holmes and Professor Challenger. The Berlin adventure was in many ways a critical point in Conan Doyle's evolution as man of letters, and it merits a thick description.

In mid-November 1890, Conan Doyle, a 31-year-old provincial doctor in general practice with the beginnings of a reputation as a writer of fiction, decided on the spur of the moment to travel to Berlin, to attend a demonstration of a cure for tuberculosis announced by Professor Robert Koch, the celebrated German bacteriologist. "[A]t a few hours' notice," he recalled years later, "I packed up a bag and started off alone upon this curious adventure" (*M&A*, 88). He went up to London from Portsmouth, collected some letters of introduction, and hurried on to the Continent that same night, meeting on the train a smart London doctor, Malcolm Morris, who was also going to learn more about the consumption cure. In Berlin, Conan Doyle could not get into the packed hall to attend the demonstration given by Koch's colleague Professor Ernst von Bergmann, but the next day he was given access to the German doctors' wards where Koch's procedure was being tested on tubercular patients. Without delay he sent a letter to the *Daily Telegraph* in which he recorded his doubts about the so-called cure; later he wrote a longer piece for W. T. Stead's *Review of Reviews* also casting doubt on the curative properties of Koch's procedure, while heaping praise on Koch himself as a Carlylean hero of science. Returning from Berlin via London to his home on the south coast, the following day Conan Doyle gave an interview to a local newspaper about his Berlin trip, in which he announced that he was giving up his Southsea practice. He had decided to go to Vienna to further his studies in ophthalmology before setting up in London as a specialist. The last part of the story is a familiar episode of the Conan Doyle myth, and is cheerfully recounted in his autobiographical *Memories and Adventures*. Setting up in practice as an oculist in Devonshire Place, close to the classical Harley Street, Conan Doyle failed to attract a single patient to cross his threshold. Yet in the time spent vainly waiting for patients, he produced the first of the stories for the *Strand* magazine, featuring Sherlock Holmes, which would make him one of the most famous authors in the world.

In his own retrospective narrative there is another reason for paying attention to the Berlin episode. *Memories and Adventures* is, on the face of it, a genial, relaxed book. Yet in the story told of the Berlin trip, turbulence troubles the normally smooth surface of the discourse. There is uncertainty, as well as urgency, in the narrative. Neither the young Conan Doyle, nor the elder self who tells the story, appears entirely in control of what is taking place. He explains that he might well have remained in Southsea permanently, but for the consequences of Koch's announcement that he would demonstrate his cure in Berlin.

A great urge came upon me suddenly that I should go to Berlin and see him do so. I could give no clear reason for this, but it was an irresistible impulse and I at once determined to go. Had I been a well-known doctor or a specialist in consumption it would have been more intelligible, but I had, as a matter of fact, no great interest in the more recent developments of my own profession, and a very strong belief that much of the so-called progress was illusory. However, at a few hours' notice I packed up a bag and started off alone upon this curious adventure. (*M&A*, 87–8)

"A great urge", with "no clear reason" but "an irresistible impulse", seem
to signal that Doyle was under some compulsion of whose nature he was
not completely conscious. When he gets to Berlin, at least in memory,
this rather frenetic tone continues. "The great thing was to be present at
Bergmann's demonstration", but tickets were simply not to be had;
Conan Doyle "conceived the wild idea of getting one from Koch himself" and goes to Koch's house, but "Koch remained a veiled prophet".
"I was fairly at my wits' end and could not imagine how I could attain
my end." He lurks at the entrance to the lecture hall, and when Bergmann appears, he recalls, "I threw myself across his path", claiming somewhat hyperbolically to have come "a thousand miles" to see the
demonstration, only to be rudely rebuffed by Bergmann, "working himself up into that strange folly of excitement which seems so strange in
the heavy German nature" (*M&A*, 89) but which is quite in harmony
with the excitability of the narrative. All of this seems to suggest that
something momentous but not fully understood is afoot, both in Conan
Doyle's own career, and in the worldwide reaction to the news of Koch's
discovery, in which it seemed "a wave of madness had seized the world"
(*M&A*, 90). The story culminates with Conan Doyle's return home.
"Two days later I was back in Southsea, but I came back a changed man"
(*M&A*, 90). The "curious adventure" of the Berlin trip had been a crisis.
In attempting to find its meaning, I will approach Conan Doyle's Berlin
experience as a cultural as well as a personal event.

    With its tally of tragic poets and operatic heroines, tuberculosis or
consumption had a certain romantic glamour. But there was nothing
glamorous about the facts. Tuberculosis was the cause of one in seven
deaths in the mid-nineteenth century.[1] It was often a prolonged and
painful illness as well as a fatal one, and before the twentieth century
there was no remedy: a cure for consumption had something of the
meaning of a cure for cancer or AIDS in more modern times.

    The story of tuberculosis is also tied up with the fortunes of the
germ theory of disease, the most significant advance in modern
pathology.[2] Highly controversial at first, the work of pioneers like
Koch and Pasteur had assured that the germ theory was almost

---

[1] Among the disease's victims was to be Conan Doyle's first wife, Louise (Touie), who
was diagnosed in 1893, and died of tuberculosis in 1906 at the age of 49. Knowledge of
what was in store adds extra poignancy to Conan Doyle's Berlin adventure.

[2] For a lively account, see Dorothy H. Crawford, *Deadly Companions: How Microbes
Shaped our History* (Oxford: Oxford University Press, 2007), 161–83.

universally accepted in the late nineteenth century—though in a story of 1894 Conan Doyle had portrayed an old-fashioned medical practitioner whose idea of a joke is to say, in a sick room, "Shut the door, or the germs will be getting in" (*Red Lamp*, 4–5). The work of bacteriologists gave modern people quite literally a new way of looking at the world and thinking about it, with implications that spread beyond the laboratory and the clinic. "In the 1880s," Laura Otis has argued in her book *Membranes*, "because of their minuscule size and deadly effects, bacteria became a metaphor through which one could articulate fears about all invisible enemies, military, political, or economic. Smallness itself became menacing."[3]

In the competitive atmosphere of late nineteenth-century Europe it was inevitable that the language of bacteriology should become entangled with that of empire and war. "Journalistic images of the war against germs produced for mass audiences during the 1890s", according to Jennifer Tucker, "bear witness to the intensifying scientific and popular interest in bacteria and to the readiness of many scientists to exploit military and imperialist iconography and racial stereotypes to show germs as unruly tribes of deadly microorganisms."[4] Conan Doyle gives an example in the opening paragraph of his *Review of Reviews* article, where he speaks of Koch's great master mind "which is rapidly bringing under subjection those unruly tribes of deadly micro-organisms which are the last creatures in the organic world to submit to the sway of man".[5] Earlier that same year, 1890, he had had a success with the Sherlock Holmes novel *The Sign of the Four*, in which, as Otis has observed, Holmes is pitted against a deadly incursion from the East, whose perpetrators he detects as consisting of an Oriental pygmy and a working-class outlaw and murderer named Small. There was a two-way metaphorical traffic between microbes and other sources of anxiety, and figures like Koch and his great rival

---

[3] Laura Otis, *Membranes: Metaphors of Invasion in Nineteenth-Century Literature, Science and Politics* (Baltimore: Johns Hopkins University Press, 1999), 94. See also the chapter "Foreign Bodies in *A Study in Scarlet* and *The Sign of Four*", in Thomas, *Detective Fiction and the Rise of Forensic Science*, 220–39.

[4] Jennifer Tucker, "Photography as Witness, Detective, and Impostor: Visual Representation in Victorian Science", in Bernard Lightman (ed.), *Victorian Science in Context* (Chicago: University of Chicago Press, 1997), 378–408; at 394.

[5] ACD, "Dr. Koch and his Cure", *Review of Reviews*, 2 (1890), 552–6; at 552. Hereafter "Dr. Koch". In "The Dying Detective", the villainous Culverton Smith, a specialist in tropical diseases, shows Watson his specimens. "Among those gelatine cultivations some of the very worst offenders in the world are now doing time" *HLB*, 147.

Louis Pasteur were heroized, as all mankind's champions in the war against disease and death.

After military service in the Prussian army, as a young man Koch had settled down to "the humdrum life of a country doctor": the words are Conan Doyle's, in the long article on "Dr. Koch and his Cure" which he wrote for the *Review of Reviews* in 1890 after his Berlin adventure, and in which he dwells, for reasons that may seem obvious, on the obscurity of Koch's beginnings, describing him as "strong and vigorous, with all his great powers striving for an outlet, even in the unpropitious surroundings in which he found himself" ("Dr. Koch", 553). One simple meaning of Koch's story for Conan Doyle was as a model for the gifted and ambitious provincial he was himself, now increasingly restless in the confines of his general practice in Southsea. The professions provided a ladder open to the talented, and by this ladder Koch had risen from the obscure village of Wollstein to become world famous.

While still a country practitioner, he had succeeded in isolating and cultivating the anthrax bacillus, thus establishing the bacteriological cause of anthrax or splenic fever, in what has been called "perhaps the first demonstration of the cause of any infectious disease".[6] It was Pasteur, however, who enlarged upon Koch's work and developed the inoculation against the disease.[7] The rivalry between Pasteur and Koch is a theme of Conan Doyle's article, and he notes that "France has been millions of pounds the richer for the vast number of animals who have been inoculated against the plague," adding piously that this "worthy rivalry" between France and Germany is "a contest as to which should confer the greatest benefits upon mankind" ("Dr. Koch", 554). With the Franco-Prussian war still very much a living memory, Conan Doyle here seems to characterize science as something both similar to and the opposite of war—still practised by nations in competition, but with results that are wholly benign to everyone.

An involvement with photography was another very important link between Koch and Conan Doyle. The latter was a keen amateur and a frequent contributor to the *British Journal of Photography* in the 1880s. Koch's interests were professional, and his achievements in bacteriology

---

[6] Thomas M. Daniel, *Captain of Death: The Story of Tuberculosis* (Rochester, NY: University of Rochester Press, 1997), 77.

[7] Koch himself had built on work on splenic fever done by the French bacteriologist Devaine. "Devaine saw it, Koch isolated it, Pasteur tamed it." ACD, "Life and Death in the Blood", *Good Words* (March 1883), 178–81; at 180.

were made possible by advances in visual technologies, particularly in microscopic and photographic instrumentation and practice. He developed techniques of staining, and became the first to make photomicrographs of bacteria. Koch believed that the introduction of photography to bacteriology would purge microscopic investigations of subjectivity, and thus guarantee them scientific. Conan Doyle was drawn to Koch, I think, not only as a model of the scientist as hero, but as someone who had provided incontrovertible ocular proof of the otherworld of the germ. The great experimentalist was the bringer of undisputable material knowledge of what had hitherto been hidden from human sight. The germ theory was one thing: but here were photographs in which it was possible to see, and impossible to deny, the bacteria that carried disease, which could then be combated. This made a great appeal to the extraordinary literalism of Conan Doyle's intellect, a propensity which was to leave him open to ridicule, and worse, later in life, most notoriously in the case of his faith in the evidence of photographs in the affair of the Cottingley fairies, which I will discuss in a later chapter. But on the whole Conan Doyle was not a man who was comfortable with uncertainties. For all his fertile creative imagination, he quite lacked the quality Keats defined as negative capability—"that is, when a man is capable of being in uncertainties, mysteries, doubts, without any irritable reaching after fact and reason".[8] Science for him was the realm of what could be tested with the eye, he shared the widespread view that "scientific" was a synonym for "undeniably true", and seems to have admired Koch for proving the existence of the hitherto unseen as much as for the clinical applications of his discoveries.

The Berlin story recounted in *Memories and Adventures* immediately follows a passage in which Conan Doyle told of his youthful search for spiritual truth. He considered but rejected Theosophy as inadequate to his needs, he says, "for I ask for severe proof, and if I have to go back to unquestioning faith I should find myself in the fold from which I wandered" (*M&A*, 87). Like many Victorians before him, Conan Doyle seems to have turned to science for what religion was no longer able to offer. No wonder there is a hint of epiphany in his reaction to Koch's announcement that he will demonstrate the cure—"A great urge came upon me suddenly that I should go to Berlin and see him

[8] John Keats to George and Thomas Keats (21 December 1817), in *The Letters of John Keats*, ed. Maurice Buxton Forman, 3rd edn. (London: Oxford University Press, 1948), 72.

do so"—the half-understood summons, the compulsion to drop everything and hurry off to see this thing which has come to pass.

At stake here is the consolidation in the nineteenth century of science as a profession, and the concomitant establishment of a certain kind of knowledge as "scientific"—a knowledge derived from agreed methods of enquiry, and consecrated as unassailable by the profession and its protocols of proof. This kind of knowledge had proliferated enormously in the Victorian age, propagated in a veritable explosion of what Alan Rauch calls "knowledge texts", including encyclopedias and instruction manuals but also museums and public institutions.[9] And the growth of such knowledge about nature, with its practical pay-off in the development of medical therapies and technological devices, was the chief evidence, and for many people the incontrovertible proof, that modernity meant progress. Conan Doyle, at this time at least, shared this faith in the benign growth of scientific knowledge, and the sometimes triumphalist idiom that often expressed it. A. Conan Doyle, MD, CM, in a letter to the Portsmouth *Evening Mail* in July 1887, had described vaccination as "one of the greatest victories ever won by science over disease", and castigated opponents of vaccination as men "whose notion of progress is to revert to the condition of things which existed in the dark ages before the dawn of medical science".[10] Developments in bacteriology led the young Conan Doyle to feel confident that within two generations, scourges like consumption, typhus, typhoid, cholera, malaria, scarlatina, diphtheria, and measles might cease to exist.[11] A general practitioner might be a foot-soldier in the march of scientific knowledge: champions of knowledge like Koch and Pasteur were in the vanguard. Crucial to his achievement was the communicable visibility that Koch had conferred on the new objects of knowledge. He made you see. For him, as for Conan Doyle, photography was crucial to the creation and consecration of knowledge, warranting its objects as objectively true.[12] In some

---

[9] See Alan Rauch, *Useful Knowledge: The Victorians, Morality, and the March of Intellect* (Durham, NC: Duke University Press, 2001), and William H. Brock, *Science for All: Studies in the History of Victorian Science and Education* (Aldershot: Variorum, 1996).

[10] ACD, "Compulsory Vaccination", Letter to the Portsmouth *Evening Mail* (15 July 1887), *Letters to the Press*, 27–9; at 27.

[11] ACD, "Life and Death in the Blood", 181.

[12] Not everyone had an implicit faith in photographs, and "photography was a controversial new standard of objective reporting in Britain during the late nineteenth century". Tucker, "Photography as Witness", 380. Tucker's article is illustrated (fig. 18.1, 379) with a doctored photograph of 1894 purporting to show Mr Gladstone entering a public house.

obvious ways both science and photography were forms of detection, bringing things to light and knowledge in a realm of certainty, where they could be dealt with. Conan Doyle would bring the same paradigm of visibility, and the same instruments of proof, to bear on the afterlife, with a similar positivistic confidence in their ability to tell the truth.

Conan Doyle's essay on Koch—published not in a scientific journal but a literary-political one, the *Review of Reviews*—is preceded by an unsigned article on the "Koch boom", illustrated with no less than three portraits of Koch (including a cartoon portraying him as an equestrian hero battling a serpent labelled "tuberculosis bacillus") and one of Berg-mann. Koch was a celebrity, and round the world the news of his dis-covery "must have sounded as the news of the advent of Jesus of Nazareth in a Judaean village".[13] Conan Doyle's own essay is illustrated with pho-tomicrographs of the bacilli that were the scientist's deadly antagonists, but contains no photographs of Koch himself, and no account of an epiphanic meeting with the heroic scientist he had come to Berlin to see. The great man was invisible to the visitor to Berlin, just as in theory the scientist was invisible in his work, at an epoch when experimental science had fully adopted impersonal protocols and claimed a detached neutrality of observation. What the *Review of Reviews* coverage does is to bring Koch back into the picture, to render him visible, and to give the process of scientific discovery the human face of a man who had under-gone personal struggles, loved mountaineering, and so on.

For Koch was now not just a celebrity, but a hero of a triumphantly modern kind for both the still new German empire and its dominant state, Prussia. In the 1880s Bismarckian Germany was beginning its acquisition of a colonial empire, and was anxious to demonstrate its powers in the world. In 1883, cholera had reappeared in Eastern Europe and spread rapidly over Egypt. The German government sent out a Cholera Commission, led by Koch, to Alexandria to investigate the disease on the spot. At the same time the French sent a team to Egypt headed by Pasteur. Neither succeeded in finding a cure, but when the outbreak in Egypt subsided Koch followed the disease to India, where it is endemic, and there succeeded in identifying the comma bacillus, the causative microbe of cholera. Pursuing the disease, which of course

---

[13] "Character Sketch: Dr. Robert Koch", *Review of Reviews*, 2 (1890), 547–51; at 547. This anonymous article, which ends "Mr Conan Doyle visited Berlin in November, and wrote this sketch for me on his return," is no doubt the work of the editor W. T. Stead himself.

knows no political boundaries, Koch (and Pasteur) had become also an instrument of foreign policy and a bearer of national prestige. Returning now to Germany, and to the University of Berlin, Koch resumed his investigations of tuberculosis.

He worked, says Daniel, "alone and in secrecy".[14] Conan Doyle too remarks on the intense privacy of Koch's domestic amenities and professional activities, joking that for the visitor to Berlin it was much easier to see the bacillus of Koch than to catch a glimpse of the man himself. In this, Koch was conforming—or Conan Doyle was catering—to a romantic expectation of the behaviour of genius, a person whose special gifts set him apart from others to commune with the source of his inspiration. Conan Doyle reports approvingly that Koch favours mountain climbing, that other occupation of the romantic solitary. But solitude is not the same thing as secrecy. In practice laboratory science is rarely a solitary occupation (Conan Doyle found fifty young men working in Koch's Hygiene Museum laboratory in Kloster Strasse) and there is something suspicious and perhaps unprofessional about scientists who work in secrecy.[15] Victor Frankenstein in his laboratory, and Henry Jekyll in his, work alone because they have something to hide.[16] The same is true of Professor Presbury, in the 1923 Sherlock Holmes story "The Creeping Man", who is trying to hide the fact that the drug he has taken for the purposes of rejuvenation has caused him to acquire the characteristics of a monkey.[17]

Robert Koch's secrecy has a less Gothic explanation, as a function of the atmosphere of personal and international competitiveness in which he worked. A cure for tuberculosis would be a boon to mankind, but would also bring glory to its discoverer. Koch had seen his anthrax work trumped by Pasteur, and had also clashed with his French rival in the search for the cure for cholera. As a young man he had served in the Franco-Prussian war, and was "profoundly nationalistic and violently anti-French".[18] He clearly had no intention of letting

[14] Daniel, *Captain of Death*, 83.

[15] Dealers in secret remedies were considered quacks by the profession. The Royal College of Physicians in Britain refused to have anything to do with Koch's tuberculin discovery because his remedy was secret. See "Character Sketch: Dr. Robert Koch", 548.

[16] In Oscar Wilde's *The Picture of Dorian Gray*, much admired by Conan Doyle, Alan Campbell, the chemist blackmailed by Dorian to dissolve the murdered Basil Hallward's corpse, later commits suicide at night in his laboratory.

[17] The tale itself is a weak reworking of *The Strange Case of Dr Jekyll and Mr Hyde*.

[18] Daniel, *Captain of Death*, 75.

the results of his research escape into the public domain where some
foreigner might take the credit for them. In the final quarter of the
nineteenth century Germany was busy becoming the third largest
colonial power in Africa, while complaining that others, the British
and the French, had already scooped up the best of the global spoils.
Koch was not prepared to see the greatest of scientific prizes, the
tuberculosis cure, snatched from his hands.

And if Koch had not been alert enough to protect his own intellectual property, there were others on hand to remind him when to
keep silent and when to publish, since more than personal issues were
at stake. Many people believed that Koch's secrecy was the result of
orders from his superiors in the German government.[19] The apparent
breakthrough was certainly announced precipitately. According to
Laura Otis the cure was not ready for human beings, and Koch "had
been forced by government ministers to announce it prematurely so
that German scientific achievements could eclipse all others at [the
International Medical Congress] in Berlin"; most scientists sympa-
thized with Koch, "knowing the pressure to which the normally pru-
dent bacteriologist had been subjected".[20]

The context for all this was a state of what could certainly be
described as bad blood in the European medical and scientific profession. German science, and scientific education, claimed pre-eminence.
There were national as well as professional rivalries and suspicions, and
at this time German–British medical relations were at a very low ebb
indeed. A recent cause of friction had been the illness of the Crown
Prince—later the Emperor Friedrich III—of Germany, Queen Victoria's son-in-law. His German physicians, led by Ernst von Bergmann
himself, diagnosed his condition as cancer of the throat, but when the
English laryngologist Morell Mackenzie was consulted he insisted they
were wrong, and that an operation for cancer was unjustifiable. A public
quarrel broke out between the English and the German doctors in the
case. By the time the Prince became Kaiser in March 1888, the condition was confirmed as cancer, and he was a dying man; he reigned for
only ninety-nine days. The Empress, who was English, was much criticized for her reliance on an English doctor, and after Friedrich's death,
the new Kaiser had to be restrained from putting Mackenzie immediately

[19] Daniel, *Captain of Death*, 83.
[20] Otis, *Membranes*, 24.

under arrest. Bergmann and his colleagues published a bulletin on the Emperor's illness which attacked Mackenzie for his misdiagnosis. Mackenzie in reply wrote a book accusing the German physicians of incompetence, brutality, and even drunkenness.[21] These furious exchanges were still fresh in the memory when Conan Doyle came to Berlin, and led him to complain that Bergmann was disposed to see "a Morell Mackenzie in every travelling Briton" ("Dr. Koch", 555).[22]

Scientific and medical expertise could confer national prestige, as well as international fame. There is every indication that Conan Doyle would not have been too shocked at the news that a national government had interfered in the conduct of scientific business. There is what looks like an instinctive patriotism in almost all his major fictional characters, however their *patria* is conceived, and he seems to have expected others too to acknowledge the paramount loyalty owed to a nation. A decade later at the time of the South African war, he himself not only put his life at some danger as an army doctor, but also put his own powers and reputation as a writer in the service of his nation's government, as an apologist for their conduct of the war. Robert Koch might have been world famous but he is commended for his love for the German mountains, and his attachment to home, his "domestic turn of mind", and indeed his Germanness is inscribed for Conan Doyle in his appearance, being "of a thoroughly German type" ("Dr. Koch", 552). The German scientist was a German before he was a scientist, and he was a Prussian state functionary. The idea of the lone heroic independent researcher was a pleasantly romantic one and might have had some plausibility in an earlier age of gentleman amateur investigators.[23] (It can be sustained, more or less, by Conan Doyle in the fictional figure of his Professor Challenger only through some sleight of hand.[24]) But it had no place in a world of expensive laboratory science, academic appointments, public funding, and government accountability. And besides, why should not a scientist who was proud

---

[21] See Theo Aronson, *The Kaisers* (London: Cassell, 1971), 149–95, 210–11.

[22] Conan Doyle said that he learned only afterwards about the Bergmann–Mackenzie feud (*M&A*, 89–90).

[23] Charles Darwin, a transitional figure in this respect, was a self-financing passenger on board the *Beagle*, 1831–6, but had at his disposal the amenities of a naval ship and a government-financed expedition.

[24] The ambiguity of Challenger's scientific appointments will be discussed in the following section.

of his country put his talents at the service of that country, as any other professional would—indeed, as would a consulting detective, who was always willing to oblige when national duty called?

Koch's story shows that nationalism and internationalism are not opposites, but dialectical partners. (A further illustration of this truth is to be found in the "revival" and internationalization of the Olympic Games, an idea conceived by Baron Pierre de Coubertin in that same year, 1890.[25]) For Koch's fame was now worldwide, but Koch's lymph, the fluid tuberculin, was obtainable only in Berlin, the imperial centre, and he kept its nature secret.[26] The wonderfully titled Prussian Minister of Worship and Public Instruction himself had announced that an administrative department would be created to manage the production, sale, and distribution of Koch's remedy: it had in effect already been nationalized.[27] Tuberculosis was global, but Koch's tuberculin was Prussian. Such was the scourge of tuberculosis that it was inevitable Koch's discovery should be touted in the press as a miracle. "A wave of madness had seized the world," wrote Conan Doyle years later, "and from all parts, notably from England, poor afflicted people were rushing to Berlin for a cure, some of them in such advanced stages of disease that they died in the train" (M&A, 90).

On 3 August 1890, in a lecture to an audience of 8,000 physicians at the 10th International Medical Congress in Berlin, widely reported in the international press, Koch announced his new lymph inoculation had been successful in destroying the tubercle bacillus *in vitro* and in affected tissues of guinea pigs. His paper on tuberculin appeared in the German scientific press on 13 November 1890, and was reprinted in the *BMJ*, in German, on 15 November. Andrew Lycett says this is what

[25] Kristine Toohey and A. J. Veal, *The Olympic Games: A Social Science Perspective* (Wallingford: CABI, 2000), 30–6. A French patriot and strongly anti-German, De Coubertin saw sport as a way for France to leave behind the effeminate and over-intellectual habits that had led to defeat by Prussia in 1870–1, and regain its pre-eminent place in Europe, but also as a way to promote international harmony and cooperation. See also Alfred E. Senn, *Power, Politics and the Olympic Games* (Champaign, Ill.: Human Kinetics, 1999), 19–33. The Olympics remain both internationalist and thoroughly nationalistic.

[26] "As regards the origin and the preparation of the remedy I am unable to make any statement, as my research is not yet concluded; I reserve this for a future communication." Robert Koch, "A Further Communication on a Remedy for Tuberculosis", *BMJ* (22 November 1890), 1193. A footnote to this article gives an address in Berlin where the remedy can be bought, though such was the immediate demand that it was unobtainable by foreign physicians for many weeks.

[27] "Character Sketch: Dr. Robert Koch", 551.

sparked Conan Doyle's interest, and that he set out for London that same day.[28] He boarded the train in London that evening, and spent most of the night on the continental express talking to Malcolm Morris. Conan Doyle must have forgotten Morris, though, when he claimed later to have had the good fortune to be "the first English physician to arrive in Berlin after the announcement of Koch's discovery" ("Dr. Koch", 555).[29] He cannot have arrived in Berlin earlier than the following day, which would be 16 November if Lycett is right about the date of his leaving London, and he remembered that Bergmann's lecture was scheduled for the day after his arrival (M&A, 88). But a BMJ report says Bergmann's "anxiously awaited address and exhibition" took place on Sunday evening, 16 November.[30] After missing Bergmann's lecture, Conan Doyle was taken the following day to visit the tubercular wards and saw some of the patients Bergmann had lectured about ("Dr. Koch", 556). His letter to the Daily Telegraph, addressed from Berlin's Central Hotel and describing his visit to the wards, is dated 17 November, that same day. What all this adds up to is that Conan Doyle left England earlier than 15 November—probably a day earlier—and therefore not prompted by Koch's German paper in the BMJ, but by accounts in the daily press.[31]

It is a detail that neatly symbolizes a larger issue, whether Conan Doyle's Berlin adventure is essentially a story about medicine or about journalism—and a further question yet, that of who the young man on the continental express thought he was and what profession he was following. This period can be seen in retrospect as one in which Conan Doyle was undergoing the metamorphosis from doctor to writer in

[28] Lycett, Conan Doyle, 156. The 15 November BMJ is also credited as Doyle's motive by Rodin and Key, in Medical Casebook of Doctor Arthur Conan Doyle, ed. Rodin and Key, 105.

[29] According to a note in the BMJ dated Tuesday 18 November, Morris seems to have been present in Berlin at 8.45 a.m. on 16 November, when a patient under his care was inoculated, in the presence of Koch himself. "The First English Case of Lupus Treated by Koch's Method", BMJ (22 November 1890), 1197.

[30] In "Dr. Koch" Conan Doyle correctly states that the lecture was given "upon the Sunday night" (555) but in later years he remembered it as taking place at noon (M&A, 89).

[31] The Daily Telegraph, for example, published articles on Koch and "The Consumption Cure" every day between 11 and 19 November—that is, starting before Koch's scientific paper appeared. Conan Doyle's letter to the editor, published on 20 November, is headlined "The Consumption Cure" to signal its place in this suite of reports in the paper. There is also a question whether Conan Doyle's knowledge of scientific German was sufficient to navigate Koch's scientific paper.

his own self-conception. Yet in November 1890 these two roles, and
vocations, were still quite evenly balanced. While still working hard at
his general practice, he was at the same time acquiring the trappings of
the professional writer, including a typewriter, and a literary agent,
A. P. Watt. He was certainly behaving as a professional writer, rather
than a doctor, when he passed through London on his way to Berlin
and called on W. T. Stead, editor of the new *Review of Reviews*, to ask if
he could supply him with letters of introduction to Koch or to Bergmann. If he succeeded in meeting them, these medical men would
have quite different responses to a man with a letter of introduction
from a magazine editor, and to someone introduced as a professional
colleague. But it seems the decisive meeting was the fortuitous one
that came about when Conan Doyle met Malcolm Morris on the
continental express.

Conan Doyle was 31 years old, Morris 41. As they talked through
the night they must have discovered that they had much in common.
Both were born into Catholic families, both had begun their career in
general practice in the provinces (like Robert Koch). Morris's ambition had brought him back to London where he had studied, and by
1890 he was one of the leading dermatologists in the country, well
launched on a career of medicine and public service that would bring
him a knighthood in 1908 and many professional honours. *Who's Who*
gives his address as 8 Harley Street, London W1. His studies in diseases
of the skin had been widened by frequent visits to Vienna, Berlin,
Hamburg, and Paris, underlining again the busy traffic between the
scientific centres of Europe among the upper orders of the profession.
Although primarily a consultant in dermatology, Morris had a secondary specialism in tuberculosis, which explains why he was hurrying to
Berlin in November 1890. He was taking with him a long-term patient
suffering from lupus, and was sufficiently well connected to have the
patient inoculated with the revolutionary treatment, under Koch's
personal supervision, upon arrival in Berlin.[32]

Morris was an eloquent, stylish, and cosmopolitan travelling companion. When he had met Stead earlier that day, Conan Doyle was
grateful for the great editor's kindness to "this big unknown provincial
doctor" (*M&A*, 88), and he may at first have been rather overawed in

---

[32] Lupus is tuberculosis of the skin. Koch's work of 1882 had proved the presence of the
tubercule bacillus in lupus.

the presence of Morris, an already distinguished man of "virility and decisiveness" who "did not suffer fools very gladly".[33] Morris however seems to have taken a shine to the younger man, and treated him to some vigorous advice, telling him that he was wasting his life in the provinces, and had "too small a field for [his] activities".

He insisted that I should leave general practice and go to London. I answered that I was by no means sure of my literary success as yet, and that I could not so easily abandon the medical career which had cost my mother such sacrifices and myself so many years of study. He asked me if there was any special branch of medicine on which I could concentrate so as to get away from general practice. (*M&A*, 90–1)

Conan Doyle replied that he was "interested in eye work" and Morris then prescribed six months' study in Vienna followed by setting up as an eye specialist in London. "Thus you will have a nice clean life with plenty of leisure for your literature" (*M&A*, 91).

Conan Doyle was to follow this recommendation, almost to the letter. But the main burden of Morris's advice is not the satisfactions of ophthalmic surgery as a career. The argument is what you might expect from a metropolitan consultant. Get out of general practice, move to the capital, exercise your powers. It was the story of Malcolm Morris's own career, and of course of Robert Koch's, and behind it lies the great bourgeois ambition of self-realization that had brought likely lads on the make from provincial obscurity to triumph or disappointment in the great city, in countless nineteenth-century novels since Balzac. With examples like Koch and Morris before him, Conan Doyle's world of local medical practice and provincial culture (such as was embodied by the Portsmouth Literary and Scientific Society, and the Portsmouth Football Club) was losing its savour.[34] Under the pressure of an ambition very much of its time, he was ready to enact that late-Victorian transition described by José Harris as "a subterranean shift in the balance of social life away from the locality to the metropolis and the nation".[35]

In urging him to quit general practice and set up as a specialist, Morris was inviting Conan Doyle to make the move he himself had

---

[33] Obituary, Sir Malcolm Morris, KCVO, FRCS Ed, *BMJ* (1 March 1924), 407, 408.

[34] Conan Doyle's social and cultural milieu at Southsea is described in detail in Stavert, *A Study in Southsea*.

[35] Harris, *Private Lives, Public Spirit*, 19.

already made so successfully, from the subordinate grade of family medicine in the provinces to the more modern, more scientific (and lucrative) practice of specialist medicine informed by the latest international research. The Harley Street address, the hospital consultancies and memberships of learned and professional societies, the scientific publications, the easy familiarity with the languages and institutions of European science—these added up to social and cultural capital that marked Morris, as Koch was marked, as one of the aristocrats of professional society.[36]

The advice of Malcolm Morris was decisive. Yet the older man was only recommending a plan that had been in Conan Doyle's mind since 1888, two years earlier. In a letter to one of his sisters that year, he had broached the idea of going abroad to "study the eye", then returning to set up as an eye surgeon in London, while continuing to earn money from his writing, for, he added, "If I were successful as a general practitioner it would be fatal to me as a writer."[37] Yet it seems it was only when Morris endorsed this ambition that Conan Doyle felt confident enough to put it into practice. Like so much else in the Berlin adventure, it is as if ideas and decisions long incubating in his mind suddenly become manifest, and active; or as if Berlin was the optical instrument that brought matters sharply into sight and focus. After the pleasant provincial obscurity of Southsea here was a different and invigorating culture, articulated in the talk of successful professional men.

Conan Doyle had much to think about when he stepped off the train and began his strange frenetic adventure in Berlin. He was quickly to discover that not all medical mandarins were as friendly as Malcolm Morris. The contacts Stead had given him were of no help. Koch himself was completely inaccessible to a lowly practitioner, though he met Morris. Putting himself "in the position of a German medical man who was seeking information in London", Conan Doyle says he thought it best to go straight to Bergmann and explain his difficulty, a tactic that would have succeeded, he says naively, in ninety-nine cases out of a hundred ("Dr. Koch", 555). Bergmann's rebuff is developed into an anecdote about nation and ethnicity. Bergmann, "notoriously gruff to our fellow-countrymen", is violently rude about Englishmen. In "Dr. Koch", he shouts, and roars. In *Memories and Adventures*, where

---

[36] See Perkin, *The Rise of Professional Society*.
[37] ACD to Lottie Doyle, n.d. (1888), in *Arthur Conan Doyle: A Life in Letters*, 252–3.

the memory casts a longer shadow and, besides, a terrible war with Germany has supervened, "he fairly spat out the word 'Englishmen'", and then "rushed on with his court all grinning at the snub which the presumptuous Englishman had received"; this is taken as evidence of the strange "folly of excitement" evident in the "heavy German nature" (*M&A*, 89, 90), though Conan Doyle was aware that some of it was kindled by rancour over Morell Mackenzie. In "Dr. Koch", the report of this rudeness is sarcastically cross-headed "The Courtesy of Von Bergmann" and Conan Doyle, with his editor's knowledge, is taking what revenge he can on the reputation in London of the great man who, in squashing an unknown young English doctor, had unwittingly offended one of Stead's reporters. To complete this little international allegory, the ethnic dimension is added in the form of an American gentleman, a Dr Hartz of Michigan, who, despite his German name, steps in to assist Conan Doyle, "on the good old principle that blood is thicker than water" ("Dr. Koch", 555–6). The next year, 1891, Conan Doyle would publish the book he considered his masterpiece, *The White Company*, under the inscription "To the hope of the future, the reunion of the English-speaking races."[38]

With the help of Hartz, and after studying Hartz's notes on the lecture from which he himself had been excluded, next morning Conan Doyle was looking at the very patients of Bergmann's who had been the subject of his demonstration, and at other tubercular patients under two other German professors. Probably on the same busy day he visited Koch's public laboratory at Kloster Strasse, and looked through the microscope at prepared slides on which pathogenic bacilli could be observed. In the journey from his medical backwater in Southsea to the vortex of scientific and clinical discovery, he had now penetrated, in effect, the most important place in the scientific world. He had reached, not the pinnacle of the profession, but the place where that pinnacle was. In the afternoon he went back to his hotel and wrote his letter to the *Daily Telegraph*. It is an impressive document, remarkable for his usual speed and decisiveness, but also for the self-confidence with which this medical nobody gives, for national publication, a critical account of the shortcomings of the tuberculin cure. He may well have been relaying misgivings voiced to him by Morris, or Hartz, or

---

[38] For the idea of a global "Britannic Confederation", to which Conan Doyle subscribed, see Young, *The Idea of English Ethnicity*, 196–241.

other scientific men he encountered in Berlin, but the opinions are presented as his own, those of "an English physician who has had good opportunities of seeing the recent development of the treatment for tuberculosis in Berlin".[39]

What Conan Doyle had accomplished was, in effect, a journalistic scoop, and he was proud of it. It was also his very first appearance in print in a national newspaper.[40] Later in life when he was a famous author, he was to be a frequent writer of letters to the press, seeing it as part of the role of the man of letters to comment on events and issues of the day. In *Memories and Adventures*, recalling his *Daily Telegraph* letter, "I rather think," he claimed, "that this letter was the very first which appeared upon the side of doubt and caution," adding, "I need not say that the event proved the truth of my forecast" (*M&A*, 90). Indeed the "consumption cure" was discredited within a year, though Koch was to go on to other discoveries and honours. But at the time, Conan Doyle's scepticism was bold indeed, the more so since he was a young and unknown provincial doctor, who had not actually attended Bergmann's demonstration, still less spoken to or even laid eyes on Robert Koch.

One explanation of the breathless tone of Conan Doyle's Berlin adventure is that it was less a matter of intellectual excitement over a scientific discovery than the fervour of a writer in pursuit of a story. When he returned to the subject in *Memories and Adventures* in the 1920s, he recreated that excitement in a new narrative, while at the same time downplaying the investment of his younger self in the scientific issues involved. He now claimed that, besides having no specialist knowledge about consumption, he had, as a matter of fact, "no great interest in the more recent developments of my own profession, and a very strong belief that much of the so-called progress was illusory" (*M&A*, 88). That scepticism about scientific progress belongs more to the older writer of 1923–4 than to the young physician of 1890. It concomitated a rougher handling not only of the rudeness of Bergmann, but also of Koch, whom Conan Doyle had described in 1890 as "the noblest German of them all" ("Dr. Koch", 556). The hyperbolical

<hr />

[39] ACD, 'The Consumption Cure', letter to the *Daily Telegraph* (20 November 1890), in *Letters to the Press*, 35–7; at 35.

[40] His earlier published letters had appeared in local newspapers, in the medical press, and in the Spiritualist publication *Light*. In Berlin he had met national journalists such as Lowe of *The Times* and Saunders of the *Morning Post*.

respect of the 1890 writings has disappeared in the 1924 account. Koch is now said to have "announced that he had discovered a sure cure for consumption" (*M&A*, 87): in 1890 Conan Doyle had been careful to point out that Koch had made no such sweeping claim.

Going on to describe his visit to Berlin and his reaction to the consumption cure, Conan Doyle remembered that he "had the temerity to disagree with every one and to come to the conclusion that the whole thing was experimental and premature" (*M&A*, 90). Although in 1890 he had been inclined to sympathize with Koch who, he said, was "compelled, in order to prevent widespread disappointment, to give his discovery to the public rather earlier than he would otherwise have done" ("Dr. Koch", 555), now he was much more frankly critical of the human cost of Koch's haste. Although he still believed in the legitimacy of the demands a nation made on its great men, the story he was now telling, about not only Bergmann but also Koch, was one of scientific arrogance and national pride with a distinctly post-war inflection. In the aftermath of the Great War Conan Doyle's views on Germans were unambiguous. More importantly, he no longer had a simple faith in scientific progress, and here was an example of how the modern dogma of the impersonal scientist, invisible in his work, seemed to have led to actions in which the ethical responsibilities of science and medicine had themselves become obscured, and these famous men, in their pursuit of prestige and pre-eminence in research, had lost sight of the effect of their vanity on ordinary people caught up in the "wave of madness" they had created.

The mimetic nervousness noted before in Conan Doyle's narrative, its strangely keyed-up but also dreamlike pace and tone, may be read as the sign of an ethical turbulence that troubles this retrospection about the events in Berlin towards which the young Conan Doyle had hastened with all his energy and professional ambition, desperate not to miss a thing. And those other travellers "from all parts, notably from England", those "poor afflicted people . . . rushing to Berlin for a cure, some of them in such advanced stages of disease that they died in the train" (*M&A*, 90): who spared a thought for them? For Koch had not been the only invisible presence in Berlin. When he went to the great man's house in his desperate search for a ticket for the demonstration, Conan Doyle had seen a large sack full of letters, bearing every sort of stamp in Europe, emptied on the floor, "a sign of all the sad broken lives and wearied hearts which were turning in hope to Berlin" (*M&A*, 89). Koch's discoveries about tuberculosis were a scientific triumph, but the vaunted tuberculosis cure of 1890 was an ethical disaster which cruelly raised and then dashed the hopes of many thousands of sufferers—a result, some might well say, of the way onrushing advances in the science of medicine might come at the expense of the humanity of the physician's calling.

To understand and practise scientific research as a professional and international competition, yielding to the mounting pressures that profession and nation brought to bear on the practitioner, might entail losing sight of what science was for in the first place, with tragic consequences for real people. If scientific men, and scientific medicine, had in this case failed in their ethical responsibility, other professions had responsibilities of their own. And after all Conan Doyle's own part in this drama, including his several accounts of it, is not that of a scientist or physician, but is entirely consistent with the role of man of letters—writer and public intellectual—as he was to come to conceive of it. Writing, as we have seen, had become a profession. One of the tasks of that profession as Conan Doyle understood and practised it was to create something like a common knowledge, at a time when knowledge itself was not only proliferating as never before, but dressing itself as a specialist expertise intended to daunt and exclude the non-professional public.[41]

Meanwhile he took the advice of Malcolm Morris, gave away his Southsea practice, and set off with his wife for Vienna to study ophthalmology. As it approaches its end, the story of his medical career seems to speed up. Morris had suggested six months in Vienna; *Memories and Adventures* remembers a stay of four months; but Conan Doyle's diary shows they were there for a little more than eight weeks.[42] Despite his year's study at Feldkirch in 1875–6, he now struggled to follow the rapid and technical German of the lecturers at the Krankenhaus.

---

[41] The effect of professionalization and specialization on the work of novelists of the generation before Conan Doyle's is examined in Joseph Murtagh, "George Eliot and the Rise of the Language of Expertise", *Novel: A Forum on Fiction*, 44/1 (2011), 88–105. Murtagh finds in George Eliot "a social mediator who could bridge gaps in the public understanding that had been brought about by an increasingly specialized division of labour" (103), but also a critic of the excesses of professional discourse.

[42] Russell Miller, *The Adventures of Arthur Conan Doyle* (London: Harvill Secker, 2008), 128.

Meanwhile the glamour of Viennese society was distracting. He enjoyed Vienna but felt that, as far as eye work was concerned, he had not learned much there.

Returning to England, he recalls that the consulting rooms he took in Devonshire Place cost £120 a year, which suggests that his unsuccessful specialist practice lasted for some time. The permanently empty waiting room makes a good story, but in fact he was in practice as an ophthalmologist for less than a month, 6 April to 4 May 1891, at which point he fell seriously ill with influenza. He recovered, to give up his medical career for full-time writing in June. It is hard to believe that he had been really serious about a career as an eye specialist, and there is no indication he did much at all to forge the connections, and propagate the reputation, on which a specialist's career entirely depended. The novel *Raffles Haw*, dedicated to Malcolm Morris, was written in those weeks in Vienna.[43] In his consulting room in London he conceived and produced the first of the Sherlock Holmes stories for the *Strand* magazine.[44] In Devonshire Place, this was where the action was. He seems only to have been going through the motions as a medical consultant. The die had been cast, and it was cast in Berlin. A straight line ran from the false discovery of the consumption cure to the launching of a career in a different profession, with its own discoveries, triumphs, and responsibilities.

In Berlin something other than the microbe had been brought to light. Describing Robert Koch's time as a provincial doctor, Conan Doyle had written of the young German's "great powers striving for an outlet" ("Dr. Koch", 552). When he himself returned, "a changed man", from Berlin, he remembered, "I had spread my wings and felt something of the powers within me" (*M&A*, 90). The important revelation for him was the result of an introspection, but it was one brought about by all the encounters of the Berlin adventure—self-belief, an understanding of his own capabilities and responsibilities, the confirming of his second vocation, the move from the profession and practice of science to that of storytelling.

---

[43] ACD, *The Doings of Raffles Haw* (London: Cassell, 1892). Conan Doyle includes Morris's address, 8 Harley Street, in the dedication.

[44] However, his first contribution to the *Strand* was "The Voice of Science", *Strand Magazine*, 1 (March 1891), 312–17.

Monsters and committees

The ambitious young fellow on a journalistic commission, after receiving some friendly advice from a senior man of science, finds himself in the presence of a famous professor of volcanic temperament, and is rudely insulted and dismissed as unworthy even to listen to the great man. Conan Doyle did not forget his rebuff by Professor Ernst von Bergmann in Berlin in 1890. It still rankled when he came to tell the story again in *Memories and Adventures* in 1923–4. But the memory had returned, usefully and in very different form, in 1911 when he began to write *The Lost World*, the first and best known of several stories about the irascible scientist Professor Challenger. The narrator, the journalist Edward Malone, is commissioned by his editor to interview the notorious Challenger. Most unwisely, he decides to get access to his subject by pretending to be a student of science. (There may be some residue here of Conan Doyle's discomfort among the giants of the scientific profession at Berlin.) Challenger has no trouble in exposing Malone as an ignorant fraud.

> "I suppose you are aware," said he, checking off points upon his fingers, "that the cranial index is a constant factor?"
> "Naturally," said I.
> "And that telegony is still *sub judice*?"
> "Undoubtedly."
> "And that the germ plasm is different from the parthenogenetic egg?"
> "Why, surely!" I cried, and gloried in my own audacity. (*LW*, 19)

The upshot of this exchange is that the scientist seizes the young man with a roar and throws him out of the house, the butler (who has seen this sort of thing before) opening the door just in time to facilitate this expulsion.

Certainly Challenger, like Sherlock Holmes, is a character who had more than one real-life model.[45] But the precedent of Bergmann's rebuff helps to show us something about how Conan Doyle's invention worked, and about the genre of romance. First, there is the boyish

---

[45] Conan Doyle mentions the Edinburgh Professor of Physiology William Rutherford as a model (*M&A*, 24–5). The highly distinguished Rutherford was in fact insane for part of his career. Challenger's name may owe something to the oceanographic *Challenger* expedition of 1872–6, led by Professor Charles Wyville Thomson, under whom Conan Doyle later studied at Edinburgh.

innocence of the scene, which will colour the whole narrative of *The Lost World*: here there is a good deal of violence, but no lasting harm. The Bergmann incident may not have been of very great account, but for the young Conan Doyle it was embarrassing and humiliating, whereas the boisterous ejection of Malone is simply farce. Just as noticeable is the hyperbole of romance, its pleasurable extremism. Conan Doyle in Berlin was rather out of his depth, but Malone out-Doyles him as a scientific ignoramus and a rank impostor. *Memories and Adventures* recalls Bergmann as "bearded and formidable", "all beard and spectacles" (*M&A*, 89, 90). Challenger has a large head, "the largest I have ever seen upon a human being", and "the face and beard which I associate with an Assyrian bull; the former florid, the latter so black as almost to have a suspicion of blue, spade-shaped and rippling down over his chest", and while Bergmann had roared at Conan Doyle, Malone reports that "a bellowing, roaring, rumbling voice made up my first impression of the notorious Professor Challenger" (*LW*, 18). There will be occasion to think further about Challenger's appearance, and his gigantism, but at this point it is enough to say that *The Lost World* is a romance of science—far more befitting that description that the scientific romances of H. G. Wells—and in romance everything is bigger and simpler and more vivid, the colours are sharper and the shapes more clear-cut, and both ideas and feelings are stronger and more exciting than in the everyday world.

For the Victorian that Conan Doyle was, there was no incompatibility between romance and science.[46] Scientific discovery was every bit as exciting as voyages of exploration—which were often themselves, of course, expeditions sponsored by some scientific institution, as the Challenger expedition is. The romance of science was an educational cliché in countless knowledge texts, and in 1905 one of the first Nobel prizes for literature had been awarded to that great poet of engineering and technology, Rudyard Kipling, whose poem "The King" memorably exploded the idea that modernity in the age of steam has killed off romance—"Confound Romance!...And all unseen | Romance brought up the nine-fifteen." When in an article of 1883 he imagined

---

[46] The gamut of Victorian publications runs through Philip Henry Gosse's popular *The Romance of Natural History* (London: James Nisbet, 1861) to the Christian Knowledge Society's *Romance of Science* series, begun in 1889. In 1910, Conan Doyle gave a speech at St Mary's Hospital Medical School on the subject of "The Romance of Medicine".

a microscopically reduced man braving the perils of a voyage through the human bloodstream, Conan Doyle was drawing on research done by Robert Koch and others in bacteriology, work which he said had revealed "a romance world" of living creatures, sublimely small and terrifying, just as exotic and deadly as the savage tiger or venomous cobra.[47] These latter were creatures to bring a thrill to the Victorian drawing-room and nursery from accounts and pictures of Britain's ever-widening empire. The romance of empire and that of science went hand in hand—as, again, in *The Lost World*—and sometimes spoke the same language, as they do when Conan Doyle, celebrating the great conquests of the germ by Koch and Pasteur, was able to look forward to a time "when these countless myriads, who had maintained their independence so long, should at last be forced to acknowledge man as the lord of creation".[48] Science was man's empire over nature. Imagination might be scorned as the offspring of ignorance by some men of science, such as Ainslie Grey in "A Physiologist's Wife", who opines that "Where science throws her calm, clear light there is happily no room for romance" (*Red Lamp*, 135). But schoolboys knew different. The frontiers of science promised as many adventures as the Khyber Pass.

Malone's quest for adventure begins in the prosaic newspaper office of his boss McArdle, the kindly but crabbed old news editor of the *Daily Gazette*, who assures the eager young man that the blank spaces in the map are all being filled in, "and there's no room for romance anywhere" (*LW*, 10).[49] But from this unpromising beginning Malone is soon to be transported to a new domain thousands of miles from home, opened up for him by a very different symbolic father, the aptly named Challenger, where the incredible becomes possible. *The Lost World* arrives late and a little whimsically to join the procession of boyish adventure tales stretching back to Henty, Haggard, Stevenson, Marryat, and Ballantyne.[50] Like dreams, the romance world is one of desire, surprise, and exaggeration, and like dreams it has childish as well as

---

[47] ACD, "Life and Death in the Blood", 178.

[48] ACD, "Life and Death in the Blood", 179.

[49] The passage from the realism of the newspaper office to the romance of the trackless frontier had already been travelled in Kipling's brilliant adventure story "The Man Who Would Be King" (1888), and the romance of blank spaces on the map had, of course, inspired the young Marlow in Joseph Conrad's "Heart of Darkness" (1902).

[50] See Martin Green, *Dreams of Adventure, Deeds of Empire* (London: Routledge and Kegan Paul, 1980).

libidinal qualities. But though its idiom may be highly coloured, romance has a serious cultural function, and a part to play in helping its readers reflect on and familiarize themselves with the modern world.[51] In particular, *The Lost World* is grounded in, or takes off from, an understanding of the profession of science that has as much to tell us as the story of its author's youthful visit to Berlin.

The question of profession is as tricky in the case of George Edward Challenger as it was in the case of Sherlock Holmes. Holmes was both a professional detective and an amateur. Challenger too seems to be at the same time the consummate academic scientist, and a gentleman dilettante. Perhaps we should think of him as something of a throw-back (in this as in other ways), an embodiment of the affluent, individualistic, self-supporting researchers and explorers of earlier times, a kind that was certainly fading by the Edwardian age, when important scientific work had largely passed into the hands of institutions of government and education, and the word "amateur", as applied to scholarly activity, had already acquired the connotation of "second-rate". The scientific profession, like its medical relative, had been busy consolidating and institutionalizing itself, agreeing on protocols, standards, practices, and qualifications designed to ratify the professional status of some practitioners while excluding others. Is Challenger inside the profession, or an outsider?

He is entitled Professor and addressed as such by other scientists. But there is no indication that he has an academic appointment. Is his professorship simply a courtesy title? When not doing fieldwork, he appears to work from home, and there is no mention of an office or laboratory, research assistants or ancillary staff. This makes him similar to his near-contemporary, the phonetician Professor Henry Higgins in Bernard Shaw's *Pygmalion* (1913), except that Higgins has students, or former students, like the unpleasant Neppomuck. Challenger's rival, Professor Summerlee, has a large class of students in London, who will be left in the charge of a *locum tenens* when he goes abroad (*LW*, 114–15); but Challenger seems to have none.[52] His wife berates him as "a man who should have been a Regius Professor at a great University

---

[51] See Daly, *Modernism, Romance and the Fin de Siècle*, 24–9.

[52] Much later in his career, we are told that he had a position as a lecturer in Physiology at the London School of Sub-Tropical Medicine, but lost it as a consequence of two personal assaults. ACD, *The Land of Mist* (London: Hutchinson, 1926), 9. Hereafter *LM*.

with a thousand students all revering you" (*LW*, 23), but for his boorish and scandalous behaviour. McArdle's information about him, which seems to be gleaned from his entry in *Who's Who* (*LW*, 10–11), shows that he belongs to no clubs, unusually for a prominent professional man. He lives in an imposing porticoed house in Kensington which to Malone "gives every indication of wealth" (*LW*, 17), which is unlikely to have been inherited by an alumnus of Largs Academy, but may have come with his wife.

To be sure, this is a genre that has a licence to be cavalier about the mundane data of schedule and income on which realism browses so patiently. And yet *The Lost World* does offer some detail about Challenger's scientific career. His early education at Largs Academy indicates he is Scottish, but not from a family wealthy enough to send their son to a public school. Edinburgh University gave him his scientific training (in a later story it appears he studied in the medical school; he would have been some four years behind Conan Doyle), and he is to be found working as an assistant in the British Museum at the age of 29, and Assistant Keeper in the Comparative Anthropology Department the following year, a promising job for a young scholar in an exciting period for the discipline, but cut short within a year by his resignation following "acrimonious Correspondence" (*LW*, 10). On the information available, this seems to be the beginning and end of his career in paid employment, so it seems reasonable to suppose his household and activities are supported by his wife's capital. (In the 1892 novel *Beyond the City* we meet a doctor who, after a large inheritance from a grateful patient, takes early retirement to turn his attention to research, another professional-amateur, able to indulge "the more scientific part of his profession, which had always had a greater charm for him than its more practical and commercial aspect".[53] But this good fortune hardly seems to fit Challenger's far from ingratiating profile.[54])

He certainly has the means to keep abreast, and ahead, of developments in the field, has won the Crayston Medal for Zoological Research, and is a member of numerous academies and scientific associations in Europe and the Americas as well as in Britain. He

[53] ACD, *The Great Shadow and Beyond the City* (Bristol: J. W. Arrowsmith, 1893), 165.

[54] Much later, however, Challenger is indeed left a huge sum in the estate of a millionaire with the provision that it should be used in the interest of science, and this enables him to finance the experiment described in "When the World Screamed". ACD, *The Maracot Deep and Other Stories* (London: John Murray, 1929), 263. Hereafter *Maracot*.

attends international congresses and, like the pugnacious Thomas Henry Huxley, relishes controversy.[55] He has a long list of scholarly publications to his name, mostly in zoology and anthropology: when Malone meets him he is at work on "a great and monumental work upon zoology which will be [his] life's justification" (*LW*, 27) but in a later story he is learned in geology and has begun "a volume upon the earth" (*Maracot*, 302). But though he seems to be a scientist ahead of his time, he is no specialist—unless it can be said of him that his specialism is omniscience, like Mycroft Holmes—and indeed he will later reveal what seems like an unmodern scorn for scientific specialization.

> I will not conceal from you that my opinion of experts is not a high one, and that I have usually found that a man who, like myself, has a well-equipped brain can take a sounder and broader view than the man who professes a special knowledge (which, alas, is so often a mere profession), and is therefore limited in his outlook. (*Maracot*, 258–9)

As a matter of fact his knowledge of many branches of science is one thing he has in common with his great rival Summerlee, the Professor of Comparative Anatomy. It is worth adding that a nineteenth-century student of evolution might find his studies leading him all over the disciplinary map, from geology and zoology to anthropology and statistics: evolution was interdisciplinary.

Challenger publishes in the scientific literature and has an international reputation, though he is certainly a maverick and many regard him as a fraud or at the least, in Tarp Henry's word, a "faddist" (*LW*, 13). Apparently without a university appointment, in some respects Challenger is a non-academic gentleman scientist in the traditional mode of Darwin and Wallace.[56] One reason why he is regarded with suspicion within the profession is that his findings lack institutional ratification and have to be taken on trust. He is a fieldwork scientist, and has undertaken an expedition to South America to verify some conclusions of the naturalists Alfred Russel Wallace and Henry Walter Bates. But his

---

[55] Challenger's recreations are listed as walking and Alpine climbing. Conan Doyle had earlier speculated on an analogy between scientific thought and mountaineering, an enthusiasm Challenger shares with scientists like the physicist John Tyndall and the bacteriologist Robert Koch. See ACD, "Dr. Koch", 552.

[56] Wallace was not independently wealthy like Darwin but made some money from the sale of zoological specimens, and from his writing. Later in life he was awarded a government pension. See Michael Shermer, *In Darwin's Shadow: The Life and Science of Alfred Russel Wallace* (Oxford: Oxford University Press, 2002).

expedition was a solitary one, and when he returned, no one believed the fantastic claims he made. He had taken some photographs—the camera, as we have seen, was a vital instrument of scientific proof—but the undeveloped film was spoiled in an accident, along with his only zoological specimens, and the scientific community back in England assumes the resultant images are fakes, and so are the bones he has brought back. "If you are clever and know your business," Tarp Henry tells Malone, "you can fake a bone as easily as you can a photograph" (*LW*, 38). (Challenger has also brought back sketches of extraordinary beasts made by the explorer Maple White but these, of course, have no status at all as scientific evidence.[57])

Faced with the disbelief and ridicule of the profession, Challenger withdraws the public claims he has made about the discovery of the lost world and its amazing fauna. Yet it seems nonetheless he does need the ratification of the profession: knowing himself to be in the right is not enough. Scientific knowledge has to be public knowledge, whether or not the public deserves or understands it. Natural selection, famously mulled over by Darwin for years, did not begin its career as scientific knowledge until institutionally consecrated in the reading of a paper at the Linnean Society in 1858, a ritual consolidated by the publication of *The Origin of Species* the following year. The reading of the paper at the same time asserted Darwin's (and Wallace's) ownership of the discovery, and offered it for adoption by the scientific community. The same need for professional recognition is the motive that leads Professor Challenger, in spite of the Nietzschean contempt he is apt to voice for the stupidity of scientists and the ignorance of the lay public, to accept an invitation to speak at a meeting of the Zoological Society at their Hall, a meeting which brings together all the main characters of the story, and sets in motion the expedition to find the lost world.

The meeting of the Zoological Society, in which Challenger clashes with his scientific enemies to the delight of a large, boisterous crowd, is one of the funniest passages in Conan Doyle's writing. He himself, though it seems he had no natural facility for it,[58] was well accustomed

---

[57] Early editions of the book included fake and composite photographs, including some purportedly of the Lost World plateau taken by Challenger and Malone, and a photograph of Challenger himself, in fact Conan Doyle in a false beard. See *The Annotated Lost World*, ed. Roy Pilot and Alvin Rodin (Indianapolis: Wessex Press, 1996), Appendix B.

[58] See Daniel Stashower, *Teller of Tales: The Life of Arthur Conan Doyle* (London: Allen Lane, 1999), 66, 184.

to public speaking, in a culture in which meetings, and oratorical controversy, figured very largely in a way that has entirely vanished in the
television age. Parliamentary and other public debates were reported
extensively and often verbatim in the press, as well as in their own
official proceedings, the words of the speaker punctuated by the reac-
tions of the listeners—"Cries of 'Shame!'" and the like—in a way
mimicked by Conan Doyle (or by Malone) in his report of the Zoological Society meeting. But in another sense the bruising encounter
between Challenger and the paladins of the Zoological Society, before
a well-informed and good-humoured audience, is simply a sporting
occasion, a scientific prizefight. Challenger has a public notoriety, and
the audience is popular as well as scientific. Tarp Henry fears the meeting may prove to be "no end of a rag" if the medical students turn out
for it and indeed, as Malone says, "it became evident to us as soon as
we had taken our seats that a youthful and even boyish spirit was
abroad in the gallery and the back portions of the hall" (*LW*, 39). We
can recognize that spirit as precisely that of the romance adventure,
invading the more staid genre of scientific debate and preparing to
turn it into a circus, as the carnivalesque exuberance of the audience
interrupts and mocks the professional pomposity of the scientists.
There is a similar narrative performance in the last chapter.

A more specific antecedent is suggested by Owen Dudley Edwards,
who points to the contests for the office of Rector at Edinburgh University, two of which took place while Conan Doyle was a student
there, in 1877 and 1880.[59] The Rector at Edinburgh was a public figure
not on the staff, elected by the students to chair the University Court.
It was a position with almost no real functions or responsibilities, and
the contests for the Rectorship used to be fairly evenly split between
Liberal and Tory supporters. The initial formal challenge in the contest
was made at a meeting which could be very rowdy, and Edwards quotes
a report in *The Scotsman* of a meeting on 5 November 1877, at which
Conan Doyle was almost certainly present, which indeed reads quite
like Malone's account of the meetings of the Zoological Society. Some
rectorial campaigns, and candidates, were more serious than others,
then as now. But the election of a Rector by the student body in the
older Scottish universities was an odd flash of democracy in institutions
not otherwise famous for egalitarianism and stakeholder-participation.

[59] Edwards, *The Quest for Sherlock Holmes*, 185–9.

In *The Firm of Girdlestone* Conan Doyle had described his *alma mater* as
an old woman, "grim and grey", with "little sentiment or romance in
her composition", indifferent to the welfare of her youthful charges:
Edinburgh was "a great unsympathetic machine" for the processing of
youthful raw material into professional men, "learned divines, astute
lawyers, and skillful medical men".[60] Not unlike Darwin's nature, the
university was an austere system that did not care who survived and
who did not. In this unforgiving and highly competitive institution,
the antics of the rectorial campaigns were like a rude word scrawled in
a ledger of accounts.

And the hilarious return of a similarly festive atmosphere in the
report of the meeting of the Zoological Society in *The Lost World*
makes its own point about a scientific professoriate which had spent
the nineteenth century segregating itself, in its institutions and its language, from the lay public and from the junior echelons of its own
profession. Conan Doyle had experienced that cold shoulder from
Professor von Bergmann in Berlin, and earlier as a student he had
been overawed by the stiff and lordly Edinburgh medical professors.
Now in *The Lost World* he exposed the scientists, right and wrong, to
the mockery of the gallery. Challenger, who has rudely interrupted an
earlier speaker, now finds his monologue reduced to a carnival, or
music-hall, turn.

"Creatures which were supposed to be Jurassic, monsters who would hunt
down and devour our largest and fiercest mammals, still exist." (Cries of
"Bosh!" Prove it!" "How do *you* know?" "Question!") "How do I know, you
ask me? I know because I have visited their secret haunts. I know because
I have seen some of them." (Applause, uproar, and a voice, "Liar!") "Am I a
liar?" (General hearty and noisy assent.) "Did I hear someone say that I was
a liar? Will the person who called me a liar stand up that I may know him?"
(A voice, "Here he is, sir!" and an inoffensive little person in spectacles, struggling violently, was held up among a group of students.) "Did you venture
to call me a liar?" ("No, sir, no!" shouted the accused, and disappeared like a
Jack-in-the-box.) "If any person in this hall dares to doubt my veracity, I shall
be glad to have a few words with him after the lecture." ("Liar!") "Who said
that?" (Again the inoffensive one plunging desperately, was elevated high into
the air.) "If I come down among you—" (*LW*, 44)

---

[60] ACD, *The Firm of Girdlestone* (London: Chatto & Windus, 1890), 32, 33. The novel
contains an account of a rectorial election.

The offer to "come down among you" is not an endorsement of the populist ethos of carnival but a threat of violence, though to the students it just adds to the fun. Of course in the context of the fiction Challenger is in the right. Jurassic monsters *do* still exist. Further, he can give as good as he gets, and is happy to insult the audience in his turn, as he has already insulted his professional opponents.

Challenger's official role in the meeting is to move a vote of thanks to the lecturer, a naturalist of some popular repute, and he takes the opportunity to pour scorn on successful popularizers "who exploit for fame or cash the work which has been done by their indigent and unknown brethren" (*LW*, 43–4), a perennial theme of professional discourse. What happens next is of interest. In the uproar following Challenger's repeated claim to have seen in South America animals believed long extinct, he issues, appropriately, a challenge.

> "...I claim that I have opened a new field of science. You dispute it." (Cheers.) Will you accredit one or more of your own number to go out as your representatives and test my statement in your name?" (*LW*, 45)

The sceptical Professor Summerlee agrees to go and Challenger promises to furnish him with the information needed to find the place, adding that it is only right that, since Summerlee is going to check Challenger's statement, there should be one or more others to accompany him and check his. This is the point at which both Lord John Roxton and the adventure-seeking Malone volunteer. Challenger moves that they be elected, as representatives of the meeting, to accompany Summerlee, and this is done by acclamation.

As Challenger himself specifies (*LW*, 46), the expedition party is in fact an ad hoc committee, a "Committee of Investigation" (*LW*, 176). While science was advanced by the propagation of theory and experimental discovery it also depended on professional bureaucratic practices which functioned like a technology. Scientific associations, such as the Royal Society, the Royal Geographical Society, or the Society for Psychical Research, commissioned and sponsored groups of qualified persons to undertake research which would be reported back to the Society.[61] This case is a little different, in that the meeting of the

---

[61] See *Philosophical Transactions of the Royal Society of London*; Robert Hugh Mill, *The Record of the Royal Geographical Society 1830–1930* (London: Royal Geographical Society, 1930); and Renée Haynes, *The Society for Psychical Research 1882–1982: A History* (London: Macdonald, 1982).

Society elects a committee to represent it, constituted of members of the meeting (not necessarily themselves members of the Society). The technology of scientific bureaucracy is brought to bear on the research question which is the testing of Challenger's claims. The committee comprises a scientific member (Summerlee), and two lay persons, Roxton, whose knowledge of the geography of South America will be practically useful, and Malone, whose function is that of an independent witness who will also act as record-keeper of the committee's activities.

Once again, what is at stake here is the status of data as scientific knowledge. A hypothesis can be tested, an experiment repeated for confirmation or disproof, and the *imprimatur* of a professional institution is another important dimension of the consecration of data as knowledge. Indeed this gatekeeping or quality-control function, of persons and practices, is the main *raison d'être* of professional bodies. The claims made for the consumption cure were debated in the scientific literature, and tested in clinical practice. Challenger's claim, that creatures believed by scientists to be extinct still existed on earth, is to be subject to the same process as the claims of Madame Blavatsky, the *monstre sacré* of Theosophy, to have witnessed and produced paranormal phenomena—astral forms and the like—which the Society of Psychical Research formed an ad hoc committee to investigate in 1884. In that case the committee of six, including both sceptics and others more favourably inclined to Theosophy, made a preliminary report, upon which the Council of the SPR decided the matter warranted sending one of their number, Richard Hodgson, to India, to the Theosophical shrine at Adhyar. Returning from this expedition, Hodgson produced the final report that declared Blavatsky a fraud, and the report was adopted by the SPR.[62] With the delivery of its report, the ad hoc committee ceases to exist.

A committee is an organ of a larger collective body. It is also a way of doing things, which is why I described it above as a bureaucratic technology set to work by an institution. (The great constitutional

---

[62] See *Proceedings of the Society for Psychical Research*, 3 (December 1885), 201–400. See also Haynes, *The Society for Psychical Research*, 140–4, and Peter Washington, *Madame Blavatsky's Baboon: Theosophy and the Emergence of the Western Guru* (London: Secker and Warburg, 1993), 82–4. Conan Doyle had been interested in Blavatsky and Theosophy in Southsea, but his confidence was very much shaken by the Hodgson report (*M&A*, 86–7).

precedent for committee work was Parliament itself, with its standing and ad hoc committees.) A committee has a task and a mandate, and it has hierarchy, disciplines, records, and established practices. Anyone who has served time on a committee knows that it can also be cumbersome, slow-moving, internally divided, open to manipulation. In the phenomenon of the scientific committee we can see a profession borrowing a tool from bureaucracy for the delegation of tasks and responsibility and a form of collective action. For some tasks a committee can do more than any individual, however charismatic.

The fictional apotheosis of the scientific committee had been reached, as a matter of fact, in a novel published fifteen years earlier, its first formal meeting described by its secretary in these terms in her journal.

30 September.—When we met in Dr Seward's study two hours after dinner, which had been at six o'clock, we unconsciously formed a sort of board or committee. Professor Van Helsing took the head of the table, to which Dr Seward motioned him as he came into the room. He made me sit next to him on his right, and asked me to act as secretary; Jonathan [Harker] sat next to me. Opposite us were Lord Godalming, Dr Seward and Mr Morris—Lord Godalming being next to the Professor, and Dr Seward in the centre.[63]

This is, of course, the vampire-combating task force in *Dracula*, published in 1897 by Conan Doyle's friend Bram Stoker. It is amusing that Mina Harker's journal describes the committee as being formed "unconsciously", as if one might talk of a bureaucratic unconscious, deeply ingrained below the level of deliberate thought in these late nineteenth-century people. Professor Van Helsing, the chairman, and Dr Seward would certainly be familiar with committees as part of their scientific profession, and the others may have had experience of service on business boards or charitable committees.[64] The first half of the Dracula story is all about the triumphs of the vampire. Only when the ad hoc committee is formed does the monster meet his match. Indeed in the face of the terrifying powers of the irrational, ancient, and

[63] Bram Stoker, *Dracula* (1897) (Harmondsworth: Penguin, 1979), 282. Like every committee secretary, Mina Harker knows the importance of the seating arrangements in a committee.

[64] It is possible that only the American Quincey Morris is a novice at this sort of thing. He interrupts this meeting to go outside to shoot at a lurking bat. No experienced committeeman would do such a thing without first asking permission of the chairman.

unknown, the committee is a formidable modern weapon, as Van Helsing says, setting out its terms of reference.

Well, you know what we have to contend against; but we, too, are not without strength. We have on our side power of combination—a power denied to the vampire kind; we have resources of science; we are free to act and think; and the hours of the day and night are ours equally. In fact, so far as our powers extend, they are unfettered, and we are free to use them. We have self-devotion in a cause, and an end to achieve which is not a selfish one. These things are much.[65]

Nicholas Daly has described Dracula as "an origin-tale for a new professional class", a story of the emergence and triumph of a new formation, the team of professional expert men.[66] In the novel, the institutional expression of this formation is the committee. They have the powers of organization and teamwork, the resources of science, intellectual mobility, and an impersonal dedication to a collective task. This committee is self-constituted and is not an organ of a larger body, except insofar as it works as the representative of the forces of goodness and modernity threatened by the vampire. We could see the story, in terms soon to be expounded in the sociologist Max Weber's *Economy and Society* (1922), as one of the triumph of modern "bureaucratic" society over the atavistic challenge of earlier forms of authority and action, embodied in the powerfully "charismatic" Dracula.[67] While Van Helsing's committee reports only to itself, it—like the entire novel—is obsessed with information and record-keeping in various media.[68] *Dracula*, while it shares the propensity of the Gothic novel to disturb and fragment narrative flow, is a compendium of archival resources, from oral testimony to letters, journals, shorthand and typewritten and phonographic records, telegraphic messages, newspaper cuttings, case histories, and scientific and historical literature. As with other nineteenth-century Gothic novels, the narrative form of *Dracula* dramatizes

[65] Stoker, *Dracula*, 285.

[66] Daly, *Modernism, Romance and the Fin de Siècle*, 26: see also 30–52.

[67] "*Rationally regulated* association within a structure of domination finds its typical expression in bureaucracy.... The *charismatic* structure of domination rests upon individual authority which is based neither upon rational rules nor upon tradition." Max Weber, *Economy and Society* (1920), 2 vols., ed. Guenther Roth and Claus Wittich (Berkeley and Los Angeles: University of California Press, 1978), ii. 954.

[68] For an elaboration of the novel's general fascination with different media see Ronald R. Thomas, "Specters of the Novel: *Dracula* and the Cinematic Afterlife of the Victorian Novel", *Nineteenth-Century Contexts*, 22 (2000), 77–102.

a struggle over the language in which disturbing experience should be narrated, and might be contained.[69] Van Helsing is constantly praising Mina Harker for her secretarial endeavours, and he is right: the success of the committee's work rests on the collection, assessment, and organization of data, the creation of the knowledge necessary to defeat the terrifyingly mysterious ghoul, and the keeping of a full and accurate record of their doings. Meanwhile the members contribute their individual expertise, interests, and knowledge—Seward the alienist, Quincey Morris the experienced hunter, and so on.

The committee formed in *The Lost World* is smaller, but quite similar. Professional expertise is provided by the scientist Summerlee. Roxton brings to the table local knowledge of the Amazon, proven leadership qualities, and firepower. Malone, who applied for membership as an unprejudiced witness, is the record-keeper. His record of the adventure, which is the book itself, is an account of the proceedings of the committee, though it doubles as journalistic dispatches sent back to McArdle, and further overflows into an autobiographical story—the comic courtship of Gladys—which would certainly be out of place in the minutes of a committee, and in a set of newspaper articles about an exploring expedition.

Having proposed the setting up of the committee to investigate his claims, Challenger now quite properly withdraws from the business, just like Robert Koch who remained modestly invisible while his discovery was being scrutinized by his international peers in Berlin. Challenger after all is the object of the committee's investigation and it would be improper for him to be a member. But it turns out that in this matter too, Challenger has no intention of following scientific or bureaucratic convention, and he materializes to everyone's astonishment in Manaos, to claim leadership of the expedition since, as he points out, he is the only person who knows where they are going. His appearance is transgressive, and not only because it is, in the expressive bureaucratic phrase, "out of order".[70] He turns up in a round, boyish straw hat with a coloured ribbon, hands in his pockets and his canvas shoes daintily pointing as he walks—almost dandyish, dressed for

---

[69] See Ronald R. Thomas, *Dreams of Authority: Freud and the Fictions of the Unconscious* (Ithaca, NY: Cornell University Press, 1990), 71–81.

[70] "Charisma is self-determined and sets its own limits. Its bearer seizes the task for which he is destined and demands that others obey and follow him by virtue of his mission." Weber, *Economy and Society*, ii. 1112.

flamboyant adventure, and not for sober bureaucracy. It transpires that from the first he had determined himself to "preside over [the] investigation" (*LW*, 61), and he loses no time in bossing the others about. They are obliged to co-opt him into the expeditionary committee and accept his leadership, "for," says Malone, "he was prepared to abandon the whole expedition rather than modify the conditions upon which he would guide us" (*LW*, 63). Some committees are authorized to co-opt new members but it is highly unlikely the Zoological Society would approve of its investigative committee being chaired by its investigatee.

Professional bureaucracy has suffered a *coup d'état* at the hands of an older, charismatic practice, and the expedition is wrested from the control of the sceptical realism (indeed naturalism) of the prosaic Summerlee to that of the heroic romance of Challenger, so that it promises to prove as boyish and colourful as that jaunty straw hat. Science and romance, after all, are far from incompatible, and Summerlee like Challenger is credited by Malone with that highest type of bravery, the bravery of the scientific mind. "Theirs was the spirit which upheld Darwin among the gauchos of the Argentine or Wallace among the head-hunters of Malaya" (*LW*, 68). Still, the travellers will continue to behave as a committee, though a fractious one. Summerlee even challenges Challenger on a point of order, refusing to recognize his leadership. "You are a man whose veracity is upon trial, and this committee is here to try it. You walk, sir, with your judges" (*LW*, 72). Procedurally Summerlee is quite right, but he has to accept that he has been out-manoeuvred by Challenger; the two men continue to bicker endlessly, a phenomenon not unknown in committees. But they address the project for which they have been commissioned, periodically debating how to go forward, assigning special tasks to individual members, keeping a record of their proceedings.[71] The same powers that the Van Helsing committee mobilized to defeat Dracula—combination, intellectual versatility, and the rest—enable these men to emerge triumphant from the monstrous dangers of the lost world. They return to London to give an account of themselves, having agreed not to speak to the press before meeting the members of the Zoological Institute, "since as delegates it was our clear duty to

---

[71] Challenger tries, improperly (and unsuccessfully), to suppress any mention of his resemblance to the ape-men from Malone's record (*LW*, 147–8). Malone, a conscientious secretary, tells him the record will keep "well within the truth".

give our first report to the body from which we had received our commission of investigation" (*LW*, 175).[72]

What they return with is, of course, a piece of ocular proof of the most conclusive kind, as Challenger, in answer to a question after his speech in the Zoological Institute and with a showman's instinct, releases a live pterodactyl into the hall. While the climax of the story is a moment of brilliant farce, it happens to contain a fantasy of some importance to Conan Doyle. Challenger's claims are vindicated comprehensively as scientific fact by material, embodied evidence, the actual pterodactyl, which he intends to make his audience see. Conan Doyle described himself, while discussing his doubts about Theosophy, as a man who required "severe proof" before he would accept any claim as true (*M&A*, 87). He attributed this to his scientific training. He was able to give a precise date (16 June 1887) to the moment when a spirit message convinced him of the truth of Spiritualist beliefs. "This message marks in my spiritual career the change of 'I believe' into 'I know'."[73] But he was to have little success persuading others to accept his beliefs as scientific facts. An incontrovertible manifestation witnessed by hundreds, like the pterodactyl in the Queen's Hall, was devoutly to be wished. But of course in *The Lost World* too, the evidence proves elusive. The creature escapes, proof of the Cretaceous fauna of the lost world goes literally out the window, leaving the people in the hall unsure what they have seen. As to the fate of the London pterodactyl, "nothing can be said to be certain on this point" (*LW*, 186).[74] It may have perched for a while on the roof of the Queen's Hall like the gargoyle it resembles, it may have frightened a guardsman outside Marlborough House, it may have set a desperate course for home and perished somewhere in the wastes of the Atlantic. In other words, far from furnishing a scientific proof, this fabulous creature returns to the immeasurable world of the Gothic and a magical or fantastic order of knowledge, where the protocols of verification do not reach.

[72] The Zoological Institute is the research division of the Zoological Society of London. The meeting to receive the report of the Challenger expedition takes place in the large Queen's Hall, for reasons of space, and is chaired by the Duke of Durham.

[73] See Lycett, *Conan Doyle*, 130.

[74] The fate of the London pterodactyl escapes scientific and journalistic discourse, just as the suicide of Winnie Verloc, another instance of the Gothic sublime, escapes from the realistic protocols of Conrad's *The Secret Agent* under the journalistic rubric of "an impenetrable mystery".

Van Helsing and his committee drew the terrible Dracula out of the shadow-world of rumour and monstrosity and vanquished him in the daylight of science and organization. But the London pterodactyl escapes the scrutiny and scope of scientific knowledge, to live or die in an uncertain, indeed indescribable existence, "something between a flying goat and a monstrous bat" (*LW*, 186). How many spirit manifestations must Conan Doyle have seen also recede into the inconclusive or grotesque. Meanwhile the meeting, its professional business unfinished, breaks up in enjoyable confusion and becomes a carnival parade, in which the travellers are borne aloft through the streets amid a crowd of 100,000 people. But the existence of living primeval animals on a plateau in South America, though known as an empirical fact to the four adventurers, is never consecrated as scientific knowledge, any more than were the manifestations of the spirit world which Conan Doyle knew to be true because he had seen them. Satisfyingly, though, at the end of the story a second expedition is being planned.

Given the close relationship between adventure stories and empire in the hands of precursors like Rider Haggard, what Malone calls "the peaceful penetration" of the lost plateau had been surprisingly free of the overt trappings of imperialism (*LW*, 99). Challenger generously names the plateau Maple White Land, after the American pioneer who discovered it. No flags are planted, no patriotic speeches made. In romance everything is personal. The science itself seems subject to none of the political pressures which men like Koch and Pasteur were expected to bear. The disputes of Challenger and Summerlee are conducted in an academic rhetoric which is very much *ad hominem*. The only thing they wholeheartedly agree upon is their poor opinion of another scientist, Dr Illingworth of Edinburgh. As for the ethical responsibilities of scientists, which had come to trouble Conan Doyle when he thought of the thousands given false hope by the news of Koch's consumption cure, in *The Lost World* this is an issue that appears to be confined to the question of whether or not Challenger has faked the evidence of the existence of the Lost World. This is the question the investigative committee is sent to rule upon, but it is obvious to any reader right from the start that Challenger is telling the truth: the question triggers the action but is of no actual ethical interest.

Yet ethical issues certainly do arise from the story, even if the fictional scientists are scarcely troubled by them. Romance infantilizes the story of science—or puerilizes it—but at the same time the novel tells a story about science that could hardly be more grown-up. For all its attempts to form institutions and practices that would make it an autonomous activity answerable to its own profession, science lives in a world of human power, a condition that applies to Challenger and Summerlee as much as it did to Bergmann and Koch. If science is mankind's empire over nature, *The Lost World* simply enacts that enticing metaphor as the scientific expedition to acquire knowledge of a place slips easily into the shape of an imperial expedition to assert power over it. It was a pleasing thought to the British to suppose they had never set out to acquire an empire, but had "conquered and peopled half the world", as the historian Seeley famously told his Cambridge undergraduates in 1881, "in a fit of absence of mind", while busy doing something else (trade).[75] Perhaps with a similar absent-mindedness, the party which goes to the Lost World on a scientific mission find themselves, without quite intending it, "in truth masters of the plateau" (*LW*, 161). The project which began in geography ends in genocide, as the scientific party with their modern weaponry help to finish off the plateau's indigenous ape-men, exterminating the males, destroying the towns, driving the females and the children away to live in slavery.[76] The white men become the political masters of the place they have given a European name, in uneasy alliance with their subalterns the local Indians, but with their weapons ready for any emergency. The present and the future of the plateau are in their hands. Its natural wonders and scientific interest aside, Lord John's discovery of diamonds on the plateau is enough to guarantee it will not be left alone by the pursuers of material interests.

The dark other that haunts the romance of *The Lost World* is the real story of the Congo. Europeans penetrated Maple White Land in the name of science. The Congo was opened in the name of philanthropy—that "masquerading philanthropy" against which Joseph Conrad protested indignantly[77]—specifically the extirpation of the

---

[75] J. R. Seeley, *The Expansion of England* (1883), ed. John Gross (Chicago: University of Chicago Press, 1971), 12.

[76] E. Ray Lankester, in one of Conan Doyle's chief sources of information about the prehistoric world, writes of "the so-called Pithecanthropus, or monkey-man", adding that "it is now certain that a higher race followed the earlier one" in human evolution. E. Ray Lankester, *Extinct Animals* (London: Archibald Constable, 1909), 88–9, 90.

[77] Joseph Conrad to T. Fisher Unwin (22 July 1896), in *The Collected Letters of Joseph Conrad*, i: *1861–1897*, ed. Frederick R. Karl and Laurence Davies (Cambridge: Cambridge University Press, 1983), 294. Conrad wrote about the Congo in "An Outpost of Progress" (1896) and "Heart of Darkness" (1899).

slave trade, but the result was a campaign of spoliation, genocide, and depopulation amounting to what Conan Doyle called a crime on a scale unprecedented in the whole course of human history, in 1909.[78] *The Crime of the Congo*, Conan Doyle's indictment of the most infamous episode of the Scramble for Africa, had been published only two years before he wrote *The Lost World*, and the novel is full of memories of the Congo. Lord John Roxton is partly based on Conan Doyle's friend Roger Casement, who as British consul in Leopoldville had written a report exposing the brutal ill treatment of local labourers under the King of the Belgians' Congo Free State (and later, like Roxton, championed the cause of the Putumayo Indians of Peru). The journalist Edward Dunn Malone resembles, at least in name, the journalist Edmund Dene Morel, founder of the *West African Mail* and of the Congo Reform Association, and another friend of Conan Doyle: the three Congo campaigners had dined together on 24 June 1910.[79] At this time Casement spoke of his impending journey up the Amazon to investigate reported atrocities against the Putumayo Indians at the hands of the Peruvian Amazon Company, and Conan Doyle sketched for him his idea for "a sort of wild boy's book" about the region.[80]

Malone in the story notes that in the Amazon, the rubber tree flourishes, "and has become, as in the Congo, a curse to the natives" in the form of forced labour under European overseers (*LW*, 58). Malone knows that the intervention of the Challenger expedition in Maple White Land has left it henceforth "the prey of hunter and prospector" (*LW*, 174). The Congo is something like the political unconscious of Maple White Land, however innocent (if that is the word) its scientific explorers may be of the political consequences their discovery is bound to entail now the Lost World is found. The scientific profession had fought to establish its autonomy, and scientific knowledge might be pursued for its own sake by independent, impersonal, and altruistic researchers with protocols that in theory insulated it from political and material interests. The Berlin adventure had shown that autonomy to be questionable in fact. Now the story of the fate of the lost plateau, with

---

[78] ACD, *The Crime of the Congo* (London: Hutchinson, 1909), 13. Hereafter *Crime*. See also Adam Hochschild, *King Leopold's Ghost: A Story of Greed, Terror and Heroism in Colonial Africa* (London: Macmillan, 1999).

[79] ACD, *The Annotated Lost World*, p. xvii.

[80] Lycett, *Conan Doyle*, 326.

a species driven to extinction and a local population and fauna awaiting exploitation, shows that Conan Doyle understood it to be an illusion.

There is a further aspect of science as humankind's empire over nature that emerges from Conan Doyle's portrayal of scientists and of Challenger in particular. The scientists in his stories are nearly all men. The scientific expedition in *The Lost World* is a journey into wholly masculine territory, though in Malone's case it is undertaken, absurdly enough, as a chivalric quest to prove himself worthy of Gladys, his suburban damsel, who proves her own worth while he is away by promptly marrying a solicitor's clerk called Potts.[81] Challenger's wife is a more formidable proposition, scolding her husband roundly for his appalling behaviour, but he deals with this interference by scooping her up and putting her, literally, on a pedestal, where she must sit, her feet dangling and her body rigid with fear, until she has calmed down. It is an apt enough image of the way she is treated as a domestic goddess and at the same time a child. She plays no further part in the story of *The Lost World*.

Science, men thought, was for men. All the characters in Conan Doyle's Berlin adventure had been men. When Francis Galton surveyed the profession in 1874, his study of 180 scientists was published, naturally, as *English Men of Science*. With occasional extraordinary exceptions like Maria Skłodowska (who had become Marie Curie in 1895), medicine was the branch of science in which women first began to make incursions. These often met the alarm and resistance of their male colleagues, satirized, as we have seen, in Conan Doyle's comic tale "The Doctors of Hoyland" (1894) in *Round the Red Lamp*. Not only was the profession masculine in personnel, according to Galton science was also masculine in nature, as we saw earlier. Statistics showed, he explained, that most scientists were influenced by their fathers, few by their mothers. "In many respects the character of scientific men is strongly anti-feminine; their mind is directed to facts and abstract theories, and not to persons or human interests.... In many respects they have little sympathy with female ways of thought."[82] Science spoke a

---

[81] The chivalry of Malone is a send-up of a theme Conan Doyle had treated seriously in *Sir Nigel* in 1906. Michael Dirda suggests that the Pottses are meant to recall the Pooters of the Grossmiths' *The Diary of a Nobody*. Michael Dirda, *On Conan Doyle* (Princeton: Princeton University Press, 2012), 36.

[82] Galton, *English Men of Science*, 207.

masculine language, of penetration, conquest, and possession, a language
of strength and size. Like Challenger, and Bergmann, scientists seemed
big. Conan Doyle in 1883 was writing excitedly of Pasteur's "gigantic"
intellect, and of Koch's "gigantic" discoveries.[83] Science was given to
seizure and command. "I am by temperament nothing but a conquistador," wrote Sigmund Freud to Wilhelm Fleiss in 1900, a few months
after he published his own discoveries about the lost world of
dreams.[84]

The scientific expedition to the Lost World proves to be, as his
Gladys prescribed, a test of manhood for the young Edward Malone,
his very name in the possession of the enormously patriarchal Professor George Edward Challenger. The natural world itself, through
which the four men make their determined way, can be found to enact
a gendered natural history, with its strong tall dark straight trees twined
about with a weaker, more beautiful, devious, and fanciful growth.

Vivid orchids and wonderful coloured lichens smouldered upon the swarthy
tree-trunks, and where a wandering shaft of light fell full upon the golden
allamanda, the scarlet star-clusters of the tacsonia, or the rich deep blue of
ipomoea the effect was of a dream of fairyland. In these great wastes of forest,
life, which abhors darkness, struggles ever upwards to the light. Every plant,
even the smaller ones, curls and writhes to the green surface, twining itself
round its stronger and taller brethren in the effort. (*LW*, 67)

The travellers may admire this beautiful if parasitic vegetation, and
Malone piously records that the jungle fills them with an awe reminis-
cent of Westminster Abbey. But their task is to hack on through it.
They have a job to do in a dangerous place.

Addressing the Royal Geographical Society whose president he was
in 1920, the explorer and imperialist Francis Younghusband made the
argument that, however much science might discover, "the characteristic
of the face and features of the Earth most worth learning about, knowing and understanding is their beauty".[85] But while most scientists—
including Challenger and Summerlee—could enjoy the beauties of
nature, their priority was not to appreciate but to master the natural

[83] ACD, "Life and Death in the Blood", 179, 180.
[84] Sigmund Freud to Wilhelm Fleiss (1 February 1900), in *The Complete Letters of Sigmund Freud to Wilhelm Fliess, 1887–1904*, ed. Geoffrey Moussaieff Masson (Cambridge,
Mass.: Belknap Press of Harvard University Press, 1985), 397–8.
[85] Francis Younghusband, "Natural Beauty and Geographical Science", *Geographical
Journal*, 56/1 (July 1920), 1–13; at 3.

world. The fertile but inert jungle is an obstacle for the travellers to surmount, and on the plateau the lumbering or grotesque monsters from the past must be brought, like Koch's micro-organisms, "to submit to the sway of man" ("Dr. Koch", 552).

The committee, and the profession that sponsored it, do nothing to check Challenger's conquistador instincts, which indeed they are inclined to share, speaking the same language of mastery. This drive of science to control and dominate nature, and its gender coding, is most fully on view in a later Challenger story, "When the World Screamed", published in the *Strand* in April and May 1928, and later in the volume *The Maracot Deep*. Here the great man, while reprising his performance of arrogant intolerance, reveals to the narrator, an engineer called Peerless Jones, his belief that "the world upon which we live is itself a living organism, endowed…with a circulation, a respiration, and a nervous system of its own" (*Maracot*, 268). At first Jones thinks him mad, but he soon succumbs to the great man's charismatic vision. Challenger sets about testing this theory by sinking an enormous shaft eight miles deep into the earth's crust, at a spot on the Sussex Downs, and now proposes to follow this with the violent insertion of a sharp drill, a hundred feet long, driven by an electric motor. Here is a strange literalization of the figure of mother nature as not only life-giving but sentient. The extraordinary violation to which he intends to subject the earth can be read as a ferocious satire on the phallic rapacity of science, even if Challenger himself is entirely unaware of this. As ever, he acts at once like a gleefully anarchic child—here preparing to act out a fantasy which would hold no surprises for Freud—and a Nietzschean overman exercising his will to power.

With reluctant help from Jones, Challenger makes his preparations with gusto, and summons a huge audience to witness the event.[86] At the site, the nerves of the earth are laid bare, as it were. "A dark purple fluid appeared to pulse in the tortuous anastomoses of channels which lay under the surface. The throb of life was in it all" (*Maracot*, 304). In due course, as Jones tells it, "my iron dart shot into the nerve ganglion of old Mother Earth and the great moment had arrived" (*Maracot*, 305). This maternal wounding or rape results in an explosion, expelling the apparatus of penetration, followed by a geyser of defiling fluid, a "gush

---

[86] The scene on the Downs is reminiscent of another display of manliness before a huge crowd, the prizefight at the climax of *Rodney Stone*.

of putridity" (*Maracot*, 308). Nature asserts a last sublimity in a terrible, indescribable scream—"No sound in history has ever equalled the cry of the injured Earth" (*Maracot*, 306)—a scream of pain and protest at once echoed by every volcano around the world. Challenger's hypothesis is proved, and he complacently accepts the admiration of the onlookers, including Peerless Jones, overawed by "the mighty achievement, the huge sweep of the conception, the genius and wonder of the execution" of what they have witnessed (*Maracot*, 309).

This crass and revolting triumph over a feminized nature is an appropriate apotheosis for the phallic scientist—"Challenger the super-scientist, Challenger the arch-pioneer, Challenger the first man of all men whom Mother Earth had been compelled to recognize" (*Maracot*, 309–10)—and on the site, we are told, the Royal Society have appropriately erected an obelisk. There is no doubt who is the monster in this extraordinarily powerful story. The intervening century has shown in ample measure what an irresponsible science can do to the natural world: this late Challenger tale is in this respect prophetic, while at the same time consistent with Conan Doyle's earlier objections to the ruthless pursuit of scientific discovery and the arrogance of scientists. In the name of the disinterested quest for knowledge about nature, Challenger may not be the last man of science "to set the whole world screaming" (*Maracot*, 310).

Thinking like a scientist

Arthur Conan Doyle was well read, intellectually curious, the holder of a doctoral degree and professional qualifications, an international traveller, friend of some of the leading writers and artists of his time. He could also be described as provincial, or rather suburban, often un- or anti-intellectual in an English way. "I wanted to say that if I were advising a young man who was beginning life, I should counsel him to devote one evening a week to scientific reading," he writes in *Through the Magic Door*, but hurriedly advises such a young man not to "choke himself with the dust of pedants", for "a very little reading" in geology, zoology, botany, archaeology, and so on will be enough to allow him to take an informed interest in the world around him.[87] He is almost, at

---

[87] ACD, *Through the Magic Door* (London: Smith, Elder, 1907), 248, 249.

times, Mr Pooter, the late-Victorian *homo suburbanus* satirized by the
Grossmith brothers in *Punch* and in *Diary of a Nobody*. He puts on a
Pooterish performance when he tells this anecdote against himself in
Through the Magic Door, just after recommending the popular science
writings of Samuel Laing.

I had met someone at a *table d'hôte* or elsewhere who made some remark
about the prehistoric remains in the valley of the Somme. I knew all about
those, and showed him that I did. I then threw out some allusion to the rock
temples of Yucatan, which he instantly picked up and enlarged upon. He
spoke of ancient Peruvian civilization, and I kept well abreast of him. I cited
the Titicaca image, and he knew all about that. He spoke of Quaternary man,
and I was with him all the time. Each was more and more amazed at the full-
ness and accuracy of the information of the other, until like a flash the explanation crossed my mind. "You are reading Samuel Laing's 'Human Origins'!"
I cried. So he was, and so by a coincidence was I. We were pouring water over
each other, but it was all new-drawn from the spring.[88]

These Pooterish aspirations to a general scientific knowledge are
amusing, as they are intended to be, but they speak to a desire he
shared with his educated contemporaries to keep up with scientific
developments. These moments, and hundreds like them, in Conan
Doyle's writing are a reminder of the centrality of science to the culture of ordinary life in Victorian times, and not just in the classroom.
Conan Doyle, who was a scientist before he was a writer of fiction,
never saw any contradiction between scientific and imaginative ways
of seeing. On the contrary, science and imagination should, in his view,
be allies in the war against materialism. The passage about scientific
reading, discussed above, ends with a characteristic exhortation to the
young to use scientific knowledge "to appreciate the order, beauty, and
majesty of that material universe which is most surely the outward sign
of the spiritual force behind it".[89] Science was to be held in suspicion
only when it was reductive. In *Sartor Resartus* Thomas Carlyle, Conan
Doyle's early master, has his hero Teufelsdröckh condemn "that progress
of Science, which is to destroy Wonder, and in its stead substitute Men-
suration and Numeration".[90] But Teufelsdröckh himself is learned in
all sciences and *Sartor Resartus* itself is described as "in reality a treatise

[88] ACD, *Through the Magic Door*, 252.
[89] ACD, *Through the Magic Door*, 249–50.
[90] *A Carlyle Reader*, ed. G. B. Tennyson (Cambridge: Cambridge University Press, 1969),
170.

upon the great science of Things in General, which Teufelsdröckh is
supposed to have professed at the university of Nobody-knows-
where".[91] Carlyle's championing of spirit against the encroachments
of materialism, his insistence that the material world was the vehicle of
the spirit, set the intellectual tenor for Conan Doyle's life early and set
it fast. But in truth Carlyle was only reaffirming a conviction about the
supremacy of spirit which had been urged upon Conan Doyle by his
Jesuit teachers at Stonyhurst, and earlier still by his artist father.

It was obvious that scientific and literary activity were not at odds
since both produced forms of knowledge. Poetry has always claimed to
tell a kind of truth and in the nineteenth century novelists, producing
the great literary form of the scientific age, with its commitment to
mimetic realism and its focus on contemporary actuality, were sometimes inclined to advance truth claims of a quasi-scientific kind for
their work. Balzac's *Comédie humaine* is proposed as a vast anthropology
of modern France. Later, naturalists like Zola applied a meticulous,
detailed observation of social and material phenomena with an apparent scientific detachment. In England George Eliot, herself learned in
science and closely associated with scientists, famously described her
fiction as "simply a set of experiments in life—an endeavour to see
what our thought and emotion may be capable of".[92] She saw her fiction as a laboratory in which ideas and feelings could be set in motion
to see how they would behave, always in the context of a duty of
education and improvement. Her science was practical, and empirical.
"I become more and more timid—with less daring to adopt any formula which does not get itself clothed for me in some human figure
and individual experience, and perhaps that is a sign that if I help
others to see at all it must be through that medium of art."[93]

Conan Doyle would certainly have been shy of describing his fictional writing in such terms, and often he is content to claim for his
stories nothing more than amusement and a temporary diversion.
Nonetheless there are important continuities in his work, and life,
between scientific and aesthetic practice, evidence of the comfortable
place occupied by science in the culture in which he wrote, as well as
of the fact that, after he had made the decision to concentrate on the

---

[91] *A Carlyle Reader*, ed. Tennyson, 335.
[92] George Eliot to Joseph Frank Payne, 25 January 1876, *The George Eliot Letters*, vi:
1874–1877, ed. Gordon S. Haight (New Haven: Yale University Press, 1955), 216.
[93] *The George Eliot Letters*, vi. 216–17.

career of a writer, he continued in interesting ways to think like the scientist he was educated to be.

Science, in an ideal frame, was the creation and management of knowledge of natural phenomena which could be observed and measured. In laboratory conditions, an isolated, immobilized, and complete set of data might be controlled and examined. But in many domains of knowledge, and particularly those with a historical dimension, the evidence available was partial, gappy, unreliable, or compromised, and in such domains the investigator was obliged to develop protocols of reconstruction, of gap-filling, in order to arrive at knowledge which could then be presented as a hypothesis subjected to testing and liable to disproof. Origins, above all, could not usually be observed. The origin of species, of languages, of the cosmos, or of human societies, these great etiological obsessions of nineteenth-century research, were not witnessed or recorded. They must be pieced together by inference and imagination from fragments of evidence. There was, in a peculiarly Victorian sense, an archaeology of knowledge.

Such protocols of reconstruction are being exemplified, clearly enough, every time Sherlock Holmes ransacks a crime scene for clues, or elicits testimony from a client or witness, searching for what is absent from the record or hidden in the manifest evidence.[94] "One of the most striking aspects of the Sherlock Holmes stories," in Nicholas Daly's words, "is the extent to which the solution of the mystery lies in the proper reading of household objects"[95]—but it is a reading in which the spectacle of ordinary appearance is supplemented by what we might call speculation. The method was applied too in the process of diagnosis in the doctor's surgery, where after taking the patient's "history" and examining the patient's body (and perhaps after the ritual enquiry "What seems to be the trouble?"), the physician applied experience and guesswork to arrive at the root of the problem, and

---

[94] The effect of this evidential paradigm was also felt in the domain of law, with the development in the late nineteenth century of the "reconstructive" trial, in which jurors and other observers were encouraged to distrust appearances and to make judgements based on their interpretation of the evidence. Lindsay Farmer has studied the process in the trial for murder of Oscar Slater, a case in which Conan Doyle himself was involved. See Lindsay Farmer, "Arthur and Oscar (and Sherlock): The Reconstructive Trial and the 'Hermeneutics of Suspicion'", *International Commentary on Evidence*, 5/1, article 4 (<http://www.bepress.com/ice/vol5/iss1/art4>: accessed 25 May 2011).

[95] Daly, *Modernism, Romance and the Fin de Siècle*, 101–2.

name it. The patient did not need to be told what his symptoms were, but what caused them. Creating knowledge might be a matter of bringing what was hidden into visibility, and here the technologies of photography, microscopy, and later the x-ray might come into play. But science was not just about observing, measuring, and counting what was there. The scientist, and the detective, also needed the courage to describe what was *not there*—vanished or hidden.

Diagnosis and detection used reconstructive methods in common with scientific disciplines with a historical dimension and narrative, like geology, archaeology, historical linguistics, and evolutionary biology, methods that enabled the investigator to reconstruct the past even from fragmentary evidence.[96] To a Christian, nature was an open book, every page of which was inscribed with the glory of God. But the earth, for Charles Darwin, was a fragmentary text, a thoroughly incomplete mystery story requiring a heroic effort of editorial supplementation. The fossil record was (and remains) massively incomplete, and "infinitely numerous transitional links" between existing and extinct species were simply not to be found:

I look at the natural geological record, as a history of the world imperfectly kept, and written in a changing dialect; of this history we possess the last volume alone, relating only to two or three countries. Of this volume, only here and there a short chapter has been preserved; and of each page, only here and there a few lines.[97]

In the reconstruction of the past from partial evidence, an investigator like Lyell or Darwin was guided by a faith in the uniformity of nature—that the laws of nature working through time are unchanging—and by what John Tyndall, another of Conan Doyle's scientific heroes, called the "scientific use of the imagination" in a famous lecture.[98] If foretelling is the function of the prophet, there were retrospective prophets among modern scientists who, T. H. Huxley joked, might be described as "backtellers".[99]

---

[96] See Lawrence Frank, *Victorian Detective Fiction and the Nature of Evidence: The Scientific Investigations of Poe, Dickens, and Doyle* (Basingstoke: Palgrave, 2003).

[97] Charles Darwin, *On the Origin of Species* (1859) (Harmondsworth: Penguin, 1968), 315–16.

[98] John Tyndall, *Scientific Addresses* (1870) (Ann Arbor: University of Michigan Press, 1995), 33–74.

[99] T. H. Huxley, "On the Method of Zadig", *Collected Essays*, vol. iv (London: Macmillan, 1911), 1–23; at 6.

It is not only in the investigative methods of Sherlock Holmes that we can see such procedures at work for Conan Doyle. Holmes recreated the entire career of Watson's brother from the evidence of his pocket watch, fleshing out the bare bones of the meagre evidence, such as scratches made around the watch's keyhole, into a complete biographical narrative. Holmes is a scientific detective, as we are repeatedly told.[100] But his creator too was thinking like a scientist when he prepared to write his historical novel *The White Company*. Conan Doyle said he had devoted two years to the study of fourteenth-century life in England, reading for his projected novel set in the Hundred Years War. The period, he said in an interview in 1892, had hardly been treated in fiction at all, so that he "had to go back to the early authorities" for all his information. "I set myself to reconstruct the archer, who has always seemed to me to be the most striking figure in English history."[101] He felt that the English archer had been reconstructed inaccurately—over-romantically—in Walter Scott's fiction. Conan Doyle took the greatest pride in this imaginative restoration of the past, as can be seen from his response a few months earlier to another interviewer's question about his historical novels.

Yes, that is the only work I really fancy. *The White Company* is the best thing I have ever done. I endeavoured in that to reconstruct the whole of the fourteenth century. Indeed, I had to do it. Scott always avoided it. I had nothing to go by in the way of previous fiction concerning that period. I read up no less than 150 books in preparation for that novel alone.[102]

He puts together the past, gathering and cross-examining the scattered clues of the available evidence. Conan Doyle emphasized that this was original, pioneering research, and he was proud of the accuracy of his depiction in *The White Company* not only of material things like costume and weaponry and food, but also of human experience itself. He wrote that he had "striven to draw the exact types of character of

---

[100] Laura J. Snyder points out that Conan Doyle may have first encountered the methods of Baconian science by way of Macaulay's essay on Francis Bacon. See Laura J. Snyder, "Sherlock Holmes: Scientific Detective", *Endeavour*, 28/3 (September 2004), 104–8.

[101] Harry How, "A Day with Dr Conan Doyle", *Strand Magazine*, 4 (August 1892), 182–8, in Harold Orel (ed.), *Sir Arthur Conan Doyle: Interviews and Recollections* (Basingstoke: Macmillan, 1991), 62–8; at 63.

[102] Raymond Blathwayt, "A Talk with Dr Conan Doyle", *The Bookman*, 2/8 (May 1892), 50–1, in *Sir Arthur Conan Doyle: Interviews and Recollections*, 57–61; at 58.

the folk then living and [had] spent much work and pains over it".[103]
But a knowledge of the evidence alone was never enough to guarantee
the success of his palaeological project, which depended on the work of
the imagination to build it into narrative. "As a rule," he admitted,
"where historical novels fail is in the fact that there is too much history
and too little novel."[104] Nonetheless, he understood that a work of fiction could create knowledge, and his reconstruction of the English soldiers of the fourteenth century would, he was confident, become a real
part of the nation's memory."I knew in my heart that the book would
live and that it would illuminate our national traditions" (*M&A*, 81).

"I never guess," boasts Sherlock Holmes (*Sign*, 10); and Watson, his
Boswell, gives the title of "The Science of Deduction" to a chapter of
each of the first two Holmes adventures, *A Study in Scarlet* and *The
Sign of the Four*.[105] Yet Holmes's characteristic method is not really
deduction (the inferring of conclusions about particulars by reasoning
from general premises), nor indeed induction (the inferring of general
conclusions from the evidence of particular instances), but what
Thomas Sebeok, following the system of logic of C. S. Pierce, names as
abduction.[106] Abduction is the conjecture of possible generalities that
could account for given particulars. "The truth is," Pierce had written,
"that the whole fabric of our knowledge is one matted felt of pure
hypothesis confirmed and refined by induction. Not the smallest
advance can be made in knowledge beyond the stage of vacant staring,
without making an abduction at every step."[107] All new knowledge
depends on the formation of a hypothesis, and abduction is something
like inspired guesswork, by which a hypothesis is made intuitively on
the basis of observations insufficient to prove it. Darwin's theory of
evolution, a hypothesis derived from the application of imagination to
a set of observations not yet ready to confirm it, was, in effect, a hunch,

---

[103] ACD to Mary Doyle (11 November 1891), *Arthur Conan Doyle: A Life in Letters*,
300–1.

[104] Blathwayt, "A Talk with Dr Conan Doyle", 59.

[105] Most studies accept Holmes's claim that his method relies on deductive logic alone.
See for example Neil C. Sargent, "Mys-Reading the Past in Detective Fiction and Law",
Law and Literature, 22/2 (Summer 2010), 288–306.

[106] Thomas A. Sebeok and Jean Umiker-Sebeok, "You Know my Method: A Juxtaposition of Charles S. Pierce and Sherlock Holmes", in Umberto Eco and Thomas A. Sebeok
(eds.), *The Sign of Three: Holmes, Dupin, Peirce* (Bloomington, Ind.: Indiana University Press,
1983), 11–54.

[107] Quoted in Sebeok and Umiker-Sebeok, "You Know my Method", 16.

a yarn spun about history. Far from being unscientific, in Pierce's view abduction was the first step in all scientific reasoning.

As for Sherlock Holmes, and despite his own warnings of the danger of theorizing in advance of one's data, according to the Sebeoks his "powers of observation, his 'extraordinary genius for minutiae,' as Watson puts it, and of deduction are in most cases built on a complicated series of what Pierce would have called guesses".[108] Sigmund Freud, another great romantic scientist, compared his own procedures to the reconstructive methods of archaeologists. In the face of incomplete analytic results, he wrote frankly in the case history of "Dora", he had no choice but "to follow the example of those discoverers whose good fortune it is to bring to the light of day after their long burial the priceless though mutilated relics of antiquity", and what this meant in practice was that he had no hesitation in filling in the gaps with what he knew should be there—"I have restored what was missing."[109]

"From a drop of water," the young Sherlock Holmes wrote in the magazine article read by Watson in the second chapter of *A Study in Scarlet*, "a logician could infer the possibility of an Atlantic or a Niagara without having seen or heard of one or the other" (*Study*, 18).[110] Perhaps so, but such an operation would have nothing to do with logic. Holmes's trained faculty of building a narrative about the unknown on the basis of a creative and intuitive—in a word, imaginative—reading of limited data has been used as an instrument to expose and deconstruct an internal contradiction in the scientific positivism of the Holmes stories (Catherine Belsey's influential essay is the best example of this argument);[111] but this is to misunderstand what it meant to Conan Doyle to think like a scientist. Again and again, Holmes proceeds by conjecture, intuition, speculation, as a great scientist must. He commends Inspector Gregory, in "Silver Blaze", as a competent detective,

---

[108] Sebeok and Umiker-Sebeok, "You Know my Method", 21.

[109] Sigmund Freud, "Fragments of an Analysis of a Case of Hysteria ('Dora')", in *Case Histories 1* (Harmondsworth: Penguin, 1977), 29–164; at 41. Freud's work on the Dora case coincides exactly with Arthur Evans's controversial excavation and restoration of the Minoan palace at Knossos, begun in 1900. Both Evans and Freud have been reproached for "reconstructing" over-zealously.

[110] For a discussion of the emergence of a new paradigm of knowledge creation in the late nineteenth century see Carlo Ginzburg, "Clues: Roots of an Evidential Paradigm", in *Clues, Myths and the Historical Method*, trans. John and Anne C. Tedeschi (Baltimore: Johns Hopkins University Press, 1989), 96–125.

[111] Catherine Belsey, "Sherlock Holmes", in *Critical Practice* (London: Methuen, 1980), 109–17.

but adds that "Were he but gifted with imagination he might rise to great heights in his profession" (*Memoirs*, 9–10). Early in *The Hound of the Baskervilles*, Dr Mortimer suggests that Holmes's speculations about an anonymous note are close to guesswork, but the detective demurs. "It is the scientific use of the imagination," he declares, quoting Tyndall's lecture title, and adds, "but we have always some material basis on which to start our speculations" (*Hound*, 33). In another case, "Thor Bridge", he speaks of "that mixture of imagination and reality which is the basis of my art" (*Case-Book*, 48). In the broken narrative of the past, Holmes is able to reconstruct that fetish of Victorian palaeoanthropology, the "missing link"—sometimes to the chagrin of his interlocutors, like Inspector MacDonald in *The Valley of Fear*. "Your thoughts move a bit too quickly for me, Mr Holmes. You leave out a link or two, and I can't get over the gap" (*Valley*, 16).

In *Extinct Animals*, a book Conan Doyle was to draw on when he was writing *The Lost World*, E. Ray Lankester had practised the art of backtelling when he examined the fossil jawbone of the Miocene mastodon and speculated from it on the origin of the elephant's trunk.[112] Comparative anatomy was one of those sciences "which have been termed historical or palaetiological", Huxley had explained, "because they are retrospectively prophetic and strive towards the reconstruction in human imagination of events which have vanished and ceased to be".[113] The importance of the detective imagination to both science and history was so widely canvassed as to be virtually a commonplace.[114] The classic statement of this widely acknowledged truth was John Tyndall's lecture "Scientific Use of the Imagination" (1870), which Conan Doyle had read as a young man. Tyndall was ruthless in dismissing the Bible as a voice of any authority in scientific questions, but his lecture is a sort of secular Genesis, a hymn to the creativity of the human imagination in science. "Now there is in the human intellect a power of expansion—I might almost call it a power of creation—which is brought into play by the simple brooding upon facts. The legend of the Spirit brooding over chaos may have originated

---

[112] Lankester, *Extinct Animals*, 117–22. Rudyard Kipling had come up with a yet more imaginative etiology for the elephant's trunk in his *Just So Stories* (1902).

[113] Huxley, "On the Method of Zadig", 9.

[114] Science, detection, historiography, and imagination come together in a chapter entitled "The Historical Imagination", in R. G. Collingwood, *The Idea of History* (Oxford: Clarendon Press, 1946), 231–48.

in a knowledge of this power."[115] Here Tyndall's own palaeographic imagination troped the Creator in coming up with an origin for Genesis itself, the book of origins. But the real hero of "Scientific Use of the Imagination" was Darwin, in whom "observation, imagination, and reason combined" had constructed a complete narrative of biological succession in advance of the facts that might definitively prove it.[116] The figure of Darwin emerges, in the lecture, as exemplary, inspirational.

I described as a commonplace this idea of scientific thinking as daring, romantic, intuitive, and imaginative. It was known to every schoolboy who subscribed to *The Romance of Science*, or indeed the *Boy's Own Paper* (first published in 1879). Of course, there was another type of the scientist in the popular imagination: fact-bound, sceptical, materialistic, and pedantic, a pourer of cold water on anything that could not be observed, verified, and measured. It is a part of the success of the character of Sherlock Holmes that he participates in both these widely held but contradictory ideas of the scientist, the cold-blooded proceduralist and the dashing intuitive, in recognition of the fact that although contradictory, most people no doubt believed equally in both. (A culture's repertoire of types is not obliged to be internally consistent, any more than its repertoire of proverbial sayings.) The commonplaces of his culture were a valuable asset to Conan Doyle. Henry James, for example, might well have hesitated to weave his characters out of such homespun material; it says something of Conan Doyle's own mind, and of his close relation to his reading public, that he was happy to draw on such stock ideas (among many others) for Sherlock Holmes, and for other characters too—Brigadier Gerard, for example, has a complicated literary lineage, but part of the fun of his character is its conformity to the comic commonplace of the swaggering Frenchman.

Sherlock Holmes might be a pedantic fact-man in his manners, but when he thinks he thinks like a scientist of the other kind, and this creative-reconstructive thinking is something he shares not only with Tyndall's and Huxley's heroes of the scientific imagination, but also with Arthur Conan Doyle, that professional creator of knowledge. The imaginative faculty that enables Holmes to conjure a Niagara from a

---

[115] Tyndall, *Scientific Addresses*, 39.
[116] Tyndall, *Scientific Addresses*, 64.

water-drop, or a career of dissipation from some scratches on a pocket watch, is not just instrumental. It is a pleasure. Holmes is not just simultaneously a cold and a hot scientist. He is also, as we have already seen, both a professional and an amateur practitioner of his craft, amateur in the sense that he pursues it largely for its own sake, and for his own satisfaction. He serves the law and, on occasion, the state, but he does what he does because he wants to. The pursuit of knowledge brings pleasure and excitement. It is a stimulant, as we can see from the fact that Holmes resorts to cocaine when there is no case, and does not use cocaine when there is. Above all, it beguiles that modernity-induced lassitude and melancholy—that *ennui*, to give it its exact name—which so haunts him as to make him sound, sometimes, like the Baudelaire of Baker Street.

I cannot live without brainwork. What else is there to live for? Stand at the window here. Was ever such a dreary, dismal, unprofitable world? See how the yellow fog swirls down the street and drifts across the dun-coloured houses. What could be more hopelessly prosaic and material? What is the use of having powers, doctor, when one has no field upon which to exert them? Crime is commonplace, existence is commonplace, and no qualities save those which are commonplace have any function upon the earth. (*Sign*, 11)

Applying his mind to the dreary formlessness outside the window, Holmes had the power to conjure cases, narratives in which the seemingly commonplace material universe was revealed to be dramatic, vivid, ethically transparent, and stimulating. It is here that, through their common investment in imagination, science and art could come together against the common enemy of the prosaic and material. If it is a Carlylean science, it is a Baudelairean or Wildean art, for while Sherlock Holmes is a kind of scientist he is also a kind of artist, the artist as dandy, egotistical, brilliant, and eccentric. To think like a scientist, or like an artist, was to think creatively, to redeem experience from the commonplace, transfiguring it and showing it capable of novelty and wonder. "How a man of science can be a materialist," Conan Doyle exclaimed, "is as amazing to me as how a sectarian can limit the possibilities of the Creator."[117] All his life he had a boyish understanding of both science and art as a form of adventure.

[117] ACD, *Through the Magic Door*, 250.

5

Law and Order

Crimes and punishments

The years that produced the early Sherlock Holmes stories also saw a crisis in the history of the police. The month before Conan Doyle began to write *A Study in Scarlet*, a demonstration to protest against unemployment culminated in demonstrators attacking the gentlemen's clubs in Pall Mall and St James's, and the police were roundly criticized for allowing it to get out of hand. The following year, on 13 November 1887 ("Bloody Sunday"), in the course of a larger demonstration in Trafalgar Square, the police attacked marchers with batons; hundreds were injured and three men were killed. To the middle-class anxiety that London was vulnerable to disorder was now added a widespread anger at the incompetence and brutality of the police, and a furious campaign in the press ensued against the Commissioner for the Metropolitan Police, Sir Charles Warren, a former major-general.[1] In August 1888, the mutilated body of the first of at least five victims of the Whitechapel murderer was found. The London police proved quite unable to identify the perpetrator, who came to be known as Jack the Ripper, or to put a stop to his increasingly ghastly activities, the most sensational crime of the Victorian age. Again there was wide-spread criticism of the police, and Warren resigned as Commissioner the day before the most gruesome Ripper killing, of Mary Jane Kelly, was discovered. Sherlock Holmes came into a world in which the

---

[1] One reason for a damaging indecision and hesitancy in law enforcement in 1886 and 1887 was the still ill-defined relationship between the Commissioner of Police and the Home Office. See Victor Bailey, "The Metropolitan Police, the Home Office and the Threat of Outcast London", in Victor Bailey (ed.), *Policing and Punishment in Nineteenth Century Britain* (London: Croom Helm, 1981), 94–125.

question of the role and competence of the police was a matter for heated public debate.

But though the police were going through a distinctly bad patch in the late 1880s, the fortunes of the force as an institution improved in the course of Conan Doyle's lifetime. Here was yet another story about professionalization. The Metropolitan Police had been formed by Robert Peel in 1829 and a detective division created in 1842, which was soon to be heroized by Dickens and in the popular press. The Criminal Investigation Department was established in 1878, and the Special Irish Branch, to combat Fenian activities, in 1884 ("Irish" was later dropped from its title).[2] Police training improved, and the number of policemen increased from about 20,500 in 1861 to 54,300 in 1911: 22,000 of these were in London.[3] This meant that the number of persons per policeman in the population fell from 980 to 664, so that more people were coming into direct contact with the agents of the disciplinary state.[4] At the same time there was a change in public perception of the police. As David Taylor puts it, "the despised 'blue locust' had become the beloved 'bobby'," and in spite of setbacks like Bloody Sunday and their failure with the Ripper murders, "by the end of the century there were clear signs of growing sympathy for the police".[5] The generally sympathetic if very patronizing portrayal of the police in the highly popular Holmes stories no doubt contributed to this gradual change of attitude. The policeman on the beat served the establishment without being of it, and was regarded by the middle class whose property he protected as something akin to a servant or a tradesman—the "handyman of the streets", as *The Times* called him in 1908.[6] His main task was to prevent crime, while the detective's was to find it out. And as the repertory of detection broadened to include photography and—after 1902—fingerprinting, detectives came to be looked on as the scientists of policing. In 1936 a Home Office report

---

[2] The CID was established when the Detective Department was reorganized, after three out of its four chief inspectors were found guilty, at the Old Bailey, of corruption. See Clive Emsley, *The English Police: A Political and Social History* (London: Longman, 1996), 72.

[3] In the 1880s the Metropolitan Police area contained a sixth of the whole national population, a quarter of the crimes, and a third of the policemen. F. W. Maitland, *Justice and Police* (London: Macmillan, 1885), 110.

[4] Figures in this and the next paragraph are from David Taylor, *Crime, Policing and Punishment in England 1750–1914* (Basingstoke: Macmillan, 1998).

[5] Taylor, *Crime, Policing and Punishment*, 89, 102.

[6] Taylor, *Crime, Policing and Punishment*, 102.

argued that "in those cases where the evidence is the result of expert examination of matter or material connected with the offence the expert, by reason of his knowledge and technique, may read and interpret evidence which is not the opinion of a fallible mind but is the direct and accurate interpretation of the infallible laws of nature".[7] Here is the familiar nexus of science, expertise, professionalism, and inhumanity (or superhumanity), to which we could add the inevitable corollary, the resentment of the subordinate grade, the uniformed branch. In the Holmes stories, of course, it is the consulting detective who possesses these superior qualities and regards the official detective force, Lestrade and Gregson and the rest, as incompetent amateurs.

Trials too had become more professional in the nineteenth century, with the old oral confrontation between accuser and defendant replaced by a longer and more technical process argued out between advocates drawn from—and restricted to—a cadre of legal professionals. While it consolidated the position of this corps of specialists as the essential mediators between the citizen and the law, legal reform in the nineteenth century was in general an effort to instantiate what can be recognized as a modern idea of justice. "The notion of justice dominant in the modern 'episteme'," as Kieron Dolan summarizes it, "incorporates such Enlightenment ideals as fixed and known laws, as impartiality and universal application, as rational systems of evidence, and penalties graduated according to the gravity of the offences."[8] Punishments were changing too, and throughout the Victorian age there was a long debate about how to achieve and balance the aims of punishment—retribution, deterrence, and reform. At the beginning of the nineteenth century there were more than 200 capital crimes— almost all felonies were capital offences—though in practice relatively few people were executed and transportation to penal colonies was the major form of secondary punishment: 160,000 people were transported between 1787 and 1867. By 1860 there remained only four capital offences, but effectively it was only for murder and treason that people were hanged. Like transportation, public executions were still

---

[7] Quoted in Philip Rawlings, *Policing: A Short History* (Cullompton: Willan Publishing, 2002), 178. Rawlings points out that this mystique of scientific detection disguises the fact that the most useful tool of detection has always been a trade of information between police and criminals.

[8] Kieran Dolin, *Fiction and the Law: Legal Discourse in Victorian and Modernist Literature* (Cambridge: Cambridge University Press, 1999), 28.

being carried out in Conan Doyle's lifetime: they were not abolished until 1868. The Victorian age saw a proliferation of prisons and penitentiaries, and periodic shifts of emphasis in carceral policy between punishment, deterrence, and rehabilitation. The prison system was nationalized in 1877 and deterrence declared to be the prime purpose of locking criminals up. But in a later reaction to this severity, a liberal reform was proposed by the Gladstone Committee in 1895, leading to the 1898 Prisons Act, which incidentally completed the uniformization of the nation's prisons in a centrally controlled system. The rise in the prison population had the collateral effect of conferring an identity on a criminal class (or profession), the fact of having been in prison continuing to set certain men and women apart from their fellow citizens after their release, an identification and socialization that made them likely to re-offend.

Late in life, Conan Doyle declared himself in favour of "perpetual segregation", though under a relatively mild penal regime, for such recidivist offenders.[9] It was taken for granted that the famous author of detective stories was interested in all aspects of crime and punishment: visits to American prisons were on the itinerary of his trips to the United States in both 1914 and 1923, for example. But a curious feature of his fiction is precisely its lack of curiosity about the fate of those criminals who go off to prison. Sherlock Holmes may be interested in a prisoner like James McCarthy in "The Boscombe Valley Mystery", held in Hereford gaol on suspicion of murder, but once a criminal has been correctly identified and sent for punishment, he is of no further interest to Holmes or to Watson unless he escapes and returns to the narrative world, like Selden the Notting Hill murderer in *The Hound of the Baskervilles*, or Jonathan Small in *The Sign of the Four*. And once we notice the absence of information about prisons in the Holmes stories, we may begin to be aware of other omissions. He may be an avid reader of police reports and the newspaper account of trials, but how often, for example, does Holmes go to court? How much would we be able to glean from these tales about what the law is and how it works? Where are the magistrates, the barristers and judges and their clerks, the legislators, penal reformers, prison chaplains, police court reporters? How often do we see the inside of a police station, hear policemen talk to each other, or glimpse their

---

[9] ACD, Letter to *The Times* (20 June 1929), in *Letters to the Press*, 336.

private lives? Apart from always ineffectual crime scene investigation and jumping to obviously wrong conclusions, how much do the stories show us of police procedure? How much could we learn from them about the sort of things the police were called upon to deal with? It is immediately obvious that there could be no place in a Holmes adventure for either Bloody Sunday or Jack the Ripper.[10] In fact there is a relatively narrow suite of crimes and disturbances in Conan Doyle's fiction, and a perfunctory account of punishments. Indeed of all the cultural domains that form the subject of these chapters, on the evidence of his stories crime and punishment seems to be the one that he knew and cared least about.

What then did Conan Doyle's fiction have to tell his first readers about crime and punishment in the society they inhabited, and what does it have to tell us? It is often averred of crime fiction that it follows, consciously or not, an agenda of reassurance and the reinforcement of social norms. "As a genre, the detective story is wholly unsuited to addressing systemic problems in any sustained way. At best, it only translates them into problems of *individual* deviance and transgression."[11] Franco Moretti put the case influentially in *Signs Taken for Wonders* when he declared that detective fiction "exists expressly to dispel the doubt that guilt might be impersonal, and therefore collective and social".[12] Ronald R. Thomas argues that it is Sherlock Holmes's consistent inclination to replace a political explanation of a crime with a private one.[13] The successes of a clever detective show us that wrongdoing may exist, but is manageable; it can be identified, contained,

---

[10] Subsequent writers have attended to this omission and there is a shelf of more recent books in which Holmes is called upon to solve, or in at least one case perpetrate, the Whitechapel murders. Conan Doyle took an interest in the case but it was a kind of crime that could not possibly have featured in his fiction. See Peter Costello, *Conan Doyle Detective* (London: Constable and Robinson, 2006), 79–94. In an interview in 1894 Conan Doyle obligingly gave Holmes's ideas on the Ripper case. See Orel (ed.), *Sir Arthur Conan Doyle: Interviews and Recollections*, 72–3.

[11] Stephen Arata, *Fictions of Loss in the Victorian Fin de Siècle* (Cambridge: Cambridge University Press, 1996), 143.

[12] Franco Moretti, *Signs Taken for Wonders* (London: NLB, 1983), 135. Genre criticism of popular forms can tend towards the dogmatic, sharing Todorov's belief that "the masterpiece of popular literature is precisely the book which best fits its genre". Tzvetan Todorov, *The Poetics of Prose*, trans. Richard Howard (Oxford: Blackwell, 1977), 43.

[13] Thomas, *Detective Fiction and the Rise of Forensic Science*, 224. Thomas argues that forensic science is deployed in the first two Holmes books to shift attention from the political to the private, and—at the same time—from domestic to foreign culpability.

righted, or at least punished. Even though we may be aware that crime is produced out of social or systemic causes—want, ignorance, injustice, misfortune—detective fiction may allow us to believe, or at least feel, that when the criminal is exposed and rendered harmless, the rest of society has been purged and redressed. Like a scapegoating ritual, crime fiction identifies and expels the abnormal: in proving someone guilty, it proves everyone else not guilty, and so is engaged, in D. A. Miller's phrase, in "producing a social innocence".[14] In *The Novel and the Police*, Miller moved backwards from detective fiction to the novel itself, to argue that novels like Dickens's *Oliver Twist* or Wilkie Collins's *The Moonstone* were themselves agents of social regulation. Snooping into private lives, meticulously amassing circumstantial details, reinscribing the offices of detection in everyday life itself, submitting everything to its regime of knowledge, approving norms of behaviour and seeing that their violation was punished—the novel, Miller argued, was a function of a phenomenon Michel Foucault had described as the diffusion of the work of discipline into the community itself—"the genre of the novel *belongs* to the disciplinary field that it portrays".[15] The detective story itself, coming into its own with Conan Doyle and others towards the end of the nineteenth century, simply now located that disciplinary power in the figure of the single gifted investigator, though still usually an unofficial one—Sherlock Holmes, Hercule Poirot, Lord Peter Wimsey, and the rest.

A Study in Scarlet made little impact at first. *The Sign of the Four* did well. But the extraordinary publishing phenomenon of Sherlock Holmes really began with the short stories that started to appear in the *Strand* in 1891, and were later collected the following year in the volume *The Adventures of Sherlock Holmes*. I now want to examine the four earliest of these, to test the above theories of detective fiction, and to see what these tales know, and say, about crime and punishment.

Consulted by a masked man in "A Scandal in Bohemia", Sherlock Holmes easily sees through the disguise, and treats his royal client with minimal respect. He is scornful of the King of Bohemia's arrogance, and privately amused by his majesty's indiscretion. The King has had a liaison with Irene Adler, an opera singer described as an adventuress,

[14] D. A. Miller, *The Novel and the Police* (Berkeley and Los Angeles: University of California Press, 1988), 34.
[15] Miller, *The Novel and the Police*, 21.

and now that he is betrothed to a royal princess, it is imperative that he recover a compromising photograph from his abandoned mistress. There is indeed a threat to social order in this story, but it does not come from the adventuress. She has refused money in exchange for the photo, so the King has had her house burgled twice, her luggage diverted and ransacked, and she herself has been twice waylaid by men in the King's employ. These royal and masculine misdemeanours are not the only crimes committed in the story. Irene Adler is completely law-abiding throughout, while it is the men ranged against her—the King, and later his agents Holmes and Watson—who break the law. Holmes will organize an affray in the street and commit an act of attempted burglary, and Watson will throw an incendiary device into Irene's house. So a hereditary ruler and his agents have no hesitation in committing crime to secure the reputation of the monarch which he has compromised by sexual indiscretion. Holmes carries out this commission despite his contempt for the King and his growing admiration for Irene Adler. European stability is maintained, the King's marriage will proceed, Holmes is rewarded. But in terms of what it says about law and order, the first Sherlock Holmes tale is both satirical and frankly anarchistic. Royalty is propped up, in a story that demonstrates royalty to be both undeserving and abusive of its powers.[16] Holmes cynically puts his skills at the service of the hereditary leadership of a bullying patriarchal political establishment for which he has no respect. The police, meantime, are nowhere to be seen. It is hard to map this tale in any straightforward way to the conservative ideological agenda that is often attributed to the genre of crime fiction. It is not a social innocence that this tale produces. The only innocent character is this society is the cosmopolitan adventuress who has no place—and seemingly no rights—in it.

"A Case of Identity" is the second story in the *Adventures* and begins with a young woman seeking help to find her bridegroom, who disappeared on her wedding day. Holmes quickly establishes that the mysterious groom was none other than the girl's stepfather in disguise, contriving to make sure she will not marry anyone else and take her inheritance with her. "It's not actionable," blusters the caddish stepfather

---

[16] The contemptible King is of course a foreigner. But there was a very good chance that a late nineteenth-century royal would be related in some way to Queen Victoria.

Windibank when his trick is exposed, and he is right (*Adventures*, 45). It was a cruel deception, but no crime has been committed. Holmes does not even reveal the solution of the case to the victim, for he says—anticipating Marlow with the Intended in "Heart of Darkness"— that it is ill advised to snatch a delusion from a woman. (If there is any disciplinary regime involved here, it has to do with the regulation of behaviour of and among men: Holmes threatens to horsewhip Windibank for his unmanly conduct in deceiving and hurting a young woman. But the deceived girl, like Kurtz's Intended, is "out of it": after consulting Holmes, she withdraws from the action—it is like the moment in a dinner party when ladies "withdraw" from the table— and the story is resolved in masculine society.)

"A Case of Identity" is a detective story without either crime or punishment. Its point is hermeneutic only: interpreting the facts, uncovering the underlying story. Holmes's skills *effect* nothing here: as in "A Scandal in Bohemia", his interventions are redundant. Here there is no penalty for the wrongdoer, no redress for the victim, no safeguarding for the community or production of social innocence. The only satisfaction derived is Watson's, and the reader's, as we see the puzzle solved, through access to Holmes's extraordinary powers of vision, his ability to find the astonishing which lies disguised in the commonplace. He expounds this to Watson at the start of this tale.

If we could fly out of that window hand in hand, hover over this great city, gently remove the roofs, and peep in at the queer things which are going on, the strange coincidences, the plannings, the cross-purposes, the wonderful chains of events, working through generations, and leading to the most *outré* results, it would make all fiction with its conventionalities and foreseen conclusions most stale and unprofitable. (*Adventures*, 30)

This kind of intimate and privileged knowledge of people's lives is closer to a doctor's knowledge of his practice than a detective's of his. And though it follows Holmes's restatement of the commonplace that truth is stranger than fiction, it is above all similar to a fiction-writer's manifesto, a claim to take the ordinary muddled materials of life and discover in them coherence, consequence, and excitement, and thus to rescue the sharers of that vision from the banalities of existence. We have seen, in an earlier chapter, that the Holmes tales are sometimes about justice. But the first two tales in the *Adventures* have nothing to do with justice, and neither of them offers the spectacle of crime being dealt with, which is supposed to be both the narrative and the ideological staple of the detective story.

A similar theme, of the discovery of the *outré* within the commonplace, motivates the next case, "The Red-Headed League". Watson is invited into the case because, Holmes tells him, "you share my love for all that is bizarre and outside the conventions and humdrum routine of every-day life" (*Adventures*, 49): for strange effects and extraordinary combinations, life can always offer something far more daring than imagination. The story begins with the prosaic pawnbroker Jabez Wilson, who "bore every mark of being an average commonplace British tradesman, obese, pompous and slow" (*Adventures*, 50). Wilson's idea of the good life is one in which nothing happens. His ambitions are to live quietly, keep a roof over his head, and pay his debts, but into this orderly and mildly entropic world (the business seems to be failing) has come a disorderly and inexplicable element, the mysterious League for the welfare and propagation of redheads, and the sluggish Wilson finds himself propelled into narrative. His ignorance of the outside world has made him gullible, and it seems appropriate that the League entice him out of his shop into a job that requires him to copy out the *Encyclopaedia Britannica*, starting at the letter A, in a sort of parody of the self-improvement in knowledge that many others saw as an instrument to lever them out of a lower social class. But Wilson knows nothing and learns nothing. When the League, and his job, one day disappear, he goes to Holmes, not to report a crime or claim redress, but just for an explanation of what is going on.

From this unpromising material Holmes sets about producing knowledge, immediately observing that his client is a Freemason, has done manual labour, been in China, and so on. Wilson's narrative, and a visit to the neighbourhood of his shop, is all Holmes needs to piece together the story, and to predict and forestall the crime, a bank robbery. Wilson is an ignoramus, but Holmes is a master of knowing, and can transform information into knowledge in the form of stories, of the past, and what is to come. His knowledge of histories is underwritten by his knowledge of the topography of the city—"It is a hobby of mine to have an exact knowledge of London" (*Adventures*, 64)—which also informs the tales in which he appears, which teem with geographical data: in "The Red-Headed League" we find Baker Street, Pope's Court off Fleet Street, Coburg (or Saxe-Coburg) Square in the City, King Edward Street near St Paul's, St James's Hall, Regent Street,

Aldersgate Underground station and Aldersgate Street, the Strand, Kensington, Hyde Park, Oxford Street, Scotland Yard, Farringdon Street, and—further afield—Lebanon, Pennsylvania, and China. Holmes always knows just where he is and he knows where things and people are to be found.

From Wilson's description of his assistant, Holmes immediately recognizes the criminal John Clay. Clay is also known to the police but, Inspector Jones confesses, "we never know where to find the man himself" (*Adventures*, 67). Holmes not only knows who and where Clay is, he knows just where he will be (tunnelling into the bank vault) on a particular night. Jones, the official police agent, is only brought in to the case once Holmes knows everything that has happened and what is about to happen, and he is brought in not to investigate the crime but to deal with the criminal, a job Holmes is almost always prepared to leave to the official force. Importantly, Holmes is always the *first* to know, to the chagrin but also to the admiration of Watson. "Here I had heard what he had heard, I had seen what he had seen, and yet from his words it was evident that he saw clearly not only what had happened, but what was about to happen, while to me the whole business was still confused and grotesque" (*Adventures*, 65).

"The Red-Headed League" is a crime story which ends conventionally (yet unusually among the stories in the *Adventures*), with the identification and arrest of the miscreant.[17] Yet in the story the question of justice and retribution seems secondary, as Holmes's (and the tale's) carelessness about the subsequent fate of John Clay suggests. This insouciance about the machinery of justice suggests some complacency: the police may be flatfooted and need to be corrected by Holmes, but then the institutions of law and order can be confidently left to get on with their business. If this was indeed Conan Doyle's view, it was later to change. Here, since Clay is known to be a murderer, presumably he will be convicted of this and other crimes and go to the gallows, but his punishment lies off the epistemological map of the story. We are not invited to take an interest in it. A similar partiality is to be found in the geography of what Franco Moretti calls "Doyle's city of crime": Moretti took the trouble to plot the locations of crime scenes in the Holmes tales and compare these with Charles Booth's

---

[17] It is the only one of the first dozen Holmes short stories to end in this conventional way. See Arata, *Fictions of Loss in the Victorian Fin de Siècle*, 147.

1889 Descriptive Map of London Poverty, and showed that the tales focus almost entirely on the West End and the City of London, and almost never venture into those parts of the metropolis where actual crime was endemic.[18] This is not simply a matter of class. Moretti's point is that crime fiction requires crime to be mysterious, while there is usually nothing very enigmatic about crimes committed in areas where social conditions produce a high crime rate. The Sherlock Holmes stories always centre on a puzzle, even when they do not contain a crime. In "The Red-Headed League", the point of the story is to bring a queue of ignorant people—Watson, Jones, Merryweather the banker, Jabez Wilson the pawnbroker, and the reader—into the same state of knowledge as Holmes (and, incidentally, the criminal John Clay). This is actually more important than the distribution of punishments and rewards.

As Simon Joyce has noted, criminals from the comfortable classes in Conan Doyle often turn out to be impostors, mad, or foreign.[19] This is not the case with the blue-blooded John Clay, though he is presumably illegitimate. The son of a royal duke but also a thief and murderer, Clay is out of place, a disruptive element, a disturber of order. (In this, he resembles another character in the *Adventures*, Neville St Clair in "The Man with the Twisted Lip", the gentleman who makes a living as a beggar, whom Holmes unmasks and firmly replaces in the suburban bourgeois culture from which he has strayed: unlike Clay, St Clair has not broken the law, but he has violated social order.) In "The Red-Headed League" Holmes's activities, which are cybernetic (having to do with the management and deployment of knowledge), succeed in containing that threat, and order is restored. But what Clay's disruption leaves behind as a trace, like a footprint in a flowerbed, is the story itself, and it is the story that is Holmes's reward, and Watson's, and ours. Watson will write the story down, but Holmes is really its author, for he has produced and organized the knowledge that allows the story to emerge from a chaos of noise, puzzlement, banality, and apparent insignificance. Watson still thinks Holmes deserves a fuller recompense, and he declares the great detective a benefactor of the human race. But Holmes says he has been amply rewarded "by having had an experience

---

[18] Franco Moretti, *Atlas of the European Novel 1800–1900* (London: Verso, 1998), 134–6.
[19] Simon Joyce, *Capital Offences: Geographies of Class and Crime in Victorian London* (Charlottesville, Va.: University of Virginia Press, 2003), 8.

which is in many ways unique, and by hearing the very remarkable narrative of the Red-Headed League" (*Adventures*, 72). This is not quite accurate. He has not so much heard the narrative as made it, brought it into knowledge. In doing so, he has redeemed for a while the commonplaces of existence. It is the reward of the Baudelairean dandy, or of the reader. "'It saved me from ennui,' he answered, yawning" (*Adventures*, 74). This is hardly the way we would expect to hear a police officer or a judge summing up a day's work.

Sherlock Holmes is not addicted to cocaine.[20] For him it is a recreational drug, and he stops using when he has an absorbing case to work on. He is not even addicted to crime; quite a few of his cases contain none. His addiction is to knowledge, and specifically to those strings or sequences of information that constitute a story. When their right place in such a sequence is found, the most prosaic and uninteresting of details—the label in a coat, a smudge of paint, a dog that didn't bark—become clothed in shining significance, as if they were angels. Holmes may be the guardian of law and order in his world, but he is dependent on a continuous supply of teeming chaos, in the form of challenges to order and meaning, delivered to Baker Street in the opening pages of each tale, from which knowledge can be created by his signal powers. Like any craftsman, he is dependent on his materials, and he grumbles about the poor quality of the modern criminal. But a drop in the crime rate is the last thing he wants. Jack the Ripper was a serial killer, and Sherlock Holmes was a serial detective. There have been many copycats.

"The Boscombe Valley Mystery" is the fourth story in the *Adventures*, and my last example. The case takes Holmes and Watson to the Wye Valley in the west of England. Moretti has observed that crimes in Conan Doyle tend to become more violent outside London. In "The Copper Beeches", when Watson declares the English countryside to be a haven of peaceful beauty, Holmes is quick to stamp on this pastoral

---

[20] Conan Doyle had watched his own father's addiction to alcohol, and in a tale of 1904, "The Missing Three-Quarter", he has Watson say that he has weaned Holmes from "the drug mania" (*Return*, 243). But in my opinion he does not portray Holmes as *dependent* on drugs. There is rather whimsical support for this view in Edgar W. Smith, "Up from the Needle", in Philip A. Shreffler (ed.), *Sherlock Holmes by Gas-Lamp: Highlights from the First Four Decades of the Baker Street Journal* (New York: Fordham University Press, 1989), 67–70. For a different opinion, see J. Thomas Dalby, "Sherlock Holmes's Cocaine Habit", *ACD: Journal of the Arthur Conan Doyle Society*, 4 (1993), 12–15.

cliché: he sees the rural scene as simply an extensive opportunity for wrongdoing, opining "that the lowest and vilest alleys in London do not present a more dreadful record of sin than does the smiling and beautiful countryside" (*Adventures*, 280).

Though "The Boscombe Valley Mystery" is another tale that does not end with the identification and punishment of the criminal, it does conform to the classic paradigm of the detective story in that it is mostly about research. On the train to the West Country, Holmes has brought with him an "immense litter of papers" (*Adventures*, 76), and he sets to work on this improvised archive, with intervals of note-taking and meditation, to organize the known facts of the case, in which James McCarthy has been arrested for the murder of his father. It seems several people in the neighbourhood believe in the young man's innocence, including Alice Turner, daughter of McCarthy's neighbour and fellow Australian, and they have retained Inspector Lestrade, of Scotland Yard, to work out the case in his interest; Lestrade, inevitably, has consulted Holmes for a second opinion, though the policeman himself is quite sure the arrested man is guilty.

Watson is inclined to agree, but Holmes warns him that circumstantial evidence may mislead, for "it may seem to point very straight to one thing, but if you shift your own point of view a little, you may find it pointing in an equally uncompromising manner to something entirely different" (*Adventures*, 78). Good narrative is not just a string of incidents, but depends on their being seen from the appropriate modality or point of view. This seems borne out by the various stories Holmes goes to work on. The institutions of the law—the police investigation, the coroner's inquest, Lestrade's own enquiries—all make up a narrative pointing unambiguously to the youth's guilt. Holmes's secondary researches, however, including his brilliant reading of clues at the scene of the crime, allow another story to emerge, one in which Alice Turner's father is the killer, and the victim his blackmailer. In due course this is confirmed by Turner himself: he murdered McCarthy when the latter extended his blackmailing activities to demand that Turner's beloved daughter be made to marry his son, "with as little regard for what she might think as if she were a slut from off the streets" (*Adventures*, 99). The sexual subjugation of a woman seems to have been the worst thing Conan Doyle could think of: it mitigates the commission of murder in *A Study in Scarlet*, "The Abbey Grange", and here.

When he has disentangled the story, a number of contrivances enable Holmes to tie it up again in a satisfying conclusion. Turner has an incurable illness and will soon be dead. His daughter and young McCarthy do in fact love each other; McCarthy has formed a rash attachment to a barmaid in Bristol but she releases him as soon as he is in trouble. Holmes's unofficial *locus* in the case leaves him disinclined to judge Turner, especially since the latter has only a few months to live, and he decides not to use Turner's confession, provided young McCarthy is acquitted at the Assize (as he is, on the strength of objections drawn out by Holmes). This forbearance means that young McCarthy and Alice Turner will get married and live happily in ignorance of the fact that her father made his money from armed robbery, his father blackmailed him, and her father bludgeoned his father to death. A poetic justice is served in this melodrama: innocence inherits from guilt.

Once again, Holmes features in the adventure as an interpreter of the facts, but hardly at all as an agent of law, even an unofficial one. There will be no trace of his activities in the official record of the case. "The Boscombe Valley Mystery" is hardly a ringing endorsement of the institutions of law and order, which for their part would certainly have sent an innocent young man to his death on the gallows. But the story is not so much critical of these institutions; rather, they are strangely unfocused, as if irrelevant to it. Holmes and Watson gather all preliminary information about the case from newspapers, including a verbatim report of the inquest. Extraordinarily, at no point in his visit to the West Country does Holmes have any contact with the local police. Lestrade is on the scene. We are told Lestrade has been retained by some neighbours to investigate the case in the interests of the accused young man, but this is a solecism: as Richard Lancelyn Green points out, it would have been illegal to retain an inspector from Scotland Yard for a fee (*Adventures*, 328 n. 78). Conan Doyle's carelessness about police procedure is interesting: he was thinking in terms of rival consultants in a different profession. In any case, Lestrade appears to do nothing at all, except frequently to repeat his belief that his client is guilty. Remarkably, nothing is shown in this story of the official operations of the organs of law and order. The inquest appears only as a newspaper report. The police—in Herefordshire where the murder took place, and in Australia where McCarthy led his earlier life of crime—are invisible. Lestrade is an ineffectual joke. Holmes's visit to McCarthy in gaol is not narrated, and the trial at the Assizes takes place offstage. A student of the institutions of law and order in late nineteenth-century England would find slim pickings indeed in this tale.

After "The Boscombe Valley Mystery" comes "The Five Orange Pips", a story in which Holmes solves the mystery, but is unable to prevent the murder of John Openshaw or to apprehend his murderers (who escape England, but are lost at sea). And so on. The triumph of law and order, in the identification, arrest, and punishment of the offender, is by no means an inevitability in the Sherlock Holmes stories. In fact, it is a narrative sequence that does not occur in the majority of the tales. The most famous of crime writers, in his fiction Conan Doyle seems not to have been very interested in nor particularly knowledgeable about how law and order actually worked in the society of his time.[21] "A Scandal in Bohemia" was a cynical story about the misbehaviour of the established and powerful, from which a resourceful woman was lucky to escape: Sherlock Holmes colludes unhesitatingly in that misbehaviour, for a fee. "A Case of Identity" removed the roof on a pathetic tale of a young girl's exploitation by her family, but left her ignorant of why her lover had disappeared, and unaware of how she had been tricked by those closest to her, who go unpunished. "The Red-Headed League" was a delightful fantasy that grafted an intricate practical joke onto the tale of the thwarting of a bank robbery. The non-criminal plan to get Jabez Wilson out of his shop bulks very much larger than the actual heist, and the officials of the law (and of the bank) are brought in only when Holmes is ready to deliver the would-be criminals into their hands. And "The Boscombe Valley Mystery" is a detective story that shows very little interest in law and order; the law that governs it is the law of melodrama, in the service of a justice that is not national, but poetic. Sherlock Holmes is far more interested in bringing transgression to light and making it knowable, than in the real business of the apparatus of law and order, the apprehension and punishment of criminals, the maintenance of order, and the prevention of crime.

---

[21] In contrast with Dickens, for example, who frequented the legislature and the courts, visited and wrote about prisons, befriended police officers, and frequently joined them in their patrols.

Edalji's eyes

In December 1906 Conan Doyle became involved in the case of George Edalji, a young Birmingham solicitor recently released from prison after serving three years of a seven-year sentence for the crime of maiming animals. The critical moment in the Sherlockian paradigm— the moment of knowing—came at the very first interview or consultation between Edalji and Conan Doyle, at the Grand Hotel in Charing Cross. Literally at first sight, it was plain to Conan Doyle that Edalji must be innocent of the charges brought against him.

After his release, which was accompanied by neither a pardon nor compensation nor indeed any explanation, Edalji had sent Conan Doyle cuttings of articles about his case from the magazine *Umpire*, and asked for his help. The facts in the case were these. George's father, the Revd Shapurji Edalji, a Parsee originally from Bombay, had been Anglican vicar of Great Wyrley in Staffordshire since 1876. His wife was English and they had three children. Shapurji became the victim of a series of anonymous letters, which began in 1888 when George was 12, and resumed in 1892 to 1895. There was also an outbreak of obscene graffiti, and some malicious practical jokes, including orders sent to tradesmen, and letters to the local press, in Edalji's name. The vicar felt obliged to publish a letter in *The Times* in August 1895 cautioning people that correspondence purporting to come from him might be a hoax.[22] The local police investigated inconclusively, but seem to have been convinced that the culprit was George. In February 1903 the area witnessed the first in a gruesome series of mutilations of animals—cattle, sheep, and horses being attacked, usually in the field at night, and wounded with a sharp instrument. Anonymous letters incriminating George Edalji in this outrage began to appear on 1 July, and after a ninth ripping took place in the night of 17 August, he was arrested and charged under the Malicious Damage Act of 1861. He was tried before a jury at the Staffordshire Quarter Sessions, found guilty, and sentenced to seven years penal servitude.[23] At Great Wyrley, the

---

[22] Costello, *Conan Doyle Detective*, 110–11.

[23] The county Quarter Sessions was a court with high criminal jurisdiction, and could try all crimes save an excepted class reserved for yet higher courts. See Maitland, *Justice and Police*, 85.

mutilations did not stop, and nor did the anonymous letters. Letters and mutilations were to continue intermittently until 1914. A campaign led by the barrister Roger Yelverton (an advocate of the setting up of a Court of Appeal), gathered 10,000 signatures for a petition for his release, and George Edalji was let out on ticket-of-leave in October 1906. But he was not pardoned, and therefore could not be reinstated on the Roll of Solicitors and resume his legal career. It was at this point that George Edalji wrote to the creator of Sherlock Holmes for help.

It was not unprecedented for a writer to take up what was perceived as a case of injustice. In 1895 W. T. Stead had championed the cause of Dr Charles Augustus Bynoe, imprisoned for forgery, with a sixpenny booklet entitled *Wanted: A Sherlock Holmes!* More recently, articles in the *Daily Mail* by George Sims, a journalist friend of Conan Doyle's and a fellow member of the Crimes Club, had helped to clear Adolph Beck, a Norwegian engineer wrongly imprisoned for robbery.[24] The great precedent, however, was that of the French novelist Émile Zola and his championing of the wretched Captain Alfred Dreyfus, a victim of injustice at the highest levels of the state, in a case that split French society down the middle and foregrounded the role of intellectuals in the formation of public opinion.

Conan Doyle was aware that it was his celebrity as author of the Holmes stories that had caused Edalji to turn to him. He was also anxious not to give the impression that he was an interfering amateur and "a universal busybody".[25] Nevertheless, once he had read the papers sent to him, and concluded that he was "in the presence of an appalling tragedy, and that [he] was called upon to do what [he] could to set it right", he did not hesitate to involve himself publicly in the case (*M&A*, 216–17). The swiftness with which he went to work on Edalji's behalf is an indication of his awareness of the public responsibilities of the writer—he was the historian and apologist of the British military campaign in South Africa, an indefatigable committee man, twice a parliamentary candidate, and an increasingly frequent writer to the correspondence columns of national newspapers, notably *The Times*—but also of the self-confidence with which he was ready to engage in a field in which he was, after all, no professional. Two motives

---

[24] See Lycett, *Conan Doyle*, 303. The handwriting expert who testified in the Beck trial was also retained by the prosecution in the Edalji case.

[25] Costello, *Conan Doyle Detective*, 134.

seem to have driven him in the case. The first was an indignant compassion for "this forlorn little group of people", the Edalji family,
anomalous and vulnerable in rural Staffordshire, and bullied by the
police who ought to have been protecting them (*M&A*, 218). The second motive was a broader one. He was a national author seeking to
help redress an injustice which brought the nation itself into disrepute.
"It is a story," he wrote, "which any unofficial Englishman must read
with shame and indignation."[26] In the Edalji case we can see him writing both as and on behalf of the "unofficial Englishman": he held no
state office, so he could speak out without fear or favour, yet at the
same time he did not speak only as an individual, but had some claim
to speak *for* Englishmen.

And so Conan Doyle came to meet George Edalji at the Grand
Hotel in Charing Cross, and the Sherlock Holmes moment took place.
Appropriately, given the exceptionally strong theme of visuality in the
Holmes stories and in their author's idea of scientific evidence, the
truth of the case fell into place for Conan Doyle through an observation of Edalji's eyes, even before a word was exchanged between the
two men. In the last reported ripping, the police maintained that
George had left the vicarage under cover of darkness, and walked to
the field where he mutilated a pony, then returned home. Yet it was
clear to Conan Doyle at first sight that Edalji was both myopic and
astigmatic—"practically blind, save in good light" (*M&A*, 218). It was
inconceivable that he could have found his way anywhere across country in the dark, and still less to the place where the mutilation was
committed, since this would involve crossing the full breadth of the
London and Northwestern Railway, with its rails, wires, and other
obstacles, a flight of steps and a tunnel, and hedges to be forced on
either side. Conan Doyle had himself been a specialist in the eye, albeit
briefly, and now he appealed to expert opinion in the profession to
confirm that a man with eyesight like Edalji's could never have managed the route at night as the police claimed. On the basis of a factual
observation, Conan Doyle now *knew* Edalji to be innocent. In a Holmes
story, the detective observation by itself might stand as incontrovertible
proof; once it was communicated to others, the rest of the case could

---

[26] ACD, *The Story of Mr. George Edalji* (1907), ed. Richard and Molly Whittington-Egan
(London: Grey House Books, 1985), 91. Hereafter *Story*. This volume brings together
Conan Doyle's articles and letters on the Edalji affair.

be left to the more pedestrian official agents of justice to tidy up, as they are so often left to do in Holmes's cases.

But Edalji's bulging eyes were not only a sign of his innocence. Conan Doyle was also able to read in them a clue as to why he had been presumed guilty by so many.[27] As photographs show, the young man simply looked odd. His strange and alien appearance, in Conan Doyle's opinion, must have made him "seem a very queer man to the eyes of an English village" (*Story*, 35). Edalji's eyes now become, in the eyes of the neighbours among whom he had lived all his life, a token of his queer nature, his abnormality and irreducible difference from themselves. Conan Doyle said he could find no cause for the misfortunes of the Edaljis except what he called "colour hatred" (*Story*, 114). He commented later that "the appearance of a coloured clergyman with a half-caste son in a rude, unrefined parish was bound to cause some regrettable situation" (*M&A*, 216). In his account of the case there is a certain recoil from the England of Great Wyrley, this fastness of sinister rustics and incompetent provincial officials, harbouring cruelty and even lunacy, while scapegoating the unworldly and foreign-looking family that has come among them, and protecting their own prejudices and unjust practices by a refusal to look manifest facts in the eye.

Conan Doyle's articles set out to demolish with a Holmesian briskness the wealth of material evidence adduced by the police to support their case against Edalji—things like a wet razor with blood on it, blood and saliva and hair on a coat, wet boots, and a footmark corresponding to the boot: not one single item of this evidence would bear criticism, he declared. Continuing the ocular theme, he presented a file of facsimile documents in support of his case, including the actual and alleged handwriting (in the anonymous letters) of George Edalji. He did not hesitate to dismiss the opinion of the handwriting expert, Thomas Henry Gurrin, retained by the police, who testified that all the letters were in George's hand. It is plain to Conan Doyle that one

---

[27] Andrew Lycett has suggested a further interpretation was in play, and that Edalji's bulging eyes and dark appearance had marked him out as guilty according to the criminologist Lombroso's scientific categorizations, as understood by Captain Anson, the Staffordshire Chief Constable. Lycett, *Conan Doyle*, 303. Lombroso however was of the view that sight was "generally more acute in criminals than in normal persons". Gina Lombroso-Ferrero, *Criminal Man According to the Classification of Cesare Lombroso* (1911) (Montclair, NJ: Patterson Smith, 1972), 249.

set of writing is that of an educated person and the other of an uneducated one. And beyond social class, he can confidently parse the handwriting to reveal something like moral character.

Compare the real Edalji writing with the addressed envelope of [sample] three, or with the postscript of four, and ask yourself whether they do not belong to an entirely different class. Apart from the question of educated as against uneducated writing, the most superficial observer of character, as expressed in writing, would say that one and two were open and free, while three and four were cramped and mean. (*Story*, 85)

Even the handwriting was revealing a world essentially melodramatic in its simple contours, with the unjustly punished victim, educated and open and free in his character, and the villain, revealed by his own writing to be low and underhand.

Edalji's eyes were a sign of something else too. They were a badge of his literacy. When Conan Doyle first cast eyes on him, George Edalji was reading a paper, squinting at the newsprint which he held close to his face. The portrait that emerges of him in Conan Doyle's writing is of a studious young man, his mild and intellectual life an extreme contrast to the brutal crimes of which he was accused, and the diabolical malice of the letters he was supposed to have sent. Not only was Edalji cultured and clerical in upbringing and manners, he also belonged to the professional classes. It is understandable that this point should be emphasized. After all, when Conan Doyle joined the case George Edalji was no longer in prison, but the criminal record, which had caused him to be struck off the Solicitors' Roll, still stood. This was one of the injustices Conan Doyle wanted to see righted. Even so, there is something relentless in his harping on about the young man's professional status and scholarly attainments. Edalji is "a rising professional man", "a most distinguished student, having won the highest legal prizes within his reach, and written, at his early age, a handbook of railway law"; "an ambitious young professional man", "the purblind, studious, teetotal young lawyer", "a young gentleman, distinguished already in an honourable profession", "an eminently sane young lawyer", "a well-educated young man, brought up in a clerical atmosphere, with no record of coarse speech or evil life"; "What in Edalji's studious life has ever given the slightest indications of such a [wicked] nature? His whole career and the testimony of all who have known him cry out against such a supposition" (*Story*, 45, 52, 57, 66, 70, 86, 87,

117). Until he fell foul of local prejudice and the law, George Edalji was in the process of establishing himself as a professional, a member of what Harold Perkin has described as that meritocratic "fourth class", which had started to disturb the stability of a more traditional three-class hierarchy towards the end of the nineteenth century.[28] In some respects George Edalji, from an immigrant family and making his way in the world through education and professional qualification, was an avatar of the new century and a new England. He might have expected his professional status to trump any residual stigma attaching to his ethnicity, just as in an earlier generation Conan Doyle's own membership of a profession spoke louder than his Irish and Catholic antecedents. It is significant that ranged against George Edalji are a suite of residual interests, belonging to an England that Conan Doyle was impatient with: the *ressentiment* of the locals with their "colour hatred" and (in one case at least) religious mania; the obstruction of a government bureaucracy and a police force not answerable to the public; the inherited privilege of the likes of Sir Reginald Hardy, who presided as Assistant Chairman over the Quarter Sessions and passed sentence on Edalji though he had no legal training or professional qualification,[29] and of Captain the Hon. George Anson, Chief Constable of Staffordshire and brother of the Earl of Lichfield, who had been prejudiced against George Edalji since the time of the first anonymous letters in the early 1890s.[30]

All these factors could only strengthen Conan Doyle's conviction that the Edalji case was a simple, black-and-white affair, as simple as the moral melodramas into which the Holmes stories resolved themselves once the facts were established. Edalji's eyes proved him innocent. Other facts emerged to confirm this. A Home Office committee of investigation, appointed after public pressure from Conan Doyle and others, found that he had been wrongly convicted, though confusingly they endorsed the police theory that he was the author of the anonymous letters and maintained that he had thus, in some sense,

---

[28] Perkin, *The Rise of Professional Society*, 116.

[29] An estate in land worth £100 a year, or a dwelling house assessed at £100 a year, qualified a man to be appointed a county justice of the peace, and sit on the bench as a magistrate at the Quarter Sessions. See Maitland, *Justice and Police*, 82.

[30] Conan Doyle was somewhat embarrassed to be attacking Anson, who had treated him with great personal courtesy. The relationship between the two men is one of the themes of the fictional retelling of the story in Julian Barnes, *Arthur and George* (London: Jonathan Cape, 2005).

brought his misfortune upon himself.[31] He was pardoned (but not compensated), and the Law Society readmitted him, with leave to practise. But not content with this, Conan Doyle in his enthusiasm had seen the possibility of closing the case in the classic fashion, by exposing the real culprit. A close study of the anonymous letters—their content, as well as their handwriting—and some local research convinced him that both the letters and the mutilations could be laid at the door of a Wyrley family, Royden Sharp and his brothers. He wrote a report making the case against Sharp and submitted it to the Home Office. They forwarded it to the Staffordshire police, who not surprisingly rejected it, and Conan Doyle was told there was not a prima facie case against Sharp. There, in a way unsatisfactory to most of the parties involved, the Edalji case ceased.

In terms of what we might call the practice of fictional detection, Conan Doyle had done pretty well. He had read the clues of material evidence, reconstructed the events, helped to exculpate the innocent accused, and brought the identity of the criminal (as he firmly believed) to the knowledge of the authorities. If this really had been a Sherlock Holmes story, that would have been enough, and justice could be left to complete its course. But the Edalji case failed to be one of those shapely narratives, punctuated by Aristotelian discovery and reversal and closed off with the promise of appropriate rewards and punishments, which Dr Watson was able to deliver, time and again, from his case-book. I have described such stories as melodramas, partly to indicate the usually unambiguous moral scheme that underwrites them. George Edalji's case was no melodrama in this sense. The difference was that the Holmes stories could rely on a dependable ambience of law and order to secure and ratify the knowledge produced by Holmes's detections. The consultant detective gave his opinion, and the apparatus of the law could be left to take the appropriate action: such was his confidence in that apparatus, so naturalized its working in the minds of Holmes, his author, and his readers, that usually its operations did not need to be shown, they could just be assumed. But in England, or at least in Staffordshire, in 1907, the institutions supposed to guarantee that ambience of law and order—the courts and judges and juries, the police and their commanders and their procedure, the law itself,

---

[31] Conan Doyle flatly rejected as absurd the theory that George wrote the letters, but nowhere do his writings address the basis of the police belief that he did so.

the penal system, the government bureaucracy under the oversight of Parliament—could not be relied on.

The Edalji case was a significant early moment in a shift of Conan Doyle's orientation towards the society he inhabited, catered to, and was proud of. In the first decade of the new century he was famous, honoured, popular, and increasingly affluent, and on terms with the men of the nation's governing class. He was a friend of generals and government ministers, distinguished scientists and lawyers, as well as of many of the cultural leaders of the day. If this inclined him to some complacency, it was a confidence that was shaken by what he learned in the Edalji affair. He discovered, he said, that "officialdom in England stands solid together, and that when you are forced to attack it you need not expect justice" (*M&A*, 220).

It was not just that he had encountered in rural Staffordshire a deep England of xenophobia, racial prejudice, and inexplicable violence. It was worse than that. Conan Doyle might have solved the crime, at least to his own satisfaction, but his solution was not endorsed by officialdom, and his real-life investigation was far from producing that "social innocence" that detective fiction has been credited, or reproached, with creating. The police had been not only incompetent—no surprise to the author or indeed to readers of the Sherlock Holmes stories—but actively obstructive, and manifestly uninterested in seeing that justice was done if this might involve overturning a conviction already obtained. The Chief Constable, it appeared, had made up his mind against George Edalji before the investigation of the animal attacks began. The procedure of the Quarter Sessions was questionable at best, the handwriting expert's testimony was open to challenge, Edalji's defence was incompetently handled, and the jury, "already prejudiced by the nature of the crimes, were hoodwinked into giving their conviction" (*Story*, 73). The Home Office was secretive, slow, and uncooperative throughout, and so was the Home Secretary, Herbert Gladstone, especially in referring a complaint about a police prosecution back to the police for an opinion.[32] This was not the England of justice and fair play whose early history Conan Doyle had recently been imagining in *Sir Nigel*. On the contrary, he protested, "I cannot imagine anything more absurd and unjust in an Oriental despotism than this" (*Story*, 74).

---

[32] The Home Secretary was the son of late Prime Minister W. E. Gladstone.

"The more Doyle penetrated the British system of power and privilege into which he had written himself by his defence of it," Diana Barsham has written, "the more he used fierce pamphleteering to attack its limitations of vision, justice and truth."[33] It is true that he leveraged his celebrity status to pursue the case of Edalji, and later of others—a less well-known citizen would hardly have been given personal access to a Chief Constable and a Home Secretary, for example. But it was also his national status that led him to regard cases like Edalji's, and later most notably Oscar Slater's, as national scandals, not just local ones. Detective fiction, we have seen, has been charged with taking systemic problems of crime and translating them into problems of merely individual deviance and transgression, susceptible to individual solutions. (In a similar way, perhaps, Conan Doyle in 1916 could not actually believe that his friend Roger Casement could have taken arms against Great Britain in wartime out of political principle; instead he argued in mitigation that Casement must have been suffering from "an abnormal physical and mental state", brought about by strain and long residence in the tropics.[34]) But Conan Doyle would not regard the Edalji case as an aberration, an individual misfiring of the machinery of justice. He insisted on seeing it as a stain on the nation as a whole.[35] Edalji had been wrongfully imprisoned because of a wholesale failure of the institutions of law and order, and Conan Doyle wanted them all reformed, from the Staffordshire Constabulary to the Home Office (*Story*, 77–8). He attacked them in the name of a man who, though naturally gifted and thoroughly blameless, had been victimized, he believed, because of his difference, in a betrayal of the principle of inclusiveness which underlay his own idea of the nation and empire. It was an early stage in the erosion of his faith in the institutions through which the nation expressed itself.

More was to come. The case of Oscar Slater, which was to involve Conan Doyle, off and on, for sixteen years, was a yet more egregious instance of official injustice, again involving a victim who was vulnerable because he was, or looked, different. Slater (Leschziner) was a

---

[33] Barsham, *Arthur Conan Doyle and the Meaning of Masculinity*, 233.

[34] *A Petition to the Prime Minister on behalf of Roger Casement, by Sir Arthur Conan Doyle and Others*, privately printed, n.d. (1916).

[35] "Either the man is guilty or else there is no compensation which is adequate for the great wrong which this country, through its officials, has inflicted upon him." ACD, Letter to the *Daily Telegraph* (20 May 1907), in *Letters to the Press*, 130–1.

German Jewish immigrant, described by Conan Doyle as "a man of disreputable, though not criminal habits".[36] At his trial for murder in Glasgow the Lord Advocate, prosecuting, told the jury that Slater was a man who "had followed a life which descended to the very depth of human degradation", without any evidence at all.[37] Slater was convicted on circumstantial evidence and served nineteen years in prison for a murder he did not commit. After a long campaign by Conan Doyle and others, his conviction was quashed in 1928. In 1929 Conan Doyle was reading Upton Sinclair's account of the trial of Sacco and Vanzetti in America, and concluding that police and judicial procedure and the whole criminal administration in the United States was now among the worst in the world. "We have little right to criticize," he was quick to add, thinking of the scandal of the Slater case, but "if one has protested against the one, one may be allowed to do so against the other".[38] As Harold Orel put it, "[Conan Doyle]'s hatred of Establishment influence used to create injustices in court, his contempt for lawyers who behaved abominably while covering up legal scandals and the inexcusable behaviour of police officials who assisted them in doing so, was not limited to these landmark cases [of Edalji and Slater]".[39]

In the last years of his life, as we shall see, Conan Doyle came to stand at an acute and uncomfortable angle to many of the institutions of the culture he had once cheerfully endorsed. But this is to anticipate. The Edalji case had shown the administration of justice in a questionable light, but other institutions had come out of the affair with credit. The press, for example, ranging from the obscure *Umpire* and Horace St George Voules's investigative *Truth* to the *National Review*, the *Manchester City News*, and the *Daily Telegraph*, helped to put Edalji's case. Ten thousand people, including several hundred lawyers, signed a petition for his release. In the spirit in which Holmes consulted Watson at the end of "The Abbey Grange", Conan Doyle was confident

---

[36] ACD, *The Case of Oscar Slater* (London: Hodder and Stoughton, 1912), 22.

[37] The jury were also misdirected by the judge, Lord Guthrie. See William Roughead's account of this disgraceful trial, in *Famous Trials*, ed. Harry Hodge and James H. Hodge, selected and introd. by John Mortimer (Harmondsworth: Penguin, 1984), 78–132, and Farmer, "Arthur and Oscar (and Sherlock)".

[38] ACD, *Our African Winter* (London: John Murray, 1929), 229.

[39] Harold Orel, "Conan Doyle's Sense of Justice", *ACD: Journal of the Arthur Conan Doyle Society*, 4 (1993), 128–33; at 131.

enough to have faith in the instincts of the British public, if they were in possession of the facts. The institutions of law might be fallible, but appeal could be made through the press to a higher court, which could be counted on to see justice served. "Now we turn to the last tribunal of all, a tribunal which never errs when the facts are laid before them, and we ask the public of Great Britain whether this thing is to go on" (*Story*, 78). These fine words are the statement of a man of letters who lives in a democracy. But later in life, as a Spiritualist tangling with an uncomprehending public and a hostile or mocking press, his faith in this last tribunal would waver too.

6

Army and Empire

Soldier boys

Of all his writing, Conan Doyle expressed most satisfaction with his historical fiction, and of his historical novels his own favourites were *The White Company* (1891) and *Sir Nigel* (1906). Set in the Plantagenet empire in England and France during the Hundred Years War, in the reign of Edward III which he considered the greatest epoch in English history, these two stories are interlinked and their author claimed "that they made an accurate picture of that great age, and that as a single piece of work they form the most complete, satisfying and ambitious thing that I have ever done" (*M&A*, 80–1). His pride in these books is partly an indication of the effort they cost him in historical research, and of his feeling that his portrayal was based on a new and more accurate understanding of the soldiers of the time, both humble and aristocratic. It also indicates that in his own mind, the historical novel was a genre of high prestige, and on this he rested his claim to literary reputation, a reputation which he felt had suffered because his fame as a writer of detective stories had distracted from what he thought of as his higher work. This does not mean that his historical novels were not popular:[1] indeed they rode a wave of readerly interest, for in the early 1880s began a boom in what came to be called the New Historical Novel, with more than 500 such titles being published in the next thirty years.[2] Conan Doyle was able to boast in *Memories and Adventures* that *The White Company* had passed through fifty editions, confirming

---

[1] *Micah Clarke* was Conan Doyle's most commercially successful novel and sold more copies in his lifetime than any of his Sherlock Holmes books.

[2] Harold Orel, *The Historical Novel from Scott to Sabatini* (New York: St Martin's Press, 1995), 1. For a more broadly-based study, see Richard Maxwell, *The Historical Novel in Europe 1650–1950* (Cambridge: Cambridge University Press, 2009).

his exultation on finishing it, when he had hurled his inky pen across the room, leaving a black smudge on the wallpaper: "I knew in my heart that the book would live and that it would illuminate our national traditions" (*M&A*, 81).

Conan Doyle thought these books told the truth, as never before, about the time of the Hundred Years War, but how much is to be learned from them about the time when they were written? In what sense can they be understood, as Georg Lukács described Walter Scott's novels, as "bringing the past to life as the prehistory of the present"?[3] Their author considered *Sir Nigel* the better of the two, but much of the later book repeats the successful formula of the earlier *The White Company*, which I will concentrate on here: it was Conan Doyle's own favourite and the book he most enjoyed writing.[4] In some obvious ways there are autobiographical elements in both, especially in *Sir Nigel* where we see the ambitious young hero, his father absent, his family fallen on hard times, swearing to recoup the fame and fortune of his house, inspired by a matriarch—in Nigel's case, his grand-mother—and her tales of the family's noble traditions. Both Nigel Loring in *Sir Nigel*, and the young hero Alleyne Edricson in *The White Company*, can only begin their adventures and their advancement in the world when they are released from their obligations to the Church, in the form of the Abbey of Waverley. These elements of the stories track particular aspects of Conan Doyle's early life, but in more general terms they are full of information about his own times, both in the ways the medieval past and its people are imagined, and in the way that past is presented as the foundation, and the inspiration, for a national and global future. The epigraph to *The White Company* could not be more specific about this latter intention.

TO THE HOPE OF THE FUTURE
THE REUNION OF THE ENGLISH-SPEAKING RACES
THIS LITTLE CHRONICLE
OF OUR COMMON ANCESTRY IS INSCRIBED.

Stories of the inspiring deeds of ancestors are the subject of traditional epic, and there are other signs that the Sir Nigel books have an epic agenda, though in a general sense this is something shared by Conan

---

[3] Georg Lukács, *The Historical Novel* (1937), trans. Hannah and Stanley Mitchell (Har-mondsworth: Penguin, 1976), 57.

[4] See Stashower, *Teller of Tales*, 108–9.

Doyle's other novels of English history—even, as we have seen, by the boxing novel *Rodney Stone*—and by the whole enterprise of English and Scottish historical fiction that stretches in the history-obsessed nineteenth century from Walter Scott through Charles Reade to G. A. Henty and Robert Louis Stevenson. In bringing past events to life by applying imagination to historical evidence, Conan Doyle was going about the familiar reconstructive business which links his own writerly practice to the detective methods of Sherlock Holmes and the scientific methods of Huxley's "backtellers". But the phrase "common ancestors" is a clue to the wider ambition of epic, whose author undertakes on behalf of a community to tell the story of where it came from. Conan Doyle plants an unmistakeable clue in *The White Company* in a scene in which Sir Nigel and his men listen to the Lady Tiphaine, wife of his worthy adversary Bertrand de Guesclin, a woman who has the gift of second sight, and enters a trance in which she sees the future. She predicts glorious prospects for the French nation, but when it comes to the English future, she is overwhelmed by what she foresees.

"My God!" she cried, "what is this that is shown me? Whence come they, these peoples, these lordly nations, these mighty countries which rise up before me? I look beyond, and others rise, and yet others, far and farther to the shores of the uttermost waters. They crowd! They swarm! The world is given to them, and it resounds with the clang of their hammers and the ringing of their church bells. They call them many names, and they rule them this way or that, but they are all English, for I can hear the voices of the people. On I go, and onwards over seas where man hath never yet sailed, and I see a great land under new stars and a stranger sky, and still the land is England. Where have her children not gone? What have they not done?"[5]

No doubt one trigger for this passage is the witches' vision of Banquo's royal descendants in *Macbeth*, but its epic precursor is in Book VI of Virgil's *Aeneid*, where Aeneas, descending to the underworld of spirits, is vouchsafed a vision of the glory of his descendants as the future makers of the Roman Empire. The Lady Tiphaine also foresees an empire for Sir Nigel's descendants, here accurately predicting the spread of industry and Christianity and the English language across the globe under the banner of an English-descended empire. Significantly, her vision does not include subject peoples of other races, but looks

---

[5] ACD, *The White Company*, 3 vols. (London: Smith, Elder, 1891), iii. 72–3. Hereafter *WC*.

much more like the confederation of English ethnicity to which the novel's epigraph appeals. When Conan Doyle himself wrote of (and travelled) the British Empire, it was first as a military responsibility and next as a network of white settlement, the solidarity of the mother country with the dominions of Canada, Australia, New Zealand, and South Africa and—in the hope he shared with other empire enthusiasts like Rudyard Kipling and Cecil Rhodes—some kind of future refederation with the United States of America. All this seems to be guaranteed in the Lady Tiphaine's prophecy, just as the rule of the Emperor Augustus was ratified and endorsed by being foreseen, centuries earlier, by his ancestor Aeneas in the underworld in Virgil's poem. The point of the novel, though, is that this glorious future rests on the warrant of a heroic national past, nowhere more evident than in the chivalry of Sir Nigel Loring and the martial exploits of the White Company. Both books, *The White Company* and *Sir Nigel*, close by binding the past to the communal, national present. *Sir Nigel* does this by a reminder that the landscape of the New Forest still contains, like a memory, the traces of Sir Nigel and the lives of his contemporaries. *The White Company* strikes a more martial note.

So they lived, these men, in their own lusty, cheery fashion—rude and rough, but honest, kindly and true. Let us thank God if we have outgrown their vices. Let us pray to God that we may ever hold their virtues. The sky may darken, and the clouds may gather, and again the day may come when Britain may have sore need of her children, on whatever shore of the sea they be found. Shall they not muster at her call? (*WC*, iii. 277)

Two anachronisms have been slipped into this stirring ending. The England of Sir Nigel has become the Britain of Victoria. And the sons summoned to her aid may now be found living overseas.

The story told in *The White Company* is a boisterous and light-hearted one. Alleyne Edricson has been educated in the Cistercian monastery, a clerkish and otherworldly youth now going out into the world, not unlike a medieval Candide. He falls in with the amiable giant Hordle John and later with the veteran archer Sam Aylward, the latter having returned to England from the King's wars to ask Sir Nigel Loring to assume command of the White Company in France. The White Company itself is a force of "free companions"—that is, a mercenary brigade of a kind that played an important part in the military history of fourteenth-century Europe. Conan Doyle is careful to explain that half the company has marched to Italy under the command of Sir John Hawkwood, which is why the remnant in France need a new commander. The actual White Company did indeed campaign rapaciously and with great success in northern Italy under Hawkwood, a brilliant and ruthless mercenary general who frequently changed sides, held his employers to ransom, or demanded payment to go away.[6] Conan Doyle's White Company are an innocent lot by comparison, professional soldiers out for profit and enjoyment, but capable of loyalty and self-sacrifice. Sam Aylward, a cheerful medieval materialist, gives a spirited account of the Poitiers campaign entirely in terms of the loot he amassed there. We see him return to England literally weighed down with the spoils of war, including (in a detail of whose authenticity Conan Doyle was proud) a feather bed. And yet he is devoted to the high-minded Sir Nigel, who has no interest at all in enriching himself, and who as a young man absent-mindedly missed claiming, quite literally, a king's ransom (an episode recounted in *Sir Nigel*). Nigel's motives in going to war are entirely chivalric. Alleyne Edricson, befriended on the road by Hordle John and Aylward, but picked out for his manners and learning by Sir Nigel to be his squire, passes promiscuously between the ranks of commoners and the officer class of mounted aristocracy.

Masculine companionship is a theme of much of Conan Doyle's work, from Baker Street to the Lost World, and in *The White Company* it has the familiar Conan Doyle contours of solidarity and reconciliation. The actual Company comes onstage quite late in the story, but the four men who make its nucleus—Alleyne, John, Aylward, and Sir Nigel—constitute a collective hero and perhaps, again, a somewhat autobiographical one, with a delicate spirit, strong body, stout heart, and noble mind. There are clear traces of utopian thinking in the English culture embodied by these people joined together in mutual respect and loyalty. As the first chapter of *Sir Nigel* points out, scarcity of labour caused by the Black Death had had the effect of empowering the peasantry and loosening the shackles of feudalism, and here Hordle John and Sam Aylward are quite unintimidated by their aristocratic leaders, and treated well by them. Though there is a very hostile portrayal in *The White Company* of a French rabble who mount an attack

---

[6] Their story is told in Frances Stonor Saunders, *Hawkwood: Diabolical Englishman* (London: Faber, 2004).

on the Chateau de Villefranche, "howling and dancing peasants, their fierce faces upturned, all drunk with bloodshed and with vengeance" (*WC*, iii. 104), this owes as much to the revolutionary French mob in *A Tale of Two Cities* as to the medieval Jacquerie. But as far as the English are concerned, the problem of class which squats like an incubus over the Victorian novel is for the most part absent in this book's story about a harmonious pre-capitalist community held together by mutual respect and interest.[7] Sir Nigel goes to war for glory, Aylward for loot, but they share the same professional ethics. "For with us in France", it is Aylward who says, "it has ever been fair and honest war—a shut fist for the man, but a bended knee for the woman" (*WC*, i. 264). There is little conflict between classes, or between Church and state, and the religious strife at the centre of *Micah Clarke* is centuries in the future.

If the White Company of free companions is a social utopia— simple, stable, harmonious, and honourable—the Sir Nigel novels also offer a thoroughly idealized vision of England itself.

Long ere Alleyne was out of sound of the Beaulieu bells he was striding sturdily along, swinging his staff and whistling as merrily as the birds in the thicket. It was an evening to raise a man's heart. The sun shining slantwise through the trees threw delicate traceries across the road, with bars of golden light between. Away in the distance before and behind, the green boughs, now turning in places to a coppery redness, shot their broad arches across the track. The still summer air was heavy with the resinous smell of the great forest. Here and there a tawny brook prattled on from among the underwood and lost itself again in the ferns and brambles upon the further side. Save the dull piping of insects and the sough of the leaves, there was silence everywhere—the sweet restful silence of nature. (*WC*, i. 35–6)

Conan Doyle is not at his best with this sort of thing, but the way this passage employs a predictable vocabulary of English nature writing, and incorporates its young hero so seamlessly into the natural scene, shows that this romance has its beginning in a dream of England, where the first half of the story takes place. It is a country where the colours are always bright, the weather is always kind, and the people of this landscape—it is the New Forest, which Conan Doyle thought of

---

[7] Here I differ from the view of Owen Dudley Edwards that "*The White Company* and *Sir Nigel* are ... deeply conscious of the class struggles of the reign of Edward III." Edwards, *The Quest for Sherlock Holmes*, 42. In the Victorian novel, class conflict is often translated into relations between men and women, but this too is not a significant problem in the Sir Nigel books.

as the numinous heart of English life—are thoroughly at home in it and with one another: all things are bright and beautiful to the rich man in his castle and the poor man at his gate. From this sunlit and optimistic England the martial and sporting race tumbles out to make its boyish mark on the world. The joviality of Chaucer's comic tales underwrites the dash and vigour of Shakespeare's *Henry V*. Here is a vision of the nation consisting of a profoundly natural and good-natured life at home, and victorious but principled forays overseas. Its epic adventure is grounded in pastoral.

But if this is an idealized picture of English history, it is not cliché. The White Company is part of the expeditionary army of Edward the Black Prince, but we see little of that legendary English hero in action in this book.[8] Instead of the famous victories of the Prince's wars we follow the army across the Pyrenees in the campaign in 1367 to restore Pedro the Cruel to the throne of Castile, a military episode neither well known nor particularly creditable to the English. Sir Nigel Loring, meantime, may be a perfect knight, but he is physically unprepossessing (and unlike his author), being comically short, bald, and very short-sighted, and having a soft, lisping voice. He is often reckless and ridiculous in his eagerness for chances to accrue honour and reputation, and in this he is an English Quixote—or, of course, an English Brigadier Gerard, for we can enjoy the adventures and panache of both heroes all the more for their naive vanity.

But the centre of gravity in *The White Company* is not Sir Nigel Loring, but the young Alleyne Edricson, who becomes his squire, and will be rewarded by the hand of Sir Nigel's daughter. There is a story of reconciliation and nation-building, reminiscent of Walter Scott's *Ivanhoe*, in the union by marriage of the Norman Lorings and the Saxon Edricsons. The adventure story is structured along Alleyne's journey and return, and finds its theme in his coming of age. Since Alleyne will, in effect, inherit the English world depicted in the novel, it is a question of some importance what sort of man he turns out to be. In Beaulieu, he wanted to become a monk, but at his father's behest

[8] G. A. Henty, the popular writer for boys, had published *St. George for England, A Tale of Cressy and Poitiers* in 1885. This may be one reason why Conan Doyle did not feature the Prince's most famous victories in *The White Company* (1891). In *Sir Nigel*, written later but set earlier, the young Nigel Loring fights at the battle of Poitiers. Henty was highly prolific, and published half a dozen adventure books in 1891, the year of *The White Company*.

he leaves the abbey, at the age of 20, so that he can see something of the world before renouncing it in favour of the life of contemplation. His encounter with Sir Nigel and the Company is "fated to turn the whole current of his life, to divert it from that dark and lonely bourne towards which it tended, and to guide it into freer and more sunlit channels" (*WC*, i. 297). Alleyne is a clerk, an intellectual, but the Lady Maude Loring has already lectured him on his duty to "live as others, and do men's work in the world" (*WC*, i. 279). It is not just that Alleyne becomes a soldier instead of a monk—and, incidentally, will return from the wars just in time to stop Maude entering a nunnery. This is also a social and aesthetic programme with implications for Conan Doyle's writerly practice. The clerkly Alleyne is directed outward from a cloistered existence to sociability and the world of busy action, and the fictional world constructed around him is one of that sunlit landscape through which we have seen him pass, the open road, the overseas adventure, the companionship of men in action, with little time for doubt or introspection.

Alleyne's manly vocation can be related to differing late-Victorian views about the novel itself, which I discussed earlier in terms of the debate, and the contrast in practice, between Henry James and Robert Louis Stevenson. With fiction's expanding readership and growing prestige, what form should a novel take? Before Stevenson and James took the field, this debate had already drawn in Charles Reade, Bulwer-Lytton, Margaret Oliphant, G. H. Lewes, George Eliot, Walter Besant, and others, favouring one side or another of an argument about fictional representation whose main terms shifted, without changing out of recognition—realism and idealism, realism and romance, the fiction of character and the fiction of incident.[9] Andrew Lang summed up the matter when he wrote that fiction was a shield with two sides: "the study of manners and of character, on one hand; on the other, the description of adventure, the delight of romantic narrative".[10] Henry James gave his view, in "The Art of Fiction", that the supreme virtue

---

[9] See Mary Poovey, "Forgotten Writers, Neglected Histories: Charles Reade and the Nineteenth-Century Transformation of the British Literary Field", *ELH* 72/2 (2004), 433–53, and Daly, *Modernism, Romance and the Fin de Siècle*, 16–19.

[10] Andrew Lang, "Realism and Romance", *Contemporary Review*, 52 (July–December 1887), 683–93; at 684. Lang defended adventure fiction from those critics who dismissed it as crude and even primitive. "Do not let us cry that, because we are 'cultured', there shall be no Buffalo Bill" (690).

of a novel resides in its ability to give "the air of reality"—in this way, he identified himself with the realists.[11] He was wary of being trapped into a distinction between novels that concentrated on action and those that concentrated on character (for "What is character but the determination of incident? What is incident but the illustration of character?").[12] But James's own practice showed him setting greater store by analysis, introspection, and point of view than by exciting events. It was the job and the boast of the novel, James declared, to compete with life in a way people could recognize from their own subjective experience. Novels should not exaggerate or simplify reality.

Stevenson disagreed. "The whole secret is that no art does 'compete with life'. Man's one method, whether he reasons or creates, is to half-shut his eyes against the dazzle and confusion of reality."[13] Reality, he said, is formless, complex, and baffling, and besides, we get enough reality in our everyday lives. "Idealism" in fiction sees its first task as pleasing the reader, not imitating reality. Art ought to simplify and organize reality, not reproduce it; and yet "we of the last quarter of the nineteenth century, breathing as we do the intellectual atmosphere of our age, are more apt to err upon the side of realism than to sin in quest of the ideal".[14] Realism, in other words, was an expression of the age of materialism. But realism in fiction, Stevenson believed, lacked excitement, and tended to produce boring stories in which nothing much happened. The novel of character and manners, such as Henry James wrote, dwells on the examination of psychology, and such action as it does portray is usually indoor, conversational, reflective: James himself, wrote Stevenson, "treats, for the most part, the statics of character, studying it at rest or only gently moved".[15] Against this model, Stevenson was ready to recommend a different kind of fiction, a fiction of incident. Sometimes he called it romance and at other times, the novel of adventure.

Incident—exciting action—was after all, in Stevenson's view, what children read for, though in saying this he was by no means trivializing

[11] James, "The Art of Fiction", 390.
[12] James, "The Art of Fiction", 392.
[13] Stevenson, "A Humble Remonstrance" (1884), in *R. L. Stevenson on Fiction*, 80–91; at 84.
[14] Stevenson, "A Note on Realism" (1883), in *R. L. Stevenson on Fiction*, 65–71; at 71.
[15] Stevenson, "A Humble Remonstrance", 88.

the effect of the literature of incident, for "fiction is to the grown man what play is to the child; it is there that he changes the atmosphere and tenor of his life."[16] He went on to argue that a fiction of incident, such as *The Arabian Nights*, should not be distracted by moral or intellectual interest; even the elaboration of "character", in the sense of introspection and the analysis of motive, would just get in the way. "Character to the boy is a sealed book; for him, a pirate is a beard, a pair of wide trousers and a liberal complement of pistols.... To add more traits, to be too clever, to start the hare of moral or intellectual interest while we are running the fox of material interest, is not to enrich but to stultify your tale."[17] Stevenson was thinking of his own boyhood reading, but his own fictional practice ran parallel to these essays of the early 1880s, as the mention of pirates may remind us. *Treasure Island* was begun in 1881, published in book form in 1883. More directly to the point here is Stevenson's medieval adventure *The Black Arrow*, which appeared in 1888, the year before Conan Doyle began *The White Company*.

Robert Louis Stevenson was not only a model, but a positively glamorous one, especially for a young writer from Scotland. And yet for Stevenson—who did not himself lack for cleverness—to warn against the dangers of being "too clever" was not entirely good advice. Conan Doyle's Sir Nigel novels follow the Stevensonian formula closely, and successfully, so that they repeat in their form the trope of Alleyne Edricson's choice forsaking "the dark and lonely bourne" of contemplation in favour of the unselfconscious "freer and more sunlit channels" of the life of action. These novels of medieval life have a robust and simple set of values—fair play, comradeship—but the smooth surface of their incidents is largely untroubled by the over-fastidious "moral or intellectual interest" Stevenson warned against. Yet Stevenson's frequent invocations of the child as reader and the reader as child—"fiction is to the grown man what play is to the child"— point to one of the consequences of this method. The Sir Nigel novels present a gallant, simple, childlike vision of history, and more specifically, a boyish one.[18] Yet Conan Doyle did not think he was writing a

---

[16] Stevenson, "A Gossip on Romance", 61.

[17] Stevenson, "A Humble Remonstrance", 88.

[18] Elsewhere Conan Doyle was to characterize the medieval knight, for all his savagery, as "a light-hearted creature, like a formidable boy playing a dreadful game". ACD, *Through the Magic Door*, 222. The relation between the romance revival and masculinity has been discussed in Chapter 1.

boys' book. How adequate is this simple-minded, sunny, swaggering vision of the medieval English past to Conan Doyle's epic ambitions, his confidence that in *The White Company* he had written a book that would live and that would "illuminate our national traditions" and inspire the English-speaking races of a global empire? How adequate was it, for that matter, as a basis for thinking about war and empire in the present?

The White Company was a very popular book, though it is impossible to say just how much it may have influenced the way its readers thought of themselves and their place in the world, as Conan Doyle was confident that it would.[19] Epic always offers a heroized portrait of the ancestors. Yet it must surely be dangerous for a people, or a class, to treat the world as if it were a boy's adventure tale. "Instinctively the Englishman is no missionary, no conqueror," wrote the American George Santayana in a fulsome essay about the British character. "He travels and conquers without a settled design, because he has the instinct for exploration. His adventures are all external; they change him so little that he is not afraid of them." He might have been speaking of the characters of *The White Company*, or of Henty's stories.[20] "Never since the heroic days of Greece," Santayana goes on, "has the world had such a sweet, just, boyish master."[21] But not everyone in the world found the boys so charming, in practice.

As for Conan Doyle's reputation, though he believed his position in literature would have been a more commanding one if Sherlock Holmes had not obscured his "higher work", it is possible that the real handicap was the suspicion that even in his higher work he was not in the end a writer for adults. (For many readers this uncertainty is probably kept alive by the fact that Conan Doyle is a writer they first encountered as young readers.[22]) But there is an uncertainty here that

[19] Richard Maxwell has a chapter tracing "the juvenile literature of English History", into which Walter Scott was retrospectively co-opted as a children's author, as an educational and moralizing national project from Charlotte Yonge to Henty and beyond, though unaccountably he does not mention Conan Doyle. Maxwell, *The Historical Novel*, 231–73.

[20] "A Henty boy may commit occasional social or political blunders but seldom changes in any substantial sense." Maxwell, *The Historical Novel*, 252.

[21] George Santayana, *Soliloquies in England and Later Soliloquies* (London: Constable, 1922), 32.

[22] This also helps to account for the affection in which he is held by so many readers, as well as for the somewhat camp (or romantic) Sherlockian game-playing that some enthusiasts enjoy. Both phenomena are exemplified and discussed by Michael Dirda in *On Conan Doyle*.

coincides with the explosion of children's literature—much of it read by adults—in the late-Victorian and Edwardian years. The publishing industry itself was finding it increasingly difficult to distinguish between adult and juvenile writing. In 1895, the *Publisher's Circular* "entirely gave up trying to classify literature by age group".[23] If *The White Company* and *Sir Nigel* are serious novels about nation and history (as, I would argue, they are), what does it tell us about that nation and history when these epic ambitions express themselves in the idiom of a story for boys?

Conan Doyle's best fiction about soldiers is to be found in his Brigadier Gerard stories, and one reason is that, with a French hero, they are free of the epic burden he assumed in the Sir Nigel books. The national pride expressed in his celebration of the victorious White Company is a source of sharp satirical comedy in these Napoleonic stories, with their moustache-twirling French and their stolid but sporting English.[24] The Gerard tales are breathless and ingenious in narrative and wit, the exploits of their protagonist joyfully undercut by his stupidity as a character and his vanity as a narrator (and by the knowledge that he fought on what proved to be the losing side). Behind the calculating genius of Napoleon and the open-heartedness of Gerard we may perhaps glimpse the shadows of Holmes and Watson, Owen Dudley Edwards has pointed out, and in the affectionate portrayal of Gerard another example of "the intellectual sympathy which Conan Doyle extended to persons of instinct and emotion".[25] Like much of Conan Doyle's best fiction, these stories have their feet planted firmly in the commonplace, in this case the stereotype of the national characteristics of the English (phlegmatic) and the French (flamboyant). Some of them are among the best comic short stories in the language.[26]

---

[23] Jonathan Rose, *The Edwardian Temperament 1895–1919* (Athens, Oh.: Ohio University Press, 1986), 183.

[24] See Owen Dudley Edwards, "Introduction", in ACD, *The Complete Brigadier Gerard*, vii–xxvi.

[25] See Owen Dudley Edwards, "Conan Doyle as Historian: A Starting Point", *ACD: Journal of the Arthur Conan Doyle Society*, 1/2 (March 1990), 95–111; at 104.

[26] See John Whitehead, "Gasconade: Conan Doyle's Brigadier Gerard", *ACD: Journal of the Arthur Conan Doyle Society*, 6 (1995), 103–11.

Army

More than any profession or church or association, the institution that excited Arthur Conan Doyle most was the British army. It was a life-long passion. He praised its soldiers, from Lord Roberts to Tommy Atkins: I do not think he ever wrote a negative word about it. He tried to join it. He served it in the field as a doctor. He wanted to reform it. He wrote two lengthy histories of its campaigns. He pestered the War Office and the newspapers with his suggestions for tactics and weapons and equipment. His only brother was a career soldier who became a brigadier-general.

Conan Doyle grew up in an artistic and female-dominated household, in a family that had little military tradition.[27] But an obsession with the army, and the navy, was widespread in Victorian Britain. The British maintained a small professional army—and another, of course, in India—and eschewed, until 1916, the big citizen armies and compulsory military service of other European powers. (Arthur Conan Doyle did not do national service: Marcel Proust did.) But the army, because of its role in guarding and expanding the empire, was a source of fascination to the public. Though the culture was very far from militarized, soldiers were glamorous. National heroes were mostly military men, national history taught in schools was mostly a history of military campaigns, and there was a great public appetite for military display, related to the taste among boys and men for adventure stories involving exciting action by flood and field.

Between the Indian Rebellion of 1857 and the South African war at the century's end, most British military actions were relatively small-scale colonial affairs, and very far away. Yet war in the last quarter of the nineteenth century "aroused a more intense and popular appeal than ever before over a comparable period of time".[28] One reason for this was a greatly expanded national press—the number of newspapers doubling in Britain between 1880 and 1900—and the appearance of an elite corps of journalists, the war correspondents, "prepared to endure

[27] Notwithstanding his maternal grandmother's first cousin once removed was "the dashing and spectacularly brave Major-General Sir Denis Pack", hero of the Peninsular Wars. See Lycett, *Conan Doyle*, 11.

[28] Edward M. Spiers, *The Army and Society 1815–1914* (London: Longman, 1980), 206.

the punishing demands of war reporting for the delights of its rewards".[29]
Conan Doyle was briefly one himself; Winston Churchill was another.
Though "newspaper correspondents and travelling gentlemen" were
considered a pest by a commander like Garnett Wolseley, who dismissed
them as "useless drones", war reporters are more kindly described in
Conan Doyle's story "The Three Correspondents" as representing "the
eyes and ears of the public—the great silent millions and millions who
had paid for everything, and who waited so patiently to know the result
of their outlay".[30] "Reports of war in distant and exotic parts of the
empire, focusing on the courage and carnage of battle, provided a vicar-
ious outlet for those trapped in the drab monotony of office and fac-
tory life."[31] The military dimension of empire was much more dramatic
and easier to understand than its administrative or economic business.
And Victoria's wars were also gratifyingly victorious, though the army
had an exciting tendency to begin a campaign with some blunder or
military reverse, before sweeping on to inevitable triumph.

But if the army was admired, it was admired at a distance, as Kipling
complained in the poem "Tommy". In the 1890s, soldiers were debarred
by some theatres and music-halls from occupying particular places in
their auditoriums, and were sometimes even prevented from riding in
omnibuses, if they were wearing the Queen's uniform. The officer
corps were always gentlemen, before the First World War.[32] But private
soldiers tended to be recruited from among the poor: about a quarter
of them were Irish.[33] In 1857, little more than half of them could read
and write. Venereal diseases and what we now call alcohol abuse were
widespread among soldiers and sailors.[34] Flogging was not abolished in
the army until 1881. If the Victorian public loved the army, they loved

[29] Philip Knightley, *The First Casualty: From the Crimea to Vietnam: The War Correspondent
as Hero, Propagandist, and Myth Maker* (London: Quartet, 1978), 42.

[30] ACD, *The Green Flag*, 293, 294.

[31] Spiers, *The Army and Society*, 211.

[32] Field Marshal Sir William Robertson, who had risen from the ranks to become
Chief of Imperial General Staff in 1916, was a legendary exception; but by that time there
were plenty of officers serving who would not have been given a commission upon join-
ing the pre-war army.

[33] James Morris, *Heaven's Command: An Imperial Progress* (Harmondsworth: Penguin,
1979), 407.

[34] A Royal Commission on Venereal Diseases reported in 1916, the year conscription
was introduced, that some ten million people in Britain had gonorrhea or syphilis, and that
about 80% of venereal disease was acquired under the influence of alcohol. See Henry
Carter (ed.), *The Church and the Drink Evil* (London: Epworth Press, 1922), 20.

it as a spectacle, a parade, or a stirring news item announcing another victory. But Conan Doyle, who knew more about the army, and had seen it at closer quarters, than most civilians, loved it unconditionally, all his life, with a boy's love. The first two literary heroes to emerge in his book *Through the Magic Door* are Walter Scott and Macaulay. "What swing and dash in both of them! What a love of all that is manly and noble and martial!"[35] The virile romanticism of his historical adventure stories seems to have decisively coloured his views of the army and of his country's wars, and in this he was far from alone.

Since the autumn of 1893 the whereabouts of the Conan Doyle family had been dictated by the needs of his wife Louise (Touie), who was consumptive, and late 1895 found them in Egypt, where her health seemed to respond well to the climate. They were there when war was declared against the Khalifa in the Sudan, and British troops under Sir Herbert Kitchener set out up the river Nile in pursuit of an old enemy. The Khalifa was the successor of the Mahdi, the religious leader whose rebellion had forced the British to abandon the Sudan, and had culminated in the death of General Gordon at Khartoum in 1885. This humiliation, and the martyrdom of the saintly Gordon, rankled very strongly with the British press and public, and with the army.[36] The Sudan was unfinished business, and the avenging of Gordon was the emotional motive of Kitchener's campaign against the Khalifa, which reached a climax in 1898 at Omdurman, a battle in which 10,000 of the Sudanese forces were killed, 13,000 wounded, and 5,000 taken prisoner; Kitchener's force lost 47 killed and 382 wounded. This was the engagement in which Winston Churchill rode with the 21st Lancers and took part in, and reported, the last British cavalry charge in battle. It was a crushing demonstration of the power of a disciplined professional army with modern armaments, and was in some ways the most triumphant moment of the adventures of the British fighting man in Conan Doyle's lifetime. The following year, in South Africa, the British would get into serious trouble facing a different enemy and a different kind of warfare; and the next conflict, which began in Europe in 1914, would be different again. These were Conan Doyle's wars.

---

[35] ACD, *Through the Magic Door*, 16.
[36] In the Holmes story "The Cardboard Box", first published in the *Strand* in January 1893, we learn that Watson, himself a war veteran, has hung a newly framed picture of General Gordon on the wall in the rooms at 221B Baker Street (*Memoirs*, 32).

In Egypt when war was declared, he secured permission from his wife for an absence of a month or so, and then lost no time in getting himself appointed honorary war correspondent for the *Westminster Gazette* in London, and hurried off upriver to follow the army, pausing only to kit himself out with a huge Italian revolver, a light khaki coat, riding breeches, and "the usual Christmas tree hung round me" (*M&A*, 135). With its approximation to army gear, it was the uniform of an amateur—"an amateur among professionals", in his own words (*M&A*, 140), both in relation to the hardened war correspondents on the scene, and to the soldiers themselves, both professions which he was inclined to venerate. As a well-connected tourist in Cairo, he had "joined in male society" (*M&A*, 127), hobnobbing with British military and official circles; now travelling with the expeditionary force, he settled easily into a life of homosocial companionship reminiscent of *The White Company*. Though he got as far south on the Nile as Sarras, this first campaign was a disappointment, and the month was up before he had a chance even to see a dervish, let alone any action. Kitchener himself advised this "travelling gentleman" to go home; the army would advance no further until it had enough camels. The most dangerous thing Conan Doyle encountered was probably his own beast, when it threw itself suddenly to its knees and pitched its surprised rider onto the desert sand.

But though this semi-farcical excursion had a fixed term, dictated by his invalid wife back in Cairo, Conan Doyle had time to form round hand opinions of the people about him. It was a simple picture. "The British officer at his best is really a splendid fellow, a large edition of the public schoolboy, with his cheery slang overlying a serious purpose which he would die rather than admit" (*M&A*, 137). Conan Doyle travelled with the officers and the journalists and seems to have had little contact with the men in the ranks. There were British troops in Kitchener's force, but most of the soldiers were Africans. The five battalions of black troops were fine fellows, but the Egyptians were "more inscrutable, less sporting and less lovable, but none the less their officers were very loyal to them" (*M&A*, 136). If this was the way the British officers saw things and talked to him, Conan Doyle was quite ready to adopt their boyish view of the affair, and to write of it in simple, essentializing, and melodramatic terms familiar from the fictional adventure stories of the kind he enjoyed inventing, and the British officer class were used to reading. "The Arab of the Soudan", he writes confidently, though he had probably never seen one and certainly not in battle, "is a desperate fanatic who rushes to death with the frenzy of a madman, and longs for close quarters where he can bury his spear in the body of his foeman, even though he carries several bullets in him before he reaches him" (*M&A*, 136). There is a great deal of this sort of thing in the dispatches of the professional war correspondents who reported from imperial campaigns.[37] The dashing Archibald Forbes of the *Daily News*, who had certainly seen battle at close quarters, affirmed that it was the job of war correspondents to record "how our countrymen, our dear ones, toil and thole, vindicate Britain's manhood, and joyously expend their lives for Queen and fatherland".[38] Conan Doyle at the time would have endorsed this uncomplicated idea of what a writer and a citizen owed to his nation. But Forbes's words are also an indication of the strength of what we have described in the preceding section as that vision of adventure in British culture, colouring not only what men read but also how they saw the world, themselves, and other people. And it may have been easier to imagine the dervish as a figure in a historical adventure story because he was indeed armed with a spear, though he faced an enemy—or "foeman"—who had a more efficient weapon. As Hilaire Belloc reminded his readers in 1898, the year of Omdurman: "Whatever happens we have got | The Maxim gun and they have not."[39] If the British army embodied the best of manhood and modernity, who could stand against it?

The Second South African or Boer War broke out with the attack on the British colony of Natal by forces of the Transvaal republic, in October 1899. After a month or so of hesitation—his mother was one of those who believed the Boers had right on their side—Conan Doyle declared himself a member of the patriotic party. It was a relief not to have to worry about the rights and wrongs of the cause. "As to the merits of the quarrel from the day they invaded Natal that becomes merely academic."[40] He urged his fellow countrymen to enlist, and

[37] See Knightley, *The First Casualty*. Knightley argues that even in the Great War, correspondents tended to identify themselves absolutely with the armies in the field, and faithfully reflect the higher command's interpretation of events.

[38] Quoted in Spiers, *The Army and Society*, 213. The fake medievalism of Forbes's "thole" (meaning to endure), like Conan Doyle's "foeman", is a clue that both writers are thinking of modern war in pre-modern literary terms.

[39] Hilaire Belloc, *The Modern Traveller* (London: Edward Arnold, 1898), 41.

[40] ACD to Mary Doyle, undated [25 or 26 December 1899], in *Arthur Conan Doyle: A Life in Letters*, 434.

tried and failed to join up for active service himself with the Middlesex Yeomanry. He was 40 years old, and felt he should set an example
for young men, "especially young athletic sporting men".[41] In the end,
he got to South Africa by other means, volunteering to join a field
hospital which was being equipped for service in the war by John
Langman, a family friend. By March 1900, he was with the army again,
and back in Africa. "For them the bullets, for us the microbes, and
both for the honour of the flag" (M&A, 175).

The Langman hospital was posted to Bloemfontein, newly captured
from the Boers, and there they helped to deal with an epidemic of
enteric (typhoid) which lasted a month and cost some 5,000 lives.
Memories and Adventures describes briefly but strikingly the dreadful
conditions of the epidemic—"constant pollution, and this pollution of
the most dangerous character and with the vilest effluvia"—in the
over-crowded field hospital, in a commandeered cricket pavilion
(M&A, 162). These were grim days, though consoled with the thought
that the greater the work, the more this medical mission proved the
necessity of its presence in Africa. The army is still heroized, its heroes
now including the steady and uncomplaining Tommies who suffered
through the appalling epidemic, but Conan Doyle felt he could now
take his place among them not as a pretend soldier but as a valuable
member of the enterprise, with a professional life-and-death skill of his
own. Later he reported with pride that his old comrade H. A. Gwynne,
the Reuters correspondent who would go on to be editor of the
Morning Post, told him: "I look upon your work during this terrible
South African business as quite equal to that of a successful general"
(M&A, 211).

But Gwynne was referring to Conan Doyle's practice as a writer,
not as a doctor. Before he set foot in South Africa, he had begun work
on his history The Great Boer War, much of which was written in Bloemfontein, and which was published in October 1900, before the war
was over. This was followed, in 1902, by The War in South Africa: Its
Cause and Conduct, in which he answered the critics, at home and
abroad, of Britain's prosecution of the conflict against the Boer republics. This was the service for which he was knighted in the same year
(M&A, 210).

---

[41] Arthur Conan Doyle: A Life in Letters, 434.

The Great Boer War is a distinguished piece of journalism and a lively history. Its account of the war is often highly personalized and anecdotal and it is filled with names, mostly of officers. Knowing his readership, Conan Doyle is especially attentive to battlefield famous last words—"What a pity!" (Brigadier Wauchope); "Fix bayonets, men, and let us make a name for ourselves"; "There's an end of my cricket"; "When I surrender... it will be my dead body!"[42] The wily Boer commander in the west is referred to repeatedly with a Homeric epithet as "the dark Cronje". Brigadier Wauchope, who at Magersfontein led men of his Highland Brigade at night straight into deadly musket fire in which he too lost his life, is portrayed not as a blunderer but as a figure both tragic and mysterious. "There are some who claim on the night before to have seen upon his strangely ascetic face that shadow of doom which is summed up in the one word 'fey'. The hand of coming death may already have lain cold upon his soul" (*GBW*, 138). Many of the anecdotes appear to come fresh from first-hand witnesses, and the history is written from the point of view of the army. The Boer soldiers are for the most part respected for their tactics and skill: the British soldiers are much admired, though it takes the leadership of commanders like Lord Roberts and Lord Kitchener to get the best out of them.

Roberts and Kitchener are shown to be consummate war commanders, expert in their wielding of the complex modern instrument which was the army. Yet while military professionalism was to be admired, part of the glamour of heroism—as in sport itself—lay in a kind of amateurism. Conan Doyle, like the newspaper-reading public at home, found this embodied in Colonel Robert Baden-Powell, legendary defender of Mafeking, and later the founder of the Boy Scout movement. "A skilled hunter and an expert at many games, there was always something of the sportsman in his keen appreciation of war" (*GBW*, 348). In Baden-Powell the professionalism of the British officer corps is redeemed by an amateur spirit; we have seen a similar formula in "The Croxley Master", and in the way the professionalism of Sherlock Holmes himself is mitigated by the amateur motivation of the dandy. Appropriately, Mafeking under Baden-Powell's command was defended for seven months by a group of non-professionals, for the

---

[42] ACD, *The Great Boer War* (1900), 2nd edn. (London: Thomas Nelson, 1908), 139, 162, 183, 225. Hereafter *GBW*.

town's garrison contained no regular soldiers at all apart from the officers. Like Lord John Roxton himself, Baden-Powell understood about style, and the importance of not seeming to try too hard—the quality prized in Renaissance Italy under the name *sprezzatura*. "When the Boers had been shelling the town for some weeks the light-hearted Colonel sent out to say that if they went on any longer he should be compelled to regard it as equivalent to a declaration of war" (*GBW*, 350). The Boers it seemed had no answer to this debonair spirit and Mafeking held out until relieved, "a prize of victory, a stake which should be the visible sign of the predominating manhood of one or other of the great white races of South Africa" (*GBW*, 359). Back home, the drunken celebrations of "Mafeking night" lasted for days.

The overall narrative of *The Great Boer War* takes on a pattern familiar from accounts of other British colonial wars. Although arguably they provoked the conflict, the British turn out to be hopelessly unprepared, suffer a series of early setbacks under uninspiring leadership, then recover, with a change of command in the field, and seize the initiative. When the slow-moving and over-cautious General Redvers Buller is replaced by the Commander-in-Chief Lord Roberts, the pace picks up, and a phase of incessant marching and fighting follows, punctuated by the recapture of towns and the lifting of sieges. Here are British troops marching into Bloemfontein.

Spectators have left it on record how from all that interminable column of yellow-clad, weary men, worn with half-rations and whole-day marches, there came never one jeer, never one taunting or exultant word, as they tramped into the capital of their enemies [i.e. of the Orange Free State]. The bearing of the troops was chivalrous in its gentleness, and not the least astonishing sight to the inhabitants was the passing of the Guards, the dandy troops of England, the body-servants of the great Queen. Black with sun and dust, staggering after a march of thirty-eight miles, gaunt and haggard, with their clothes in such a state that decency demanded that some of the men should be discreetly packed away in the heart of the dense column, they still swung into the town with the aspect of Kentish hop-pickers and the bearing of heroes. (*GBW*, 301–2)

For this was a victory not just for an army or an empire, but for a national character, for chivalry, fair play, and a capacity to endure. When Conan Doyle saw these same troops for himself in Bloemfontein not long after, he saw them as proof that "the spirit of the race" burned as brightly as ever, and that the real glories of the British race were yet to come—"The Empire walks, and may still walk, with an uncertain step, but with every year its tread will be firmer, for its weakness is that of waxing youth and not of waning age" (*GBW*, 317). In this he was contradicting a quite prevalent anxiety that the difficulties the British had experienced in defeating the heavily outnumbered Boers might on the contrary be a sign that the race was over the hill, and heading for the decadence and degeneration that had caused earlier empires to collapse. A yet more alarming theory of history, put forward in these years by the aged social evolutionist Herbert Spencer, that under the weight of its imperial triumphs there was a danger that the nation might be returning to brutality and barbarism, seems endorsed in the title of a book denouncing the army's scorched-earth tactics and the concentration camps, *Methods of Barbarism* (1901) by Conan Doyle's fellow Spiritualist and the editor who sent him to Berlin, W. T. Stead.[43] Conan Doyle set his face resolutely against these gloomy interpretations of events: the British army marched for progress and a better modern world.

Here, however, was no longer a colour-coded drama of modernity overcoming primitive barbarism, as the Sudan and other colonial wars had seemed to offer. In South Africa, in Diana Barsham's words, the British faced an enemy "uncannily familiar as a white imperial force with a strong racial resemblance to the British".[44] In what sense could it be claimed that history was on the side of the British, in their struggle with an antagonist of Protestant northern European stock, so like themselves? How could the Boers—brave, honest, white farmers as they were—be understood as "standing unconsciously for mediaevalism and corruption, even as our rough-tongued Tommies stood for civilization, progress, and the equal rights of men" (*GBW*, 189)? Conan Doyle found the answer to this question in a familiar place: religion.

Like most of his contemporaries, Conan Doyle did not use the word "race" with a consistent single meaning, but in his work the word usually implies a tradition of cultural practice as well as a genetic inheritance. The culture of the Boers, he argues, had been corrupted by their religious belief, which encouraged them to think of themselves as a chosen people, whose rights and interests overrode those of all others,

---

[43] See Herbert Spencer, "Re-barbarization", in *Facts and Comments* (London: Williams and Norgate, 1902), 122–33.

[44] Barsham, *Arthur Conan Doyle and the Meaning of Masculinity*, 220.

both the British settlers who were starting to outnumber them in their own republics and, of course, the black Africans who always had.[45] Their doctrinaire and fundamentalist religion made Boer government oligarchical, venal, and incompetent, and Boer culture narrow and grotesque. "To their corruption," Conan Doyle complained, "they added such crass ignorance that they argue in the published reports of the Volksraad [the Republic of Transvaal parliament] debates that using dynamite bombs to bring down rain was firing at God, that it is impious to destroy locusts, that the word 'participate' should not be used because it is not in the Bible, and that postal pillar-boxes are extravagant and effeminate" (*GBW*, 17–18).[46] When Conan Doyle attacked organized religion he usually had the Church and the priesthood in his sights, but in the Boer republics he found a whole culture, from its political leadership to the education of its children, in the grip of a "dour fatalistic Old Testament religion" that held it stubbornly in the past; this "ancient theology", armed with "inconveniently modern rifles" (*GBW*, 2), was a direct cause of the conflict, he argued, and thus he was able to present this struggle too as one in which the British army was the instrument of progress and modernity in its war with primitivism and superstition.

The War in South Africa: Its Causes and Conduct (1902) is Conan Doyle's indignant answer to critics of the war, at home and abroad. He claimed to have written it in nine days, sixteen hours a day, and he enlisted the help of publishers and newspapers, the War Office and the Foreign Office, and raised funds from donations and sales to have the book translated and disseminated internationally. It is a testimony to his reputation and network of powerful connections, but also to his sense of the role of the man of letters in national life. The book is titled as a

[45] The proportion of blacks ("Kaffirs") to whites south of the Zambezi was probably ten to one, leading J. A. Hobson to make the lonely argument that "if the principle of the greatest good of the greatest number is to prevail in South Africa, their claims should be paramount". J. A. Hobson, *The War in South Africa: Its Causes and Effects* (London: James Nisbet, 1900), 279. Hobson argued that the war was being fought to secure a cheap supply of labour for the mining industry.

[46] These Volksraad debate reports made excellent anti-Boer propaganda. "Deputy Taljaard said that he could not see why people wanted to be always writing letters; he wrote none himself. In the days of his youth he had written a letter and had not been afraid to travel fifty miles and more on horseback and by wagon to post it—and now people complained if they had to go one mile." ACD, *The War in South Africa: Its Causes and Conduct* (Toronto: George N. Morang, 1902), 17–18. On the same page, "Mr. Jan de Beer complained of the lack of uniformity in neckties."

rebuttal of the liberal J. A. Hobson's *The War in South Africa: Its Causes and Effects* (1900), and takes on a number of the chief allegations made against the British by opponents of the war—that they had provoked the conflict, specifically in their complicity with the Jameson Raid into Transvaal (Conan Doyle said the British government knew nothing of the Raid in advance); that this was a capitalists' war, fought for the profits of mining companies and their financial backers ("Such a supposition is absurd, nor can any reason be given why a body of high-minded and honourable British gentlemen like the Cabinet should sacrifice their country for the sake of a number of cosmopolitan financiers, most of whom are German Jews");[47] that Britain wanted to get its hands on the gold mines (but these belonged to companies, regardless of whose flag flew above them); that here was a strong monarchy attacking a weak republic (rather, a democracy at war with an oligarchy, and the Boer forces were the stronger at the outbreak of hostilities); that the British were seeking revenge for their defeat at Majuba in the first war between them (yet the British had shown great patience); that the Boers had no aggressive designs against the British (contradicted by public pronouncements by Boer leaders); that the British burned farms (both sides did this); that the British policy of herding the civilian population of the veldt into concentration camps was cruel (but "it became evident that it was the duty of the British, as a civilized people, to form camps of refuge for the women and children where, out of reach, as we hoped, of all harm, they could await the return of peace");[48] that many died of disease in the camps (yet there was "a consensus of opinion from all the camps that the defects in sanitation are due to the habits of the inmates").[49]

British soldiers' treatment of enemy civilians was a matter of contention, and Conan Doyle devotes a whole chapter to their defence. W. T. Stead declared that no gentleman in England would allow his servant girl to be out all night in the company of soldiers. "Why then should they suppose that when the same men are released from all the restraints of civilization, and sent forth to burn, destroy, and loot at their own sweet pleasure, will they suddenly undergo so complete a transformation as to scrupulously respect the wives and daughters of

---

[47] ACD, *The War in South Africa*, 51.
[48] ACD, *The War in South Africa*, 81.
[49] ACD, *The War in South Africa*, 84.

the enemy."[50] Against this sort of thing Conan Doyle reported Lord Roberts's statement, when asked to sum up the character of the soldiers he had led, "that they had behaved like gentlemen"; and added his own credibility-stretching testimony that in three months in Bloemfontein he only once saw a man drunk, and "not only never saw any outrage, but in many confidential talks with officers I never heard of one".[51]

There was some room for improvement, he allowed, and in the final chapter of his history he was confident in suggesting "Some Military Lessons of the War", passing judgement on weaponry and equipment, training and tactics, just like an expert. He urged that the size of the army be reduced, but that it should be supported by a militia of a million men for home defence. Modern warfare demands intelligence and individuality, so soldiers should be better paid and drawn from a different social class. There is no need for the gold lace and frippery to catch the plough-boy, or the luxurious habits that attract the sons of the rich, he argued: the modern army should be a bourgeois career and a serious profession. Yet for Conan Doyle, South Africa had demonstrated again the lesson of *The White Company*, that wars were fought and won by spirit as well as by skill. *The Great Boer War* contributes to a myth of the British army. And the army, itself an organ and expression of the nation, needed not only the brisk professionalism of Roberts and Kitchener but also the *sprezzatura* of Mafeking.

When another war came in 1914, he was widowed, remarried, and for a second time the father of a young family. He was immediately ready to offer his support for the war effort, and was soon busy writing patriotic pamphlets and articles; anti-German sentiment came easily to him, seeded at the time of his Berlin trip, and confirmed by what he remembered of unsporting German competitiveness when he took part in a motoring rally organized by Prince Henry, the Kaiser's brother, in 1911.[52] He believed that Germany's attack on France was politically senseless, and based on a deluded belief that the British character had degenerated and Britain would not come to the aid of Belgium—"the big cowardly fellow would stand by with folded arms and see his little

---

[50] W. T. Stead, *Methods of Barbarism* (London: Mowbray House, 1901), 77.

[51] ACD, *The War in South Africa*, 93, 94. For "Outrage, n.", the *OED* 2.b gives "Violence affecting others; violent injury or harm (sometimes *spec.* sexual assault or rape)".

[52] Andrew Lycett argues, however, that Conan Doyle was something of a Germanophile before 1914. Lycett, *Conan Doyle*, 331–2.

friend knocked about by the bully" (*M&A*, 312–13)—another unset-tlingly schoolboyish interpretation of history, and oddly amnesiac about what he had written of the activities of the "little friend" in *The Crime of the Congo*, as recently as 1909. But when it came to military and strategic matters, the veteran of Bloemfontein and war historian had by now assumed an authoritative voice, every column-inch a pun-dit, and he was soon offering his views in the national press—chiefly in *The Times*—on a host of questions, including volunteers, the subma-rine menace (which he had been one of the first to predict), lifebelts and lifeboats, bombardment and mining, body armour, recruitment and national service, prostitutes preying on soldiers, prisoners of war, air raids and reprisals, drink and venereal disease among soldiers, Ger-man policy, British strategy, and the need to inculcate a hatred of the enemy.[53] The last item at least may seem a shocking thing to find in the remit of a writer's practice. But Conan Doyle was now taking himself seriously as the voice of the British public at war (it was a role sought by others too, such as Arnold Bennett and H. G. Wells), and by the end of 1917 that voice was strained by three years of war with no end in sight. More fully than ever before or since, the daily press was the institution through which the nation talked to itself and formed its views, and Conan Doyle's was a voice frequently heard on matters of policy and public concern. All this busy journalistic work is a further instance of his understanding of the practice of a writer. Membership of the profession of letters gave him the right to trespass into the field of knowledge of other professions—the law, politics, the army, the clergy—and make himself heard, an amateur with a licence.

As a national writer in his own mind and that of much of the public, he seldom deviates from the official and patriotic line, and indeed per-haps no very radical wartime dissention can be expected from the Deputy Lieutenant of Surrey. But he does sometimes present the unat-tractive picture of a civilian, past military age, urging more vigorous measures against the enemy—the bombing of civilian targets, the pub-lic shaming of shirkers from military service, the rough treatment of prisoners, the propaganda of shock. The motive of these newspaper articles and letters was not just to sound off; they were intended to be a stimulus and focus for debate, and often they attracted replies, hostile or approving, in the form of published ripostes or private letters. It was

[53] See ACD, *Letters to the Press*, 364–5.

in wartime that Conan Doyle was most conscious of living in a democracy; the British government could not have gone to war without popular support, and eventual success in the war depended on the steadfastness of that support, from people at home and in the empire rallying to "the one banner which meant to each a just and liberal rule".[54] Here was a national role for the writer, in marshalling public opinion behind the work that army and navy were doing.

Inevitably, he set to work on a history of the war on the Western Front, *The British Campaign in France and Flanders*, which would run to six volumes (1916–20). The model was his own successful Boer War history, and the narrative was again to have an eyewitness quality to it, built up as it was, he said, from letters, diaries, and interviews "from the hands or lips of men who have been soldiers in our armies, the deeds of which it was my ambition to understand and to chronicle".[55] An opening chapter sets out to prove Germany entirely to blame for this war between Germanic kinsfolk: if not the German people as a whole, then the Prussian military system which, he had explained in a letter to *The Times*, had always been cruel and had now moulded all the rest of Germany in its own image.[56] But no sooner has the war begun, than an almost supernatural effect supervenes.

A just war seemed to touch the land with some magic wand, which healed all dissentions and merged into one national whole those vivid controversies which are, in fact, a sign rather of intense vitality than of degeneration. In a moment the faddist forgot his fad, the capitalist his grievance against taxation, the Labour man his feud against Capital, the Tory his hatred of the Government, even the woman her craving for the vote.[57]

Here is another national utopia of reconciliation: the squabbling palaver which the Germans had mistaken for degeneration was only the noise of democracy, and in the crisis of war, the elements of the culture set aside their differences in a common identity and cause. Again, the army in the field is the most potent symbol of this integration, comprising as it does not only men from the different nations of the United Kingdom, but also troops from the dominions—including

---

[54] ACD, *The British Campaign in France and Flanders*, ii: *1915* (1917) (Newcastle upon Tyne: Cambridge Scholars, 2009), 21.

[55] ACD, *The British Campaign in France and Flanders*, i: *1914* (1916) (Newcastle upon Tyne: Cambridge Scholars, 2009), 2.

[56] ACD, Letter to *The Times* (6 February 1915), in *Letters to the Press*, 216–19.

[57] ACD, *The British Campaign in France and Flanders*, i. 20.

"South Africa, under the splendid leadership of Botha"—and from India.[58] So powerful was this Kiplingesque vision of multinational and multi-ethnic endeavour that Conan Doyle was obliged to remind his readers, almost apologetically, that four-fifths of the army was purely English.[59] The expeditionary force which in 1914 followed in the footsteps of Sam Aylward and Hordle John has been described as "incomparably the best trained, best organized, and best equipped British Army which ever went forth to war".[60] But it was too small for industrial mass warfare. The war in France and Flanders that followed, a prolonged entrenched war of attrition between conscript armies, was one in which it was hard to find opportunities for panache.

He later described the war as the physical climax of his life (*M&A*, 311). It was also the professional climax of his career as a man of letters, when his reputation as a public intellectual was at its height. Whether or not he was right in thinking that in wartime the women of Britain forgot their craving for the vote, national history in the war years seemed more than ever a masculine affair, and the war itself a test of national manhood at home as well as at the front. No longer remote, this war was on Britain's European doorstep, its noise audible in the south-eastern counties of Kent and Sussex; and with millions of men conscripted into the fighting forces, it could no longer be thought of as a boyish adventure. And yet, with so many men away at war, women were more visible and audible than ever in wartime society and its economy. The culture was at the same time hypermasculinized and hyperfeminized. Something equally strange happened to Conan Doyle. He was a writer for whom manliness had always been important as a theme and as a part of his authorial self-conception, and he responded vigorously to this challenge to personal and national masculinity; yet this surge of manhood in the bloodstream also produced in him a flood of antibodies of a different kind.

On one hand, he continued to behave as a man of war, offering in public his opinions and suggestions about military affairs. Desperate to get to the front, but diffident about the prospect of being regarded as a civilian spectator or joy-rider, he solved this problem when he realized

---

[58] ACD, *The British Campaign in France and Flanders*, i. 21. General Louis Botha had fought the British in the Boer War, as had Jan Smuts who went on to join Lloyd George's Imperial War Cabinet.

[59] ACD, *The British Campaign in France and Flanders*, ii. 78.

[60] Spiers, *The Army and Society*, 284.

that as deputy lieutenant of a county he was entitled to wear a uniform when with troops, and so when he turned up in the British lines in France it was "in a wondrous khaki garb which was something between that of a Colonel and a Brigadier, with silver roses instead of stars or crowns upon the shoulder-straps" (M&A, 345). Yet a few months later in the same year that saw this parade of warriorhood, he made a public exhibition of himself of a different, even opposite kind, when he made a declaration of his belief in Spiritualism. This was no lightning conversion, but a conviction that had grown on him over the decades. But it came to a head in the particular conditions of a prolonged war, the death of men and the bereavement of women—"the days of universal sorrow and loss", as he put it, "when the voice of Rachel was heard throughout the land" (M&A, 396). To most people his assurances that the dead were not really dead must have seemed embarrassingly unmanly, in a pious, sentimental, irrational, self-deluding way. But the war had convinced him that people would pay attention to his words because he was famous and trusted. It was the suffering of soldiers and their families that first caused to him to embark on that public mission—the military word "campaign" also seemed appropriate (M&A, 396)—to disseminate his consoling knowledge of the afterlife as a proven fact. At the height of wartime this national writer had identified himself with a cause that, as he knew perfectly well, most people considered neither masculine, gentlemanly, dignified, nor indeed honest.

And so Conan Doyle emerged at the end of the Great War as a self-contradictory combination of establishment blowhard and alienated dissident. That latter description is not an exaggeration. His openly espoused Spiritualism, and the controversies in which this would involve him for the rest of his life, had opened his eyes to much that was repulsive in the culture, the way of life for which the troops were fighting and dying. He was far from alone in asking what the war was being fought for, for "when the War came it brought earnestness into all our souls and made us look more closely at our own beliefs and reassess their values".[61] In struggling to understand what had gone disastrously wrong to bring about this war, he concluded it was "the organized materialism of Germany".[62] But an unprincipled hostility to

---

[61] ACD, *The New Revelation* (Toronto: Hodder and Stoughton, 1918), 39.
[62] ACD, *The Vital Message* (London: Hodder and Stoughton, 1919), 19.

the spiritual, on the part of the scientific profession and the press and the law and even the churches, convinced him that competitive materialism—that old enemy—was not rampant only in Germany, but had eaten into the institutions of his own nation as well as of others. At the end of the war, he concluded in his history, it had left Europe an exhausted waste land. Soldiers on all sides had gone to war with bravery and honour, but those values of the spirit for which earlier warriors had fought had been betrayed by those who sent them into battle. "The system which left seven million dead upon the fields of Europe must be rotten to the core"; it was now time to learn its lesson, for only then was there a chance that the war of 1914 might be seen not as the beginning of a new dark ages, but as the start of "that upward path which leads away from personal or national selfishness towards the City Beautiful upon the distant hills".[63]

Empire

Conan Doyle's lifetime coincided with the zenith of the British Empire. When he was born, the British had just succeeded in quelling the great Indian rebellion (the "Indian Mutiny") of 1857–8. The empire expanded during Victoria's reign, especially in its last two decades, and again in the aftermath of the First World War. But ten years after his death, it would be everywhere embattled in another world war from which it would emerge fatally wounded.

There were two British Empires, one white and one Oriental, dramatically different. The white empire consisted of territories in which people from Britain had settled in large numbers, subduing or driving out or in some places liquidating indigenous inhabitants or earlier arrivals. This settler empire included the partially self-governing dominions of Canada, Australia, and New Zealand, and what became after 1910 the dominion of the Union of South Africa, comprising the previously separate colonies of the Cape, Natal, Transvaal, and the Orange Free State. This predominantly English-speaking empire could be described in the words of the title of Charles Wentworth Dilke's 1868 travel book, *Greater Britain*, and Conan Doyle would have

---

[63] ACD, *The British Campaign in France and Flanders*, vi: *July–November 1918* (1920) (Newcastle upon Tyne: Cambridge Scholars, 2009), 169.

endorsed Dilke's inclusion under this rubric of the former American colonies which made up the United States. This empire filled Conan Doyle with pride and with a fellow feeling for a vigorous global community, an ethnicity (for "race" for Conan Doyle and his contemporaries was a biocultural category) rooted in a shared language and strengthened by various phases of genetic mingling which he regarded as unambiguously benign—evidence, perhaps, of "a great hand blending the seeds". "It does not, for example, take much prophetic power to say that something very great is being built up on the other side of the Atlantic. When on an Anglo-Celtic basis you see the Italian, the Hun, and the Scandinavian being added, you feel that there is no human quality which may not be thereby evolved."[64] "Despite Hannah Arendt's claim that modern race theory originates in a concern for purity," Stephen Arata has remarked, "the British have always found the notion of symbolic hybridization congenial."[65]

Ireland, a European country and a part of the United Kingdom since 1801 and governed by a viceroy, but heading for independence in Conan Doyle's lifetime, was an imperial anomaly, the empire's sore thumb. The Irish were welcome to belong to Greater Britain, though many seemed reluctant; it was not until his friendship with Roger Casement, and probably in 1913, that Conan Doyle became a supporter of Home Rule, though he hoped that a self-governing Ireland would strengthen its ties with the empire.[66] His own Irish heritage remained something of an unresolved question, and the many confident statements in his work that the Irish are on the side of the angels are undercut by other hints—Moriarty's Irish name is often remarked—that their allegiance is to another party.[67]

The second British Empire consisted of people of a different colour from the British, ruled over by a small minority of administrators from Britain, and garrisoned by a mixed armed force typically including European officers and local troops. This was Britain's Oriental empire, anchored in the enormous Indian subcontinent, but with outposts to

---

[64] ACD, *Through the Magic Door*, 69.

[65] Arata, *Fictions of Loss in the Victorian Fin de Siècle*, 160.

[66] Lycett, *Conan Doyle*, 340–1.

[67] The best account of Conan Doyle's Irishness is in Edwards, *The Quest for Sherlock Holmes*. For an extended argument that Conan Doyle's engagement with British imperialism was decisively inflected by Irish nationalism, see Catherine Wynne, *The Colonial Conan Doyle: British Imperialism, Irish Nationalism, and the Gothic* (Westport, Conn.: Greenwood Press, 2002).

be found not only in Asia but, in George Orwell's useful phrase, "anywhere south of Gibraltar or east of Suez".[68] Arthur Conan Doyle travelled extensively throughout Greater Britain, but apart from his voyage along the West African coast as a young ship's doctor in 1881, and the trip to Egypt in 1895, his knowledge of the empire of the Orient was, like that of most British people of his generation, second-hand and very literary. He showed little curiosity about its government or its economic life. For him, the Oriental empire was most interesting as a problem in policing.

The Mystery of Cloomber, an apprentice piece published in 1888, offers a good example of a knowledge of the Orient drawn entirely from books. Major-General Heatherstone, late of the Indian army and a hero of 1857, is tracked down in his home at Cloomber Hall in the remote south-west of Scotland by three mysterious Indians, who exact revenge on him for his murder of a holy man forty years earlier. The story bristles with orientalist commonplaces. There were three mysterious Indians in Wilkie Collins's *The Moonstone*, a mystery story published only twenty years earlier, which also contains the motif of retribution brought home to a British officer for a crime committed years before in the Orient (the motif turns up again, but more subtly, in Conan Doyle's *The Sign of the Four*). In this case the crime was sacrilegious, and this too is a favourite topos of what Patrick Brantlinger was the first to call "imperial gothic"; Kipling's story "The Mark of the Beast" is one of the best examples, but there are plenty of others, often involving the removal or theft of a sacred object or the desecration of an Oriental temple or an ancient Egyptian tomb—other examples include Bram Stoker's *The Jewel of the Seven Stars* and Conan Doyle's own mummy tale, "Lot No. 249" (1892). Such stories encode some of the anxiety which is the dark side of a triumphant imperialism, the feeling that the British might have got their hands on something they could not understand or control.[69] But these tales also simply plunder the Orient for enjoyable and exotic thrills. The sacrilege-revenge motif

---

[68] Orwell uses the words in his essay "Marrakech" (1939), in *The Complete Works of George Orwell*, ed. Peter Davison, 20 vols. (London: Secker and Warburg, 1998), xi. 416–21; at 420, quoting the phrase "east of Suez" in Rudyard Kipling's poem "Mandalay".

[69] See Patrick Brantlinger, *Rule of Darkness: British Literature and Imperialism 1830–1914* (Ithaca, NY: Cornell University Press, 1988), 227–54. A theory of commodity and consumption in the mummy story is developed in Daly, *Modernism, Romance and the Fin de Siècle*, 84–116.

carries two of the dominant ideas that form part of popular British knowledge of the Orient which Conan Doyle's fiction was helping to create: spirituality and violence.

Violence was endemic in the Orient as the British imagined it; the well-known inherent savagery of most Oriental peoples was both an explanation and a justification for European mastery of the non-white world, which should not be left to its own pagan and lawless devices.[70] From the Zulu impi to Kipling's "Fuzzy-Wuzzies" in the Sudan, to the murderous thuggees and the disloyal sepoys of the Mutiny, and the inexplicable Boxer rebels of China, there was a broad repertoire of Oriental bloodthirstiness to be excited by, for it seemed obvious that people of colour or "natives", lacking the twin restraints of Christianity and civilized modernity, were given by nature to destructive outbursts. Conan Doyle reproduces this orientalist knowledge in his fiction, and indeed the known violence of "natives"—a topic emerging from but also justifying the practice of imperial invasion, coercion, and policing—provided an inexhaustible lode of narrative gold for storytellers like Conan Doyle (and it still does). The violence perpetrated by the three Indians in *The Mystery of Cloomber* is retributive, and mysterious, but in much popular literature of the period, Oriental violence is a given. Though in this story one of the Indians quotes Milton and has perfect manners, there is no doubt what he has come to do, just as we know perfectly well how the Egyptian mummy in "Lot No. 249", lifeless for 3,000 years, is going to behave when he is woken up. In "The Pot of Caviare" (1908), an old professor has no hesitation in poisoning the entire European population of a besieged outpost in north China rather than let them fall alive into the hands of the unspeakable Boxer rebels.[71] The savagery of the Boxers required no explanation.

---

[70] Conan Doyle's view of the world is "orientalist" in the sense given the word by Edward W. Said's *Orientalism*, yet not as crudely so as is sometimes suggested. Jon Thompson, for example, discussing the representation of the Indians in *The Sign of the Four*, has overlooked the grasping Major Sholto and Captain Morstan when he says that in that novel "the English, by contrast, are portrayed as being actuated by noble aims rather than vulgar, material ones". Thompson, *Fiction, Crime and Empire*, 70. For British fiction and orientalism, see Douglas Kerr, *Eastern Figures: Orient and Empire in British Writing* (Hong Kong: Hong Kong University Press, 2008).

[71] *A Pot of Caviare*, a one-act play adapted from this story, was performed at the Adelphi Theatre in 1910.

But if the Orient was known to be inherently violent, it was also known to wear the aspect of spirituality and immemorial wisdom. This piece of Western knowledge was also entirely compatible with an imperial way of looking at the world, for if Orientals were inclined to a timeless and spiritual life, this was in contrast to Western people who knew themselves to be modern, scientific, and executive, and it was clear which kind of person should be running things; and so for example the saintly lama in Kipling's novel *Kim* is more than happy to leave matters of government and worldly knowledge in India to the efficient British, while he concentrates on his quest for spiritual enlightenment. Oriental spirituality could be aggressive and frightening, in which case it was called fanaticism and superstition. But more often it was an object of respect and curiosity for British observers who, like Conan Doyle himself, felt that the global success and material prosperity of their own way of life had been achieved at the price of a certain impoverishment of the spirit. In his wanderings after his disappearance at the Reichenbach Falls, that stubborn materialist Sherlock Holmes spent two years in Tibet and visited the great Lama, and also travelled to Mecca and to Khartoum, in a grand tour of sites of Oriental spirituality and violence.[72]

And so, in *The Mystery of Cloomber*, the three Indians who come to Scotland to murder General Heatherstone are no mere hit-men, but adepts of an Oriental religion which has given them extraordinary spiritual and mental faculties. Not only do they have telepathic and coercive powers similar to those of the mesmerist in *The Parasite*, they can dissociate spiritual from material forms, and travel about in the astral body, faster than lightning. They also appear to be several hundred years old. The Indians are rather indiscriminately referred to as Sikhs, Parsees, Buddhists, and Hindus.[73] They belong quite clearly to that hallucinatory East conjured up in the imagination of Theosophists, who located their whole panoply of exciting spiritual effects in ancient Oriental practice. Conan Doyle spread a confection of Theosophical motifs around the Indians in *The Mystery of Cloomber*, to render them mysterious and exotic in a conventionally Oriental

---

[72] ACD, "The Empty House", in *The Return of Sherlock Holmes*, 12.
[73] They are most frequently described as Buddhists though Ram Singh is a highly unlikely name for a Buddhist and the other two, Lal Hoomi and Mowdar Khan, bear names Conan Doyle seems to have made up. Later he gave Muslim names to Sikh characters in *The Sign of the Four*.

way.[74] Their spirituality is treated with respect, even awe, by the narrator, who concludes piously that there are more things in heaven and earth than can be accounted for by the scientist, who should admit that in the East there are wise men who are many thousand years ahead of him in all the essentials of knowledge. Still, Oriental spirituality coexisted with Oriental savagery. "It was difficult for me to associate the noble-faced Ram Singh's gentle, refined manner and words of wisdom with any deed of violence, yet now that I thought of it I could see that a terrible capacity for wrath lay behind his shaggy brows and dark, piercing eyes."[75]

The Oriental empire needed to be policed, contained, and protected. It is not frivolous to observe that, when you read Conan Doyle, it is hard to see what else it is for. *The Tragedy of the Korosko* is a short novel in which a party of tourists on the Nile is captured by a band of the Khalifa's "dervishes", and then rescued by the Egyptian Camel Corps, led by its British officers. The tourists themselves, British and Americans and an Irish couple, are a demographic sample of Greater Britain, but the cruise party includes a good-natured but argumentative Frenchman called M. Fardet. The French were the rivals of the British on the Nile, and Fardet tries to recruit Headingly, an American fellow passenger, to his view that the British are unprincipled exploiters of their empire. But in the discussion that ensues, he is obliged to concede that in Egypt there is no favourable tariff for British goods, that the contract to build a railway had been given to a French company, and that the British garrison is paid by London. The British keep order, dispense justice to the locals, and guard the frontier, he has to admit, and the prosperity of the Egyptians has increased enormously under Lord Cromer's management. For all the Frenchman's bluster, Headingly concludes that the British seem to take a great deal of trouble in their imperial work, and to get very little in exchange.[76]

---

[74] Madame Blavatsky was exposed as a fraud by the SPR in 1885, causing Conan Doyle's enthusiasm for Theosophy to cool. Its author's "allowing the winds of credulity to blow very freely on his imagination in relation to Theosophy" in the story is one reason to support an early composition date for *The Mystery of Cloomber* (though it was not published until 1888), according to Owen Dudley Edwards who has argued for composition before 1885 and perhaps as early as 1882. See Edwards, "The Mystery of *The Mystery of Cloomber*", *ACD: Journal of the Arthur Conan Doyle Society*, 2/2 (Autumn 1991), 101–33.

[75] ACD, *The Mystery of Cloomber* (London: Ward and Downey, 1889), 95.

[76] ACD, *The Tragedy of the Korosko* (London: Smith, Elder, 1898), 25–31.

This opinion, elevated to a sense of tragic national destiny that same year in Kipling's imperial poem "The White Man's Burden", seems, in a general sense, to have been Conan Doyle's view also. The imperial order was its own reward. It was a utopian project, a selfless game played against nature to improve the lives of people who needed help.

All over the world war exists between Nature and the British Raj. Nature sends smallpox. The Raj sends vaccine. Nature sends the flood. The Raj sends the dam. Nature sends the famine. The Raj supplies the food. Nature sends the bellicose spirit of tribal warfare. The Raj, in the person of the Police Inspector, suppresses it. It has been a long uphill game, but the Raj usually wins. It is the greatest force for good in this world.[77]

The British, says Colonel Cochrane in *The Tragedy of the Korosko*, have a high conception of justice and public duty and were compelled by a kind of natural law, like air rushing into a vacuum, to govern India: now all over the world, "against our direct interests and our deliberate intentions, we are drawn into the same thing".[78] We have seen Conan Doyle deny that the war against the Boers had anything to do with South Africa's mineral resources, though he himself, in his career as an enthusiastic and rather swashbuckling investor, held considerable stocks in mining companies there and in Australia.[79] *The Firm of Girdlestone*, a novel about a merchant business in the African trade, hinges on a fraudulent attempt to depress and then corner the world market in diamonds. But its economic theme is at the level of fairy tale, and the novel's main focus is on the family melodrama and, particularly, on the "pseudo-religious monomania" of old Girdlestone himself. While he ruthlessly exploits his African workers and tries to cheat his young ward of her inheritance, he fills his diary with exclamations about the workings of grace within him. This is a novel in which Conan Doyle settles some of his scores with things he disliked about Scotland, including a kind of penny-pinching Calvinist hypocrisy, and there is a real interest in the connection between this kind of Protestantism, and the business practices that bring the merchant his success, and later his downfall.[80]

[77] ACD, *Our African Winter* (London: John Murray, 1929), 249–50.
[78] ACD, *The Tragedy of the Korosko*, 38–9.
[79] "If when I earned money I had dug a hole in the garden and buried it there I should be a much richer man today" (*M&A*, 239–40).
[80] As we have seen, this novel also contains his indictment of the coldness of Edinburgh University, as "a great unsympathetic machine" for turning out fodder for the professions. ACD, *The Firm of Girdlestone*, 33.

Yet there is little curiosity about the organic connection between official military and administrative policies and actions in the empire, and the interests of British trade and finance around the world.

Britain's adherence throughout the Victorian age to the policy of free trade seems to have masked and naturalized for many people the economic dimension of a global empire—though it worked to the advantage of those who controlled the trade routes, "free trade" was after all not an action, but a way of just letting things happen of their own accord. When Conan Doyle eventually came out in favour of protectionism and the "imperial preference" (reciprocal trading tariffs with the colonies) advocated by Joseph Chamberlain in 1903, his argument seems to be that Britain should take steps to benefit from its imperial possessions as it had not bothered, or found it necessary, to do before.[81] Most of the time, though, he was content to think of empire-building and empire-keeping as its own reward, and of the British Empire as a service provided to others, and a great theatre for heroic British deeds, sponsored by a nation and government that had always taken "an honourable and philanthropic view of the rights of the native and the claim which he has to the protection of the law".[82]

In 1906 Conan Doyle first turned his attention to an example of imperialism that was absolutely not honourable, philanthropic, or blind to its own profit. The Congo Reform Association had been set up in 1904 by the journalist E. D. Morel, after Roger Casement, the British consul on the scene, had substantiated allegations of slavery in the rubber plantations belonging to King Leopold of the Belgians—for the vast area of central Africa that became the Belgian Congo in 1909 had hitherto been the personal estate of the King. Morel's book *Red Rubber*, which denounced Leopold's murderous exploitation of the Congo, appeared in 1906. Conan Doyle first wrote to Morel in 1907 to offer help, shared a speaking platform with him at vast rallies for Congo reform, and offered to write a book in 1909 to further publicity and raise money for the cause. He plunged vigorously into research for the book, using Morel's own store of material, and seems to have written it in eight days; *The Crime of the Congo* was published in October 1909, sold 25,000 copies a week when it first appeared, and was immediately

---

[81] See his three letters to the *Spectator* on this subject in 1903. ACD, *Letters to the Press*, 94–8.

[82] ACD, *The War in South Africa*, 3.

translated into several languages. Once again the writer was an activist, and he had become part of what has been called "the first major international human rights movement of the twentieth century".[83]

The whole book makes clear that there was no question now who deserved the title of the Napoleon of Crime. King Leopold stood, wrote Conan Doyle, "with such a cloud of terrible direct personal responsibility resting upon him as no man in modern European history has had to bear" (*Crime*, 11). Evidence for this crime, including the authenticating "incorruptible evidence of the Kodak", was plentiful and unimpeachable, and other European powers were duty-bound to intervene, for they had made themselves responsible for the welfare of the native races in the Treaty of Berlin (which came out of the 1885 Congress which the Germans called the *Kongokonferenz*). The book is a rather different example of Conan Doyle building his knowledge of "native" countries from reading, for he draws on published sources and statistics, the testimony of travellers and missionaries. Neither the data nor the arguments of *The Crime of the Congo* were original, but Conan Doyle marshalled them with an impressive narrative energy and uncompromising indignation. The book tells the story of how Henry Morton Stanley, commissioned to open the Congo basin up for trade, had secured no less than 450 separate treaties transferring title over land to the King of the Belgians personally, from men who had no right to sell the land and no idea they were doing so. "And yet it is on the strength of such treaties as these that twenty millions of people have been expropriated, and the whole wealth and land of the country proclaimed to belong, not to the inhabitants, but to the State—that is, to King Leopold" (*Crime*, 10). A campaign to suppress the Arab-run slave trade provided the enterprise with a cover of philanthropy which, as we have seen, so disgusted Joseph Conrad (who was there in 1890).[84] Conan Doyle was even more indignant. "Tartuffe and Jack the Ripper—was ever such a combination in the history of the world!" (*Crime*, 41). He alleged that the Belgians used local troops who practised cannibalism on their enemies. It is certain that the system of labour put into practice in Leopold's Congo included *de facto* slavery and spoliation enforced with the utmost ruthlessness, with the consequence, in the best modern estimate, that during the Leopold period and its

---

[83] Hochschild, *King Leopold's Ghost*, 274.
[84] Conrad, *Collected Letters of Joseph Conrad*, i. 294.

immediate aftermath about ten million people, or half the entire population of the Congo area, disappeared.[85]

This is how Conan Doyle explained it.

The State is run with the one object of producing revenue. For this end all land and its produce are appropriated. How, then, is this produce to be gathered? It can only be by the natives. But if the natives gather it they must be paid their price, which will diminish profits, or else they will refuse to work. Then they must be made to work. But the agents are too few to make them work. Then they must employ such sub-agents as will strike most terror into the people. But if these sub-agents are to make the people work all the time, then they must themselves reside in the villages. So a capita [overseer] must be sent as a constant terror to each village. Is it not clear that these steps are not accidental, but are absolutely essential to the original idea? Given the confiscation of the land, all the rest must logically follow. It is utterly futile, therefore, to imagine that any reform can set matters right. Such a thing is impossible. Until unfettered trade is unconditionally restored, as it now exists in every German and English colony, it is absolutely out of the question that any specious promises or written decrees can modify the situation. But, on the other hand, if trade be put upon this natural basis, then for many years the present owners of the Congo land, instead of sharing dividends, must pay out at least a million a year to administer the country, exactly as England pays half a million a year to administer the neighbouring land of Nigeria. To grasp that fact is to understand the root of the whole question. (*Crime*, 29)

The analysis is sound, and the spirit of *The Crime of the Congo* entirely praiseworthy. The book is not a denunciation of colonialism or of empire, however, but of criminal malpractice in these enterprises. Because he was seeking concerted European action to end the Belgian crime in the Congo, the book has polite references to other colonial powers, to Germany with its traditions of kindly home life and "the splendid private and public example of [Kaiser] William II", and to "the generous, chivalrous instincts of the French people", whose colonial record during centuries had been "hardly inferior to our own"—though Conan Doyle was in fact still smarting from the way her European neighbours had gleefully sought advantage from Britain's troubles in South Africa (*Crime*, 6–7). Conan Doyle thrived on simplicity, and responsibility for the Congo atrocities could legitimately be laid at the door of one man, King Leopold. But after the Congo had been annexed to the Belgian state in 1908 it was clear things had not

[85] Hochschild, *King Leopold's Ghost*, 233.

got much better. The Belgian enterprise could be condemned as an absolute disgrace because there were examples to hand of how to do the thing properly. "The fact is that the running of a tropical colony is, of all tests, the most searching as to the development of the nation which attempts it; to see helpless people and not to oppress them, to see great wealth and not to confiscate it, to have absolute power and not to abuse it, to raise the native instead of sinking yourself—these are the supreme trials of a nation's spirit" (*Crime*, 86). An overseas empire was, in effect, the visible projection of a nation's character, and the terrible Belgian failure served if anything to confirm Conan Doyle's faith in the successful practice of empire by his own countrymen. In this view, he has something in common with Marlow, the narrator of Conrad's Congo tale "Heart of Darkness", who consoles himself in his contemplation of the crimes of other empires by thinking about the red (British) portions of the map, where, he can be confident, "some real work" is being done.[86] Conan Doyle could see that the Belgians had been drawn into a crime of genocidal proportions because of a fundamental misunderstanding of the nature of empire, believing it was for profit, instead of for order.

As for the British, with this satisfying confidence in the probity of their empire, they could enjoy it, as they enjoyed the army, as evidence of their global pre-eminence, and as a spectacle and an excitement at a distance. The empire lent colour and glamour to a grey north European climate and a stolid way of life. Time and again in Conan Doyle's fiction, the empire—white or Oriental—delivers a jolt of dynamism, danger, or desire to the British scene. Problems or conflicts hatched on the frontier—the Australian outback, the American plains, the mines of South Africa, the Egyptian necropolis, the battlefields of India—are imported into his stories, like so much raw material shipped from the colonies, and processed into the finished product of stories and plays. Empire might not seem (and ought not to be) obviously profitable to its masters, and in Conan Doyle's time it was becoming conventional to speak of it in terms of trusteeship, a temporary authority to protect the interests of "natives" until they should be able to manage their own affairs. But it certainly put the imperial power in possession of a rich stream of cultural treasure. The embodiment of this is Thaddeus Sholto

---

[86] Joseph Conrad, *Heart of Darkness* (1902), ed. Robert Kimbrough, 3rd edn. (Norton Critical Edition, New York: Norton, 1988), 13.

in *The Sign of the Four*, son of a soldier, but himself an aesthete and consumer of orientalia, who lolls about a suburban London apartment furnished with all manner of Eastern trophies, curtains and rugs, two great tiger-skins, and a huge hookah.

The white empire of the dominions was a good deal less exotic, but served as a different kind of affirmation of Britishness, proof that the domestic model flourished beyond its shores. Here the keynote was not violence but enterprise. And the dominions, vast and multifarious as they were, are also presented in his writings as yet more proof of the great theme of his version of the story of the nation and its empire—an essential oneness, a unity only strengthened, it seemed, by its manifest diversity. The great exemplification of this truth was to be found in the way the empire—both white and Oriental—rallied round the home country in time of war. The fiction is full of instances of the alliance, sometimes within the genetic inheritance of a single character but more often in bands of men, of Saxon and Celt, or sometimes Saxon and Norman. These dramas of integration are played out on an epic scale on the stage of the empire itself. National institutions themselves provided a model of mixture and partnership, or rather Britain's imperial work marked its national institutions with a cosmopolitan diversity of origins.[87]

It can be argued that Conan Doyle, a divided man with a divided provenance, harps too insistently on the empire as a spectacle of cooperation, harmony, and singleness of purpose. Certainly there is a didactic element to this insistence, as if in hammering home this vision of unity he could secure it in fact. Even the somewhat anomalous Irish are bound in to a single enterprise, like the bloody-minded Fenians in the story "The Green Flag" (1893) who nonetheless give their lives fighting for the British army in the Sudan. In *The Valley of Fear*, Conan Doyle underplayed the Irishness of the lawless Molly Maguires in Pennsylvania, as if to draw attention away from the potential of the Irish to disturb his vision of the unity of Greater Britain.[88] The American Revolution itself he saw as the product of a series of political

---

[87] Thus in Conan Doyle's fourth year of study at Edinburgh University, 622 of the student intake were Scots, 492 entered from England, 25 from Ireland, 89 from India, 174 from the British colonies, and 40 from other countries. See Edwards, *The Quest for Sherlock Holmes*, 180.

[88] See a fuller discussion in Wynne, *The Colonial Conan Doyle*, 42–56.

blunders. Without it, the whole of North America might have been one magnificent undivided country, independent of its parent, "yet united in such unblemished ties of blood and memory to the old country that each could lean at all times upon the other" (*M&A*, 299). The aptly named *The White Company* is dedicated, as we have seen, to the reunion of the English-speaking races, and this vision of Greater Britain is similar to the one prophesied to Sir Nigel and his friends by the Lady Tiphaine.

And unexpectedly, the white empire, like the Orient, turned out to have a spirituality of its own. Just as, he believed, every corporeal human body was inhabited by an etheric body which was its undying spiritual self, so in his later years the empire that Conan Doyle travelled tirelessly was the shell for a spiritual infrastructure which it was his mission, he was sure, to strengthen and sustain. Theosophy came wreathed in Oriental trappings, with its invocations of ancient Tibetan practices and its fabulous esotericism. Spiritualism is, by contrast, definitely homespun. Though its intellectual inheritance, mapped in Conan Doyle's *History of Spiritualism*, goes back to Swedenborg, it has its feet firmly planted in Greater Britain. With early manifestations in lowland Scotland and in the Shaker communities of the United States, Spiritualism became a movement in the 1840s when Margaret and Kate Fox, teenaged daughters of a farmer in Hydesville, New York State, achieved national fame with their claim to communicate with spirits. From this, the "Hydesville episode", the beliefs and practices that came to be called Spiritualism rapidly developed and spread across the continent, across the Atlantic, and in due course across the white empire. Empirical, prosaic, even democratic, not much interested in theory or ritual, Spiritualism did seem to bear something of what Conan Doyle thought of as an essentially British character. Though its time had not yet fully come, he was confident it was to be the greatest of the gifts of the English-speaking races to the world.

And so the last phase of Conan Doyle's life, as we shall see in the following chapter, was dominated by his mission to nurture the spiritualization of the empire. From Perth to Port Elizabeth, and from Ottawa to Auckland, he contacted and encouraged the network of Spiritualist communities, lecturing, testifying, and debating, travelling 50,000 miles and speaking face to face with a quarter of a million people (*M&A*, 397). There is no doubt of the model he was following.

St Paul, first and greatest of missionaries, in his time had travelled another empire, visiting the scattered and sometimes embattled outposts of a faith based on a new revelation, and sowing the seeds for the time to come, when that empire and the spiritual practice that he preached would be one and the same thing.

7

Spirit

Church

A young professional, setting out to make his way in the world, has the immediate task of becoming known, making a name, and setting up those networks of knowledge and practice from which an early stream of customers, clients, or patients may flow. Conan Doyle was starting from scratch in Southsea in 1882, in a one-man practice in a town where he seems to have known nobody. His own family in Edinburgh were not in a position to help, except in sending the 9-year-old Innes to keep his brother company in the house in Elm Grove. But Arthur was the family heir, the oldest Doyle grandson, and he did have other relatives willing to assist him. From London, his uncle Richard (Dicky) Doyle sent him a letter of introduction to the Catholic Bishop of Portsmouth. But Arthur made no use of this letter. He burnt it. He recalled later that his mind was so perfectly clear, and he had so entirely broken away from the old faith that he could not possibly use it "for material ends" (M&A, 66).

There were both Protestants and Catholics among Conan Doyle's Irish forebears, but all four of his grandparents were Catholics, he had been brought up a Catholic in Protestant Edinburgh, and put to school with the Jesuits at Stonyhurst. His uncle Dicky Doyle, a successful artist and illustrator and man-about-town in London, took his religion seriously enough to have resigned as a salaried contributor to *Punch* in protest against what he considered the anti-Catholic tone of the magazine's reporting of the issue of the Ecclesiastical Titles Assumptions Bill in 1850.[1] He was well connected in Catholic Church circles, and the

[1] Lycett, *Conan Doyle*, 14.

letter of introduction to the bishop which he had written for his young
nephew could have been, in Martin Booth's well-chosen word,
"a godsend".[2] There were no other Catholic doctors in Portsmouth.
To be known as a Catholic physician would certainly have brought the
young man patients at a time when he was starting his practice from
absolutely nothing. But Conan Doyle would not make opportunistic
use of this advantage to draw on the goodwill of the local Catholics to
build up his patient list. There was not an overlap of profession and
practice here after all, for he no longer professed or practised the Catholic faith and in fact had not done so since the end of his Jesuit schooling at Feldkirch.[3] Indeed, there had been a painful interview with
Uncle Dicky earlier in the year, over lunch at the Athenaeum Club, at
which the nephew's agnosticism had been the topic. We learn something about both uncle and nephew from the fact that Dicky Doyle
nonetheless wrote the letter, and that Arthur Conan Doyle nonetheless
burnt it. The gesture, a private but at the same time a melodramatic
one, was an act of identity, albeit of a negative kind. He was refusing
the chance to be identified as a Catholic doctor.

The great majority of British Victorians thought of themselves as
Christians, and for many the propagation of Christianity among the
heathen was one of the reasons for having an overseas empire. The
nation's Christian community was itself divided, not only between
Protestants and the Catholic minority, but among kinds of Protestantism, the high and low wings of the Anglican Church, the vigorous
nonconformist movement that had grown up in the eighteenth century, and the differing degrees of Evangelical belief and practice both
within and outside the Church of England. Edinburgh, a city full of
churches, was the headquarters of the Presbyterian Church of Scotland,
and had a reputation for the dour and denying kind of Calvinism associated with the great reformer John Knox.

Anti-Catholic sentiment throughout Britain had been widespread
in the age of the European wars of religion, and many still felt there
was something at least potentially treasonous in a British subject who
accepted the authority of the Pope in Rome, even if only in spiritual
matters. Catholicism also suffered among British people for its association with the Irish, a Catholic nation whose people were routinely

[2] Booth, *The Doctor, the Detective and Arthur Conan Doyle*, 94.
[3] Edwards, *The Quest for Sherlock Holmes*, 138–9.

stigmatized as backward and troublesome peasants and, in the later decades, ungrateful and violent Fenian separatists. (This suspicion could extend, as Owen Dudley Edwards says, to "persons of Irish surnames" such as Doyle.[4]) There was an acknowledgement that Protestantism was, as John Henry Newman himself called it, the intellectual and moral language of the body politic in Britain. But the position of Catholics improved in the nineteenth century, though they were still held under suspicion and routinely discriminated against by many. In 1829 the Catholic Emancipation Act had restored to them something like full civil rights, including the right to sit in Parliament. The publications of the Tractarian movement of the 1830s and 1840s, and the debate this generated, had an unintended consequence in bringing a new generation of intellectually formidable converts to Rome, of whom Newman, and later Henry Manning, were spectacular examples. Some of these advances were checked when, in 1869 and 1870, decrees of the Vatican Council declared the Pope infallible in matters of faith, a move greeted with incomprehension and disgust by most Protestants (and, incidentally, by the apostate Arthur Conan Doyle).

There is in the Victorian era, and in the work of Conan Doyle, something like an epic struggle involving science and religion, and the claims of the material and the spiritual world. The emergence of an independent scientific culture, and profession, had brought into being an ideology of scientific materialism hostile, or indifferent at best, to organized religion.[5] This is a vital part of the story of Conan Doyle and spiritual profession. It is important to note first, though, that religion came to him in the shape of the Roman Catholic Church, and specifically, in the formative years of his schooling, in "an austere and culturally defensive Jesuit education".[6]

Though there were individual priests he remembered with gratitude, Conan Doyle did not look back fondly on the years of his education at the hands of the Jesuits at Stonyhurst. To pick out his remarks about the Jesuits from the generally benign discourse of *Memories and Adventures* is to amass a comically consistent anthology of faint praises and backhanded qualifications. Father Cassidy is remembered as "more

[4] Edwards, *The Quest for Sherlock Holmes*, 62–3.
[5] See Roger Luckhurst, *The Invention of Telepathy 1870–1901* (Oxford: Oxford University Press, 2002), 9–21.
[6] Edwards, "Conan Doyle as Historian: A Starting Point", 95.

human than Jesuits usually are": at Stonyhurst, the general curriculum "like the building, was mediaeval but sound": the teaching of the classics "was no worse at Stonyhurst than at any other school": there was frequent corporal punishment, but this taught the boys not to show that they were hurt, "one of the best trainings for a hard life": the masters' constant surveillance of the boys might weaken self-respect and independence, "but it at least minimizes temptation and scandal": "I cannot remember that they [the Jesuits] were less truthful than their fellows, or more casuistical than their neighbours," and indeed they "were keen, clean-minded earnest men, so far as I knew them, with a few black sheep among them, but not many, for the process of selection was careful and long" (*M&A*, 14, 15, 16, 20). The curriculum was old-fashioned and dull—why couldn't Homer be studied in translation?—and the regime was authoritarian. The boys, he remembered, were never allowed for an instant to be alone with each other; the priests took part in all games and activities, and stalked the dormitories at night.

In some respects, by this account Stonyhurst was just another late-Victorian public school, if especially vigilant in its policing of the potential vices that schoolboy flesh was heir to. Yet the school was not just a religious foundation, but a Catholic one, and not just Catholic but Jesuit, and the case against it in *Memories and Adventures* is consistent with the mature Conan Doyle's quarrel with organized religion in general and "the old faith" especially, above all as embodied in the Jesuit order. The Jesuit teachers at Stonyhurst were strict and unbending, they had "no trust in human nature", he remembered (*M&A*, 15). Their belief was that the boys had to be constantly disciplined and punished if any good was to be got from them. The young Doyle had reacted predictably, going out of his way to do mischievous and outrageous things simply to show that his spirit was unbroken. He was frequently beaten and transgressed again, though, as he recalled, "an appeal to my better nature and not to my fears would have found an answer at once" (*M&A*, 17). But the Jesuit view of the world, and of human nature, was profoundly dark, a view reflected in the essentially penal organization of the school regime, resting on an assumption of sinfulness and the need for the mortification of the body. The young Conan Doyle was temperamentally opposed to this view of things before he was ever intellectually hostile to it.

Authoritarian, dogmatic, intolerant, and hidebound—these aspects of the religious and especially the Catholic hierarchy, against which he was to war with increasing impatience in later life, seemed prefigured, symbolized, and concentrated in the stern figure of the Stonyhurst Jesuits. In 1919 he recalled them as "athletes, scholars and gentlemen", "in all ways estimable outside the narrowness which limits the world to Mother Church".[7] And yet the narrowness was a fatal one. "In all ways, save in their theology, they were admirable, though this same theology made them hard and inhuman upon the surface, which is indeed the general effect of Catholicism in its extreme forms" (*M&A*, 20). The Jesuits were the *corps d'élite* of the Roman Church, and here we find a familiar perception of a cold hard-heartedness in that gifted, highly trained, carefully selected body of men at the top of a profession. It was the Jesuits' extremism, and their fundamentalism, that made them uncompromising and disdainful of the ordinary. As a Spiritualist, Conan Doyle was to find that his most persistent enemies were Jesuits at one end of the Christian spectrum, and Evangelicals of the Plymouth Brethren type at the other: he supposed that "the literal interpretation of the Bible was the common bond".[8] The spiritual could give faith, but the literal could kill it.

He went so far as to blame the Jesuits for ruining the old faith. Agreeing with the modernist theologian George Tyrrell, he claimed that Jesuits were behind "all those extreme doctrines of papal infallibility and Immaculate Conception, with a general all-round tightening of dogma" (*M&A*, 20)—the retrenchments, under Pius IX, which had made it so hard for a modern man to assent to Catholicism that there was now, Conan Doyle was ready to assert, not a single man of outstanding fame in science or in general thought who was a practising Catholic. Extremist dogmatism at the top of the hierarchy was also responsible for a disastrous secular policy. In a bad-tempered consideration of the Catholic Church's resistance to drink reform, its attack upon the innocent Dreyfus, its refusal to support reform in the Congo, and its "obvious leaning towards the Central Powers" in the Great War, Conan Doyle felt ready to conclude, "one would think it was ruled by a Council of lunatics".[9]

---

[7] ACD, *The Vital Message*, 188.
[8] ACD, *The Wanderings of a Spiritualist* (London: Collins, 1922), 12.
[9] ACD, *The Wanderings of a Spiritualist*, 110.

"Theology has always been the enemy of real religion."[10] He argued that the intolerance of the divorce laws, against which he campaigned, was based largely upon theological considerations.[11] The Catholic Church's own extreme stubbornness had pitched it into an unnecessary war with modernity itself, which it was bound to lose, for Mother Church "has always been wrong from Galileo to Darwin".[12] Many Protestant Christians had struggled to find ways of coexisting with the new world that science was revealing, and had been met halfway by scientists eager to explain that the theory of evolution, for example, need not be incompatible with Christian faith. Others, such as the great preacher C. H. Spurgeon, simply recommended a closed border between the spiritual and the material world and their respective authorities: "Let the scientific men keep to their own sphere, and we will keep to ours."[13] But Catholicism, according to Conan Doyle whose idea of the old faith was formed in the 1860s and 1870s by the reactionary teachers at Stonyhurst and the provocatively anti-modern papacy of Pius IX, could only try to protect itself from the modern world with an ever-thickening shell of dogma and denial. It was good for nothing. Certainly its rituals held no attractions for a man who could never remember, since reaching manhood, feeling himself the better for having gone into a church.[14]

What the Church ought to be able to offer to the modern world was its ethical, not its dogmatic teaching, and this was largely contained in the life of Christ. Conan Doyle was far from alone among Victorian apostates in his rejection of the punitive and jealous God of the Old Testament, his admiration for the ethical teaching of Jesus, and his eagerness to emancipate the latter from the former. With his gospel of love and compassion, Jesus was felt even by non-believers to be quite compatible with the liberal modern world. But Catholicism's insistence that the spiritual life had to be mediated through a central priestly authority went against the grain of modern, individualistic, secular culture. This is a view rather surprisingly put by the Puritan rebel Micah Clarke, who declares that there are stages of human progress for which

[10] ACD, *Our African Winter*, 16.
[11] See Orel, "Conan Doyle's Sense of Justice", 131.
[12] ACD, *Our African Winter*, 247.
[13] C. H. Spurgeon, *Fifty Most Remarkable Sermons* (London: Passmore and Alabaster, 1908), 472.
[14] ACD, *The Wanderings of a Spiritualist*, 32.

the Church of Rome is well suited, but that in the modern England of the seventeenth century, "a nursery of strong, thinking men", its absolute authority is no longer acceptable.[15] The Reformation, in this view, was an expression of the intellectual independence of the national character.

If Jesus remained a modern hero—and in the spirit messages of the very late *Pheneas Speaks*, Jesus appears to be restored to something like supreme spiritual authority—this was on account of his life and not his death. Everything in Conan Doyle shrank from what he saw as the Church's obsession with sacrifice and redemption by blood. Perhaps under the influence of Kipling, he attributed this obsession to the infiltration of pagan Mithraism into Pauline Christianity.[16] But it was related too to the morose regime of the Stonyhurst Jesuits, their lack of trust in human nature, their assumption of human evil, their insistence on the need for atonement by suffering. But what kind of divine Providence condemned everyone to sinfulness and demanded a blood sacrifice? Who could believe, or teach, that the Ruler of the Universe was an implacable torturer?[17] It was a view not only repugnant to human compassion, and suspect as a tactic whereby the Church could scare its flock into obedience, but also, just as interestingly, not modern. The threat of damnation was a powerful weapon in the armoury of Jesuit rhetoric: the sermon in Joyce's *A Portrait of the Artist as a Young Man* is a formidable example. Conan Doyle stoutly resisted such threats. "Providence is not so fiercely vindictive as theologians would try to make us believe," he assured the audiences of one of the popular lectures on "Death and the Hereafter" which he delivered in the years after the Great War. "And with our modern scientific knowledge of sin a great deal which seemed to the theologian to be very black and terrible is after all really a matter of heredity and environment."[18] The Jesuits were wrong. "Man is not naturally bad. The average human being is good."[19] And, as the spirit communications advised, "the average human being goes to heaven".[20]

[15] ACD, *Micah Clarke* (London: Longmans, Green, 1889), 300.
[16] ACD, *The Wanderings of a Spiritualist*, 217.
[17] ACD, *The Vital Message*, 101.
[18] ACD, *Lecture on Spiritualism* (Worthing: The Worthing Gazette, 1919), 8, 10.
[19] ACD, *The History of Spiritualism*, 2 vols. (London: Cassell, 1926), i. 14. Conan Doyle wrote this *History* with the collaboration of Leslie Curnow.
[20] ACD, *Lecture on Spiritualism*, 10.

The Christian Church had lost its way, lost touch with the real values exemplified in the life of Jesus, and lost the ability to deal with the modern world. There was a need, he came to believe, for "the reform of the decadent Christianity of today".[21] It had to be simplified, purified, made modern and humane. It could and must be reconciled with science, and restored as a moral force in the world. For Conan Doyle, Diana Barsham has argued, Spiritualism itself was no more nor less than "a revised and modernized version of Christianity".[22] It was, or should be—ironically, in view of the chronically quarrelsome history of Spiritualist and psychic institutions—an instrument of reconciliation among Christian men of goodwill. The need for such reconciliation had been expressed as far back as *Micah Clarke* (1889), a story of the Monmouth rebellion of 1685, whose hero is the son of a marriage between a Puritan and an Anglican. In the symbol of this marriage of which he is the heroic fruit, Micah finds hope for healing the nation's religious strife.[23]

And yet even in this tale, Catholicism is not included in the promise of this ecumenical utopia (indeed the Catholicism of James II was the motive for the Monmouth rebellion in the first place), and the old faith remained a nagging problem for Conan Doyle, one which he seems to have been unable either to resolve or to leave alone. In his final decade, when his remarks on Roman Catholic practices and personnel become particularly astringent, the reason lies no doubt in the attitude of the Catholic Church to Spiritualism. For while there were plenty of Christian as well as non-Christian Spiritualists, and both groups used a language saturated in Christian terms to describe their beliefs, the Catholic Church remained unreservedly hostile to Spiritualism. "Catholic publications insisted that demonic spirits inspired psychic manifestations, and séance practices threatened the spiritual and mental health of participants."[24] In the decade after the Great War, alarmed by the increase in the number of converts to Spiritualism, the Catholic Church initiated a number of campaigns to combat the baleful effect of the movement on religious life, climaxing in the formation of the Catholic Crusade Against Spiritualism in 1926. To Conan Doyle

---

[21] ACD, *The Vital Message*, 17.

[22] Barsham, *Arthur Conan Doyle and the Meaning of Masculinity*, 243.

[23] ACD, *Micah Clarke*, 408.

[24] Jenny Hazelgrove, *Spiritualism and British Society between the Wars* (Manchester: Manchester University Press, 2000), 22.

it must have seemed only the latest manifestation of the hard, hide-bound, denying regime he had first encountered as a boy, and from which he had signalled his own deliberate exile when he burned his uncle's letter.

There were upstanding Christian men in all the churches, but it was "still beyond all doubt" that Christianity had broken down because it had failed as a moral force in the world.[25] This failure had allowed a formidable antagonist to slip into the fold and begin its predatory work—for "when religion is dead," Conan Doyle wrote in *The Vital Message*, "materialism becomes active".[26] But the circumstances that unleashed the diabolical force of materialism in the nineteenth century had also, he believed, produced its redeeming spiritual opposite.

Spiritualism

"No doubt I am a materialist," declares Austin Gilroy, the young Professor of Physiology who narrates Conan Doyle's *The Parasite*.

I have trained myself to deal only with fact and with proof. Surmise and fancy have no place in my scheme of thought. Show me what I can see with my microscope, cut with my scalpel, weigh in my balance, and I will devote a lifetime to its investigation. But when you ask me to study feelings, impressions, suggestions, you ask me to do what is distasteful and even demoralizing. A departure from pure reason affects me like an evil smell or a musical discord.[27]

There are dozens of statements, and characters, like this in Conan Doyle's work. The materialist is a fixed point in his landscape, and such characters have a tendency to declare themselves, as Gilroy does here, with a sort of manifesto, often delivered with a certain aggression and even swagger that may have been learned from the champions of scientific naturalism like John Tyndall and T. H. Huxley. We have met several such characters already. Among them are Sherlock Holmes— "This agency stands flat-footed upon the ground, and there it must remain"[28]—and that somewhat autobiographical young general practitioner, Stark Munro, whose letters contain long reflections on

[25] ACD, *The Vital Message*, 192.
[26] ACD, *The Vital Message*, 193.
[27] ACD, *The Parasite* (1894) (New York: Harper & Brothers, 1895), 5, 6.
[28] ACD, "The Sussex Vampire", in *Case-Book*, 73.

science, philosophy, and religion that are useful pointers to Conan
Doyle's own intellectual development. Stark Munro believes, as did the
young Conan Doyle, in some sort of Providence, arguing that a survey
of the scheme of nature shows conclusively that there are laws at work
in it that display intelligence and power. But this conclusion, he says, is
reached by observing how nature works, and without the assistance of
faith. His Providence is nature itself, working through what he con-
ceives as a progressive evolution. Science, in young Stark Munro's view,
has gone much of the way to falsify the truths of the sacred texts of
religion, and render its churches redundant in the modern world. "The
clergy, busy in their own limited circles, and coming in contact only
with those who agree with them, have not realized how largely the
rising generation has outgrown them" (SM, 177).[29]

One thing these paladins of materialism hold in common is a pride
in their modernity. Their feet planted on the solid ground of attested
and proven scientific facts, they have little time for perceptions of what
science cannot observe and measure—intimations of the intuitive,
metaphysical, romantic, and spiritual.[30] Such matters are routinely seen,
and dismissed, by Conan Doyle's materialists as non-scientific (and
very frequently feminine) orders of knowledge, and *ipso facto* as delu-
sions which a proper modern scientific gaze would dissipate. In the
Spiritualist novel *The Land of Mist*, Professor Challenger's daughter
Enid protests that she cannot believe that her father will have no more
"life hereafter" than a broken clock; but the great man of science—
"There is something virile and manly in facing the worst"—dismisses
this as mere sentimentalism. "Four buckets of water and a bagful of
salts," he tells her with some relish. "That's your daddy, my lass, and you
may as well reconcile your mind to it" (LM, 18). With the theory of
evolution at his back—as Herbert Spencer had applied it to the progressive development of human societies—and the tools of modern

[29] Stark Munro is of the view that it is only women who keep religious orthodoxy alive,
not because they are more earnest than men, but because they follow their emotion.

[30] It is of interest in this context that when Virginia Woolf mounted her attack on what
she saw as the imaginative deficiency of the male Edwardian novelists, H. G. Wells, Arnold
Bennett, and John Galsworthy, she explained: "If we tried to formulate our meaning in one
word we should say that these three writers are materialists. It is because they are concerned not with the spirit but with the body that they have disappointed us..." Virginia
Woolf, "Modern Fiction" (1919), in *The Common Reader: First Series*, ed. Andrew McNeillie
(London: Hogarth Press, 1984), 147. The whole essay is couched in a language curiously
close to that of Spiritualism.

science in his hands, a man like Challenger might reconcile himself to individual extinction, in the context of a general progress.

Material progress brings materialism. If material progress was the badge of modern times—and the signs of technological advance and material prosperity were all around in nineteenth-century Britain, if not equally in everyone's grasp—then materialism was the religion, or anti-religion, of capitalist modernity. Materialism itself was a broad church and practice, its manifestations ranging from scientific proto-cols that recognized the existence of nothing that could not be objec-tively verified and measured, to the kind of materialism expressed in an attachment to material things, above all to money, and the relentless "getting and spending" lamented by Wordsworth early in the century. An out-and-out materialism dismissed as meaningless any talk of soul or spirit; there was no reliable evidence for such things. Materialism is one of the very big themes of the industrial age, with its huge increase in the availability of commodities for consumption and possession, in the pressure on individuals to compete to create worldly success meas-urable in material terms, and, alongside this, a weakening of those traditional cultural narratives, especially religious ones, that located value elsewhere than in material satisfaction and display. Meanwhile, it seemed to many that the world could be so impressively described, quantified, and improved by the application of science that non-materialist forms of knowledge were discounted, and discred-ited. As J. G. Frazer explained in the second (1900) edition of *The Golden Bough*, modernity was the age of science, ready to displace reli-gion as religion in its day had displaced the magical practice of primi-tive societies. Furthermore, science was beginning to cast its authority into fields of activity—social, moral, educational, and even theologi-cal—which other forms of knowledge and their purveyors had been used to having to themselves.

Materialism was the currency of a scientific culture and profession emerging fully in the 1870s, the decade when Conan Doyle was a medical student, and tangling with non-material knowledges, both residual and newly formed, in what Roger Luckhurst calls "a con-fused and confusing series of engagements over the relative value of 'spirit' and 'matter'".[31] Later in his life Conan Doyle was to come

---

[31] Luckhurst, *The Invention of Telepathy*, 12. For the context of an unevenly paced profes-sionalization of British intellectual and academic life, see Collini, *Public Moralists*.

to understand this great contention in stark and simple terms, as a struggle between the materialist and the spiritual vision. But the current of Spiritualist practice was only part of a great tide of disquiet flowing through Victorian British culture, which saw materialism as the great villain of modernity. Janet Oppenheim describes this widespread alarm.

With its partner atheism, the alarmists moaned, it uprooted churches, made a mockery of morality, undermined social sanctions, and sapped the very foundations of western society and culture. If even T. H. Huxley, that most outspoken advocate and publicist of science, shied away from the ultimate, devastating implications of materialism, it is understandable why others in this period should exert themselves to oppose the materialist stand. That, in fact, became the special task of the spiritualists in Victorian and Edwardian Britain: to deplore and combat that materialism that they perceived as all too rampant in their time.[32]

But this is to anticipate. Young Stark Munro is quite blithe in his materialism, and so no doubt was young Conan Doyle, for a while. His schooling had left him unenthusiastic about the bullying spiritual regime of the Jesuits, and he seems to have lost his Christian faith by the time he returned to Edinburgh as a medical student. His university training then immersed him in the materialities of the body, and the scientific protocols by which its ailments could be described and managed. From maternity ward to morgue, what you saw was what you got, and if anything was to survive of the body, it was only in the physical sense that matter could be transformed but not destroyed (*SM*, 179). "When I had finished my medical education in 1882," Conan Doyle recalled, "I found myself, like many young medical men, a convinced materialist as regards our personal destiny."[33]

We were under the influence of men like Professor Huxley, Herbert Spencer, Darwin, and other eminent men who did great service but all of whom were either agnostic or frankly materialistic; and naturally we were impelled in the same direction. I was a believer in Materialism. I believed that life ended in death.[34]

---

[32] Janet Oppenheim, *The Other World: Spiritualism and Psychical Research in England, 1850–1914* (Cambridge: Cambridge University Press, 1985), 61.

[33] ACD, *The New Revelation*, 14.

[34] ACD, *Lecture on Spiritualism*, 1.

And although later in life he was to identify himself so strongly with the truths of the spiritual world, he was ready to admit that the agnosticism of the Victorian materialists had performed a useful function. "For all rebuilding a site must be cleared" (*M&A*, 83). It was a thoroughly Victorian metaphor for modernization. Materialism had been instrumental in making a space for modernity, by destroying "the old iron-clad unreasoning Evangelical position" which had prevailed before (*M&A*, 83). But for the older Conan Doyle, this necessary demolition work could not be the end of the story. It produced only an empty space, a space of agnosticism, of not-knowing. That space was destined to be filled, he became sure, by a form of modern knowledge that would have perplexed and perhaps disgusted many of the scientific workers who had cleared it.

He was to produce a rival story about the emergence of modernity, one in which the triumph of materialism was not the final chapter, but a necessary step on the road to something else. "Every materialist, as I can now clearly see, is a case of arrested development. He has cleared his ruins, but has not begun to build that which would shelter him" (*M&A*, 32). The scepticism of the scientific age was useful in clearing away the pre-modern dogmatism, authoritarianism, and superstition peddled in the established churches. It prepared the way, he earnestly believed, for the emergence of a spiritual culture and nation. But to remain mired in materialism could only mean to descend lower and lower to a purely utilitarian and selfish view of the universe, with disastrous consequences. For him, the "typical materialist state" was the Germany of the Kaiser, whose self-centred arrogance precipitated the Great War.[35]

The Parasite of 1894, with which I began this section, is a good instance of an early stage of Conan Doyle's move beyond materialism. It is a story about mesmerism, in which the sceptical young professor, Austin Gilroy, succumbs to the mysterious mental powers of the exotic Miss Penelosa, who causes him to behave violently out of character, jeopardize his career, and very nearly murder his fiancée. The struggle between Gilroy and the mesmerist is cast in the form of a rivalry between a man of science and a woman possessed of psychic powers he is unwilling to admit and quite unable to resist. "This woman, by her own explanation, can dominate my nervous organism," the physiologist

[35] ACD, *The History of Spiritualism*, ii. 246.

reports. "She can project herself into my body and take command of it."[36] Miss Penelosa is a character who is marked in several ways as thoroughly other to Gilroy, ways that all seem disadvantageous to her in terms of symbolic capital: she is a woman, intuitive, foreign (a creole from Trinidad), sexually unattractive, crippled. He searches for adjectives to describe her—furtive; fierce; feline. She invades and enslaves him mentally, having first suborned his fiancée, as punishment for his refusal to believe in her powers. He is utterly unable to resist her, his scientific knowledge and professional prestige counting for nothing in the struggle between them. Only her sudden death at the end of the story prevents him from bringing his own world—rational, successful, law-governed, respectable, and smug—crashing down to irrecoverable disaster at her mesmeric command.

But to see this story as a war between scientific and anti-scientific powers is to miss some of the point signalled by the title. For a parasite is an invader, but also operates from within. As so often in Conan Doyle, physical appearance carries a broad hint of what is to come. For Gilroy confesses that, though a scientist by education, he is a highly psychic man by temperament, and he cites in evidence his nervous and intuitive boyhood, and his dark hair, thin olive face, and tapering fingers. In other words, a susceptibility to psychic forces is already there, within the scientific investigator; the presence of the mesmerist only makes it manifest. There again, Miss Penelosa is permitted, indeed invited, to show her powers in the polite drawing-rooms of a university town because there is a scientific curiosity about her as a phenomenon. First Wilson, the psychologist, takes her up as a potential research subject, then Gilroy himself, the physiologist, is persuaded to participate in an experiment to test what she can do.

We have here, in effect, a miniature history of the Society for Psychical Research. For it was the very advances made by science that produced a widespread curiosity, and a growing knowledge, about phenomena that challenged a purely material view of the world in the late decades of the nineteenth century, just as it was the consolidation of realism as a mode of representation in fiction that produced, late in the century, a great rush of tales of mystery and horror, the supernatural and inexplicable and uncanny. An increasingly assertive scientific knowledge was bound to be drawn to what Tim Armstrong has called

[36] ACD, *The Parasite*, 68.

"borderline phenomena", and beyond into the hinterland of the unknown.[37] Spiritualists and psychics, at the same time, could turn to science for a language (of phenomena such as wavelengths, ether, and of course evolution) to help them describe, explain, and legitimize their own findings. As for Conan Doyle himself, it was not long after he completed the research for his MD dissertation, and while practising medicine in Southsea, that he began his own investigations in the occult. His intellectual position at this time may have been close to that attributed to the fictional Stark Munro. But he came, after all, from a family of artists, and a Celtic one at that. He was to become an avowed Spiritualist, but he never ceased to think of himself as a man of science. There were scientists who scoffed at Spiritualism, and Spiritualists who would have nothing to do with science, but Conan Doyle was not unusual in his time in holding dual membership of these constituencies of knowledge and practice.

Miss Penelosa is not a Spiritualist, of course, but a mesmerist, even if her powers of suggestion are so strong as to challenge scientific explanation. *The Parasite* is not a supernatural story, any more than is Robert Louis Stevenson's *The Strange Case of Doctor Jekyll and Mr Hyde* (1886), which is one of its inspirations—and even though, like the Stevenson story, its villain casts a diabolical shadow that derives from the Gothic tradition. But it is a story about *telepathy*, a term coined in 1882 by the psychologist Frederic Myers to name forms of occult relation or communication between people at a distance.[38] Research into telepathy could involve the investigation of a gamut of phenomena from mind-reading and hypnotism to automatic writing, haunted houses, and messages from the dead. Conan Doyle's interest in telepathy seems to have begun with mesmerism.[39] Mesmerism, and later hypnotism, were subjects which a young physician had particular reason to take an interest in, for therapeutic claims had been made for both, though they were familiar to the general public more often in the form of stage entertainment, usually with exotic magical and Oriental trappings. A contemporary observer stated confidently that hypnotism was "known to the earliest races of Asia", but complained that the practice "which is now the subject of much intelligent and well-directed

[37] Tim Armstrong, *Modernism: A Cultural History* (Cambridge: Polity, 2005), 122.

[38] Its history has been written by Roger Luckhurst in *The Invention of Telepathy*.

[39] Kelvin I. Jones, *Conan Doyle and the Spirits: The Spiritualist World of Sir Arthur Conan Doyle* (Wellingborough: Aquarian Press, 1989), 53.

research . . . is also, unfortunately, the plaything of a class of wandering stage performers".[40] The orientalism and the taint of fraud were themes that would often haunt Conan Doyle's own later researches, as he proceeded to widen his investigations in telepathy from mesmerism to table-rapping sessions and experiments with automatic writing, to full séances of spirit communication (thus recapitulating the moving focus of psychic practices in the nineteenth century). In one sense, these things began for him as leisure activities, even rather faddish ones, and not unlike the many other hobbies, sports, and pastimes in which the young doctor bonded with his neighbours in Southsea. He attended his first séances at the house of an important patient, Thomas Harward, a retired lieutenant-general. At another level, though, they are provocations, in which the scientifically educated man lays down a challenge to the invisible world. But what is at stake is not science, but materialism.

The Society for Psychical Research was founded in 1882, the year in which Conan Doyle set up in practice at Southsea. Its mission was to investigate in a proper scientific manner the spectrum of psychic phenomena "designated by such terms as mesmeric, psychical and Spiritualistic".[41] There was certainly plenty to investigate and explain, and a gap had not yet opened between the psychological, amenable to scientific enquiry, and the psychic, usually considered beyond the legitimizing pale of science. The leadership of the SPR was drawn from that wing of the scientific community that did not dismiss such phenomena out of hand, and included distinguished scholars like the philosopher Henry Sidgwick, and the psychologists Frederic Myers and Edmund Gurney. When Conan Doyle set out his own intellectual genealogy as a Spiritualist, he habitually stressed the work of scientific investigators more than that of sensitives and mediums. In goading Professor Challenger to attend a séance, in the novel *The Land of Mist*, Edward Malone reminds him of the men of science who have embraced Spiritualism, a list that includes the naturalist Alfred Russel Wallace, the physicist Sir Oliver Lodge, and the criminologist Cesare Lombroso. The more comprehensive catalogue of those who took a serious interest in psychical research embraced a good proportion of the

---

[40] Ernest Hart, *Hypnotism, Mesmerism and the New Witchcraft* (London: Smith, Elder, 1896), 2. See also J. Milne Bramwell, *Hypnotism* (London: Grant Richards, 1903).

[41] Luckhurst, *The Invention of Telepathy*, 56.

intellectual leadership of the time, and not only in Britain; William James, Charles Richet, Henri Bergson, and Sigmund Freud were all associated with the SPR. Challenger himself, a celebrity scientist and rationalist, is courted in the story as a particularly valuable recruit to the cause.

Conan Doyle's early experiments with telepathy were carried out in domestic space, in the spirit of that "medical materialism" in which he had been trained.[42] But his own ability to convey thought without words, and the research with which he followed this up, soon convinced him, he says, to reconsider. "If thought could go a thousand miles and produce a perceptible effect then it differed entirely not only in degree but in kind from any purely physical material. That seemed certain, and it must involve some modification of my views" (*M&A*, 84). As this makes clear, the modification required was to entail a reconsideration of his purely materialistic account of existence, but not of his adherence to scientific procedures in his psychic studies. Even so, his material philosophy, as expressed in *The Stark Munro Letters*, did not easily crumble, and "the author can truly say", he wrote much later, "that year after year he clung on to every line of defence until he was finally compelled, if he were to preserve any claim to mental honesty, to abandon the materialistic position" (*M&A*, 185). It is certain that one reason for clinging onto materialism was that it was associated with the scientific advances that made the nineteenth century so obviously and vastly superior to earlier ages in terms of its knowledge and control of nature; to abandon it seemed perverse, regressive, even ridiculous. So there had been a real intellectual struggle, and he did not want people to believe that his new convictions had been arrived at without effort. They were the product of thought, not a surrender to feelings. There was no sudden conversion, or blinding revelation.

His psychic studies proceeded, year by year, a combination of experimentation and reading—Frederic Myers, Sir Walter Crookes, William Barrett, Alfred Russel Wallace, Victor Hugo, Johann Friedrich Zöllner. He studied the life of the famous medium D. D. Home, and was excited to discover that his own wife's closest friend, Lily

---

[42] The relation between domesticity and mesmeric or arcane knowledge in Doyle's work is examined in Catherine Wynne, "Arthur Conan Doyle's Domestic Desires: Mesmerism, Mediumship and *Femmes Fatales*", in Martin Willis and Catherine Wynne (eds.), *Victorian Literary Mesmerism* (Amsterdam: Rodopi, 2006), 227–44.

Loder-Symonds, had the gift of automatic writing. Conan Doyle began this accumulation of knowledge in Southsea in the years after his marriage in 1885, but did not join the SPR until 1893, and announced himself in public as a committed Spiritualist only in 1916. That announcement was prompted by the publication of Oliver Lodge's *Raymond, or Life and Death*, and in the hope of offering comfort to those mourning the loss of loved ones in the terrible slaughter of the Great War. Lodge's book provides detailed transcripts of postmortem communications from his son Raymond, a young army officer killed in battle in 1915, and others (including Frederic Myers himself, still busy on the other side). For the first principle of materialism was the uniformity of nature: nature never broke its own rules, therefore human beings and all other organisms were subject to the manifest law that life ended with death. But if materialism was discredited, telepathic communication proved, and the existence of the spirit independent of the body admitted, this made again available for belief that supreme prize, the spirit's survival after death.

As he learned more about the Spiritualist position, Conan Doyle claimed, it was some time before the religious side of the matter struck him (*M&A*, 117). This is hardly believable, but it is consistent with the story he wants to tell about his approach to Spiritualism along the path of science. He might have abandoned the religion of his family, but he was not on the lookout for a replacement faith.

Years were to pass before I understood that in that direction [psychic knowledge] might be found the positive proofs which I constantly asserted were the only conditions upon which I could resume any sort of allegiance to the unseen. I must have definite demonstration, for if it were to be a matter of faith then I might as well go back to the faith of my fathers. "Never will I accept anything which cannot be proved to me. The evils of religion have all come from accepting things which cannot be proved." So I said at the time and I have been true to my resolve. (*M&A*, 33)

This licensed him to say that he and his fellow Spiritualists founded their belief in life after death and in the existence of invisible worlds "not upon ancient tradition or upon vague intuitions, but upon proven facts, so that a science of religion may be built up, and man given a sure pathway amid the quagmire of the creeds".[43] It was observed facts, not

---

[43] ACD, *The History of Spiritualism*, ii. 247. He would certainly reject the argument, made by Jonathan Rose among others, that he "renounced rational religion for faith pure and simple". Rose, *The Edwardian Temperament*, 36.

subjective feelings and certainly not the weight of tradition, that had shown up the materialistic view of existence as inadequate.

In announcing a "science of religion", Conan Doyle was once again not putting forward an unprecedented claim. Theosophy, Spiritualism's exotic sibling, had always declared itself a science, if an esoteric one: the two movements were allies, though uneasy ones, Theosophists being suspicious of Spiritualism's need for comforting communication with the departed, while Spiritualists like Conan Doyle felt that Theosophy was not based on solid proofs as Spiritualism was.[44] But Frederic Myers himself, stalwart of the Society for Psychical Research, also hoped in his work to reconcile the domains of science and spirit and show them to be not antagonistic but, as Janet Oppenheim puts it, "the two diverse sides of one and the same coin".[45] Francis Bacon, pioneering the scientific method early in the seventeenth century, had fenced off the area of "Divine things" from scientific enquiry, but Myers believed the time had come to demolish the fence.

I claim that there now exists an incipient method of getting at this Divine knowledge also, with the same certainty, the same calm assurance, with which we make our steady progress in the knowledge of terrene things. The authority of creeds and Churches will thus be replaced by the authority of observation and experiment. The impulse of faith will resolve itself into a reasoned and resolute imagination, bent upon raising even higher than now the highest ideals of man.[46]

The fulfilment of Spiritualism was also to be the apotheosis of science, Conan Doyle believed. "We can say: 'We will meet you on your own ground and show you by material and scientific tests that the soul and personality survive.' That is the aim of Psychic Science, and it has been fully attained. It means an end to materialism for ever."[47]

This was impressive, of course, though it might be seen as evidence for what Jonathan Rose brilliantly identified as "that recurrent weakness in Edwardian thought—wishful thinking".[48] The problem came with the evidence that these material and scientific tests produced. For in the

[44] "I asked for proofs and spiritualism has given them to me." ACD, *The Wanderings of a Spiritualist*, 164. For Theosophy and Spiritualism, see Oppenheim, *The Other World*, especially 162–200.

[45] Oppenheim, *The Other World*, 154.

[46] Frederic Myers, *Human Personality and its Survival of Bodily Death* (London: Longmans, Green, 1903), 279.

[47] ACD, *The Vital Message*, 69.

[48] Rose, *The Edwardian Temperament*, 80.

disproof of materialism, the material world returned again and again in all its haunting banality. In *The Edge of the Unknown*, Conan Doyle retold the story of how, in 1871, a Mrs Guppy had disappeared from her home in Highbury in London and appeared on the table of a room in Lambs Conduit Street where a séance was being held: many people witnessed this.[49] To demonstrate the existence of life after death, the spirits of the dead summoned in séances might be prevailed upon to lift furniture and tootle trumpets, whistle or ring bells. At Southsea Conan Doyle was much impressed by a spirit message advising him not to read a book by Leigh Hunt, for he had indeed been pondering whether to do so (*M&A*, 86). Later, during the Great War, he recorded in writing that he had dreamed of the name "Piave", and sure enough there was a great battle there several months later. "There is the fact, amply proved by documents and beyond all possible coincidence" (*M&A*, 368). In Sydney, as he attested, an apport medium called Bailey materialized 138 articles under stringent conditions in a closed room. These included eight live birds, a leopard skin, seven inscribed Babylonian tablets, and an Arabic newspaper.[50] At Christchurch in New Zealand, Conan Doyle was to meet a psychic dog named Darkie, though on the whole, the meeting was not a success.[51] Spirits returned to report the existence of sports, whisky and soda, laboratories, and research libraries on the other side, but not newspapers ("There is no need. We know everything," said the spirit of the former editor of *The Times*, the late John Delane).[52] The spirit guide Pheneas, an Arabian who lived at Ur millennia ago, communicated through Jean Conan Doyle's automatic script and at one point suggested a Dictaphone, "to save you writing".[53] A session Conan Doyle had in 1919 with the spirit photographer William Hope, in which he was hoping to receive a message from his son Kingsley, produced instead a photograph containing a written greeting from the late Archdeacon Colley.[54] And meanwhile, mediums (usually female) in the hope of winning the endorsement of scientific or journalistic observers

[49] ACD, *The Edge of the Unknown* (London: John Murray, 1930), 57.

[50] ACD, *The Wanderings of a Spiritualist*, 100.

[51] ACD, *The Wanderings of a Spiritualist*, 200.

[52] ACD, *Pheneas Speaks* (London: Psychic Review and Bookshop, 1927), 35. Hereafter *Pheneas*. The presence of whisky and soda on the other side was confirmed by the late Raymond Lodge.

[53] *Pheneas*, 205.

[54] ACD and others, *The Case for Spirit Photography* (London: Hutchinson, 1922), 22.

(almost always male) more or less consented to be strip-searched, trussed in ropes or swaddled in bandages, handcuffed, locked in cabinets, and were sometimes assaulted by psychic researchers bent on testing their powers.[55] "By a strange paradox," Conan Doyle wrote in an article about ectoplasm, "the searchers after spirit have come to know more about matter, and its extraordinary possibilities, than any materialist has learned."[56] The paradox extends, surely, to an almost magical faith in material evidence on the part of the searcher after spirit desperate to emancipate himself from materialism. Some opponents objected that Spiritualists were self-deluded, simply reporting as fact the suggestions of their own thoughts and desires. The material manifestations of séances could be advanced as a counter-argument to this, but they were often trivial, grotesque, and highly suspect.

For it was not just that Spiritualist mediums were often detected in fraud. Conan Doyle was quite ready to admit this, while pointing out that individual instances of cheating did not discredit the whole enterprise, and that, however many bogus ghosts and spirit messages might be exposed, survival after death needed to be proved conclusively only once. Though it set its face against materialism, Spiritualism's lodgement in the material, known world gives it a prosaic quality which is virtually opposite to the way spiritual experience is usually conceived, especially in the Christian West. Spiritualists disagreed among themselves as to whether what they did was compatible with the beliefs of Christianity or other faiths, but Spiritualism is unlike other religious practices in its refusal to mystify. Spirits were manifest: this was a fact. There was very little that was mysterious about them. You could make an appointment to speak with them.[57] They made noises, and moved about the room, and sometimes they dispensed practical advice to the living. They could be young or old, solemn or flighty. The way they made themselves known in séances—"the heaving table or the flying tambourine"[58]—might seem sometimes trivial, but this was just a way

[55] The relationship between mediumship and the female sexual role is discussed at length in Alex Owen, *The Darkened Room: Women, Power and Spiritualism in Late Victorian England* (London: Virago, 1989). Not all, but the majority of mediums were women, whose gender, it was thought, inclined them to be "sensitive".

[56] ACD, *The Edge of the Unknown*, 217.

[57] Conan Doyle describes helping a lost soul, a "grey spirit", and making an appointment for another talk with him, in *Pheneas Speaks*, 31.

[58] ACD, *The New Revelation*, 50.

of getting the attention of the living, like a telephone bell. "We are a materialist generation, and the great force beyond appeals to us through material things."[59] There was a continuity between the world of spirit and the most banal of matter.

The spirits of the dead could be recognized, and sometimes they could be photographed. Most spirits were not significantly different after death; they had moods, a daily life, they made mistakes like getting names and times wrong, they exchanged news among themselves, they celebrated Christmas (*Pheneas*, 50), they were usually willing to help but few had been made privy to the secrets of the universe. There were Spiritualist churches, and meeting halls, but a spirit was just as likely to answer a summons amid the domestic clutter of someone's living room. Mediums were people of no particular class or education, often personally not very prepossessing, and Spiritualism had no priesthood and very little ritual. Ectoplasm was actual stuff.[60] The spirit was a body, though an etheric one, but ether itself was a substance that had been described by physicists like Oliver Lodge, and for several decades held a place in the body of orthodox scientific knowledge. The spirit world was all around, but simply inhabited a different wavelength, and so was unperceived for the same physical reasons that extremes of the spectrum were invisible to the naked eye, or certain sounds pitched beyond the capacity of the ear. The afterlife, which goes virtually undescribed in the Bible, was reported on in detail in the Spiritualist literature, a place with a landscape, weather, vegetation, buildings, activities, and institutions of its own. Its upper reaches or spheres were not really describable, but its lower slopes were reported to be in every respect a very nice place. This might seem all too mundane for some people, but what, Conan Doyle reasonably enough wanted to know, did such people themselves anticipate of heaven? "Are we to be mere wisps of gaseous happiness floating about in the air?"[61]

This wealth of knowledge about the "land of mist" might only recently have come to light, like a geographical or astronomical or microscopic discovery, but it was knowledge, attainable by quite ordinary

---

[59] ACD, *Lecture on Spiritualism*, 4.

[60] In an observed experiment in 1909 with a medium called Eva, "It was testified by witnesses, and shown by the photographs, that there oozed from the medium's mucous membranes, and occasionally from her skin, this extraordinary gelatinous material." ACD, *The Edge of the Unknown*, 217.

[61] ACD, *The New Revelation*, 79–80.

means, and freely available to the enquirer; and there seemed no reason why it should not, like other knowledges, increase. Conan Doyle came to believe that the truths of Spiritualism were simply there, like the objects visible through Galileo's telescope, and that everyone open-minded could share them. He would make this point again and again. "I don't want to convert you," he used to tell his lecture audiences. "I merely tell you what I know. What you do with it is your business."[62] The case was proven, as far as he was concerned, and the very people who continued to clamour for proofs did not take the trouble to examine the copious proofs which already existed, but seemed to think the whole subject should begin *de novo* because they had asked for information.[63] It was not a matter of faith. You only had to believe your eyes. What Spiritualists knew, and what they did, was open to all: this was, of course, one of the things that made Spiritualism especially vulnerable to both attack and derision. It was not sealed in any special mystique of ritual or language, like the knowledge and practice of most churches (and indeed professions), and nor was it mediated through an exclusive body of specialist initiates. Not everyone had psychic powers, but the mediums had, in themselves, no spiritual authority; indeed when not in trance, they usually had little enough to say. Spiritualists thought of themselves as like the earliest Christians, an egalitarian brotherhood, who met in each other's houses, before the development of a clergy and a church and a hierarchy and all that went with these things.

The last decade or so of Conan Doyle's life was dedicated to spreading Spiritualist knowledge—in effect, to missionary practice. Perhaps it was inevitable that he should go public sooner or later with these beliefs, since his idea of the role of the writer was one that involved him in public debate on all sorts of matters of importance. But it was specifically the Great War, in the midst of which he made a public statement of his Spiritualist convictions, that precipitated this action, in two ways. First, he felt he had a message of hope for all those millions who were mourning friends and relatives who had died in the war, for he could offer them "an utter fearlessness of death, and an immense consolation when those who are dear to us pass behind the veil".[64]

---

[62] ACD, *Lecture on Spiritualism*, 11.
[63] ACD, *The New Revelation*, 94.
[64] ACD, *The New Revelation*, 97.

Second, the war itself was, he believed, a symptom and result of the catastrophic spiritual crisis which only the "new revelation" of Spiritualism could resolve. So he embarked on a tireless campaign of lecturing, travels, controversy, and publications, which tested even his stout constitution. In the seventh decade of his life, this most respectable of men had become a revolutionary.

To read his Spiritualist writings in the context of the work of others to which he refers, and in particular to that of Myers and Lodge, is to understand that intellectually, Conan Doyle had not very much that was original to contribute to the cause. What he brought to it was the publicity that adhered to his fame as an author and public figure, the trust and respect in which he was held (though this was something of a diminishing asset, as he developed a reputation for credulousness), and the habitual robustness with which he stiffened the discourse of Spiritualism with an assertive masculinity. He claimed to have brought to the cause "a combative and aggressive spirit which it lacked before" (*M&A*, 398); indeed he seems to have been quite unafraid of attack, abuse, or ridicule. But amidst the many polemical and historical writings with which he tried to further the cause in that last decade, the novel *The Land of Mist* is the book that gives the fullest picture of his understanding of the place of Spiritualism in the culture of his time. Like almost all of his fiction, this novel contains a strong enough element of fantasy and what might be called wish-fulfilment to be described as a kind of romance. The education of the journalist Malone from scepticism to belief, the transformation of Professor Challenger himself, from an implacable enemy of Spiritualism to a believer and advocate, the series of spectacular—if not exactly miraculous—reversals and discoveries that bring these things about, and finally the love and marriage between Malone and Challenger's daughter Enid, which applies a sort of dynastic seal to the story of the victory of the good cause, a frequent enough trope in romance—all these things show the novel delivering a utopia, a version of the world as Conan Doyle felt it ought to be. In another sense it is a straightforwardly documentary and didactic book, which takes non-believing readers inside the world of the Spiritualists and educates them about it. As such it has the same motive, despite its fictional form, as the lectures and histories and polemical works of the final decade.

Indeed for readers inclined to blench at the great unreadable slab of *The History of Spiritualism*, or the sometimes repetitive and slapdash narratives of his lecture tours, *The Land of Mist* can be recommended as, in effect, a kind of lively encyclopedia of Spiritualism in a fictional frame. This is why I describe it here in some detail. It is clear that Conan Doyle was careful to cover all the important aspects of Spiritualist practice and beliefs, and he does so through the eyes of Edward Malone, investigating Spiritualism at first as a journalistic commission, and later as a kind of epistemological pilgrimage and spiritual quest. The story is arranged along a string of psychic events designed to show readers what Spiritualists and psychic investigators do, and is punctuated and supplemented by explanations, in dialogue, of Spiritualist lore on matters like clairvoyance, materializations and ectoplasm, telepathy and the etheric body, poltergeists, spirit guides, spirit photography, the debate about the proper relation between Spiritualism and Christianity, the spheres of the afterlife, and the prospects of the Second Coming. Meantime a number of cultural institutions are critically examined through the lens of their transactions with Spiritualists: the churches, the police and the courts, the press, psychical researchers, and the scientific profession. With much to say too about class, gender, and education, *The Land of Mist* emerges, rather surprisingly, as Conan Doyle's most inclusive social fiction, a sort of Spiritualist condition-of-England novel.

The Spiritualist set-pieces that supply the rhythm of Malone's quest show him penetrating by degrees ever deeper into spiritual experience and conviction. First, he and Enid Challenger attend a Spiritualist church. This is pretty unprepossessing. It is approached by a side-street of dull brick houses off the Edgware Road, housed in a cramped and frowsy building, and attended by a congregation of earnest, simple folk, for the most part neither distinguished, intellectual, nor smart. Small tradespeople, shopwalkers, clerks and artisans, harassed housewives, occasional young folk in search of sensation—this is the constituency of H. G. Wells's and Arnold Bennett's novels, a prosaic world of class-betraying accents and lowbrow culture, bourgeois aspirations, self-improvement, and board-school manners; not the kind of environment, Malone admits, where much spiritual revelation might be expected. And yet, as he reminds himself later, making a favourite point of Conan Doyle's, the original apostles were working men, and early Christianity was "run by slaves and underlings until it gradually extended upwards" (*LM*, 40). Whether in Hammersmith or Holland Park, a practical egalitarianism is the norm among seekers after spiritual truth. The Duchess of Rossland and Mr Bolsover the grocer fraternize at Spiritualist gatherings. "There is no such leveller of classes as Spiritualism, and the charwoman with psychic force is the superior of the millionaire who lacks it" (*LM*, 84). It is not a classless community that is depicted, for characters are carefully marked for class by codes of speech and manners that the English novel had been developing for 200 years—and nor is it one lacking class-consciousness; but it is one where the classes can meet and consort on an equal footing, and this is one of the ways in which Conan Doyle sets about showing, in his community of Spiritualists, an alternative society, a counter-culture or city-within-the-city that acts as a reproach to the busy materialistic competitive metropolis that encloses it.

In the Spiritualist church off the Edgware Road, Malone witnesses a mixed bag of practices: trance and clairvoyant mediumship, a platitudinous address from the spirit of an inhabitant of Atlantis, a message relayed from the Central Intelligence about the Second Coming—all this in the humdrum setting of the business of a small church; hymns are sung to a harmonium accompaniment, a collection is taken for the building fund. It is on this occasion that Malone receives his first shock, when the spirit of the dead Professor Summerlee, his comrade in arms from the Lost World expedition, seems to give him a message. The second psychic event takes place in yet more banal circumstances. This is a domestic or family séance without a professional medium (such as the Conan Doyles frequently undertook at home), which meets regularly in the house of Mr Bolsover, the Hammersmith grocer. Here a spirit guide, a little black girl addressed as Wee One, levitates the trumpet and tambourine so beloved of the departed, and a more mature spirit called Luke—with an educated English voice speaking "in a fashion to which the good Bolsover could not attain" (*LM*, 67)—instructs the company on love and marriage in the afterlife. Again, the democratic and ecumenical nature of the Spiritualist community, in this world and the next, is emphasized. After this, Malone is ready to experience a materialization séance with a professional medium, Tom Linden, and this is where he sees, as had Conan Doyle, the materialized form of his own dead mother. It is the first climax of the story.

Now the focus shifts for a while to the medium Linden. He receives paying clients in his home, and dispenses advice, not unlike a general practitioner. But two of these clients prove to be undercover policewomen, and Linden is subsequently summonsed to appear in court. The narrative spends much indignation on this episode, for not only has Linden been entrapped (no complaint has been made against him), but he is charged with fortune-telling under the archaic Vagrancy Act of 1824, for under this law the profession of mediumship or wonder-working is in itself a legal crime, whether it be genuine or not. The trial of Tom Linden is an occasion that shows the panoply of the law to be nothing more than institutionalized bullying. Linden is tried in a police court, before Mr Melrose, a magistrate who manifestly favours the police solicitor, and scarcely listens to the defence case. "Such men as the defendant are the noxious fungi which collect on a corrupt society, and the attempt to compare their vulgarities with the holy men of old, or to claim similar gifts, must be reprobated by all right-thinking men" (*LM*, 128), he says, before sentencing Linden to two months' hard labour without the option of a fine.

The smug summing-up does pinpoint the magistrate's assumption of the authority to speak as the conscience of society itself—"all right-thinking men". But the narrative has already shown that the police timed their arrest of Linden to ensure that he will appear before this particular magistrate, whose materialist views are a matter of record and will guarantee a conviction, and avoid others who might be more sympathetic to the medium. It is also clear that the police have gone after Linden and stitched him up in the expectation of benefiting from a subsequent fine—"If we get twenty-five pounds fine it has to go somewhere—Police Fund, of course, but there may be something over," Inspector Murphy tells his policewomen (*LM*, 118). Alas, he has miscalculated: Melrose sends the medium to prison instead. Malone is indignant, but trusts that the newspapers will ventilate this manifest injustice. He returns home, however, to read the headline in the *Planet*, "IMPOSTOR IN THE POLICE COURT", and a jeering report. The chapter ends like this.

Yes, poor Tom Linden had a bad Press. He went down into his miserable cell amid universal objurgation. The *Planet*, an evening paper which depended for its circulation upon the sporting forecasts of Captain Touch-and-go, remarked upon the absurdity of forecasting the future. *Honest John*, a weekly journal which had been mixed up with some of the greatest frauds of the century, was of opinion that the dishonesty of Linden was a public scandal. A rich country rector wrote to *The Times* to express his indignation that anyone should profess to sell the gifts of the spirit. The *Churchman* remarked that such incidents arose from the growing infidelity, while the *Freethinker* saw in them a reversion to superstition. Finally Mr Maskelyne showed the public, to the great advantage of his box office, exactly how the swindle was perpetrated. So for a few days Tom Linden was what the French call a "succès d'exécration." Then the world moved on and he was left to his fate.[65] (*LM*, 130)

This is hardly the satire of Jonathan Swift, but it could conceivably be that other Irishman, George Bernard Shaw. There is, however, a certain sourness in it, a note that creeps into Conan Doyle's writing only in his last decade, and which we may use to measure the distance between this and the work of that upstanding, good-humoured, gentlemanly establishment figure of earlier years and books. It was as if Spiritualism set a kind of examination, and these organs of national justice and formers of public opinion were seen to fail it. Immersed in his Spiritualist mission, Conan Doyle was losing faith, or at least patience, in the institutions of the nation, and was more inclined to identify himself with a different and radical community, described in the novel by the barrister Mailey.

Yes, psychic power in its varied manifestations is found in humble quarters, but surely that has been its main characteristic from the beginning—fishermen, carpenters, tent-makers, camel drivers, these were the prophets of old. At this moment some of the highest psychic gifts in England lie in a miner, a cotton operative, a railway-porter, a bargeman and a charwoman. Thus does history repeat itself, and that foolish beak, with Tom Linden before him, was but Felix judging Paul. The old wheel goes round. (*LM*, 166–7)

Malone's education continues. With Charles Mason, an Anglican priest and living proof that Spiritualism can be entirely compatible with orthodox Christian faith, and with his old friend Lord John Roxton, he spends a night in a haunted house (as Conan Doyle had done on behalf of the Society for Psychical Research); this house contains a violent and terrifying spirit, which is eventually quelled and ministered to by the priest. The theme of the troubled soul continues into the next episode, where Malone attends a "rescue circle", a séance

---

[65] Most British newspapers carried horseracing tips. Several, including the *Daily Mail*, ran a regular fortune-telling column. *Honest John* is probably intended to evoke the weekly *John Bull* whose notorious proprietor, Horatio Bottomley, was convicted of fraud (and expelled from Parliament, of which he was an elected member) in 1922, and was currently serving seven years in Wormwood Scrubs. Nevil Maskelyne was a celebrated professional magician. He died in 1924, the year before *The Land of Mist* was published.

dedicated to contacting and giving comfort and guidance to perturbed spirits who do not understand what has become of them after death, or indeed that they are dead at all. Conan Doyle had extensive experience of rescue circles.

Here in a self-contained chapter a strange interlude interrupts the story, with a dramatic shift of tone. Earlier we had met Tom Linden's brother the villainous Silas, a broken-down pugilist who tries to get Tom to teach him what he assumes are the tricks of the trade so that he can earn a living as a false medium. Now we see Silas at home, in a squalid lodging at the back of Tottenham Court Road where he lives with his second wife and the two children of his first marriage. The scene might be inspired by Dickens, or equally by the sensational and sentimental domestic melodramas of the Victorian theatre, ballads or illustrations designed to bring a tear to the eye, or the pamphlet literature or magic lantern shows of the temperance movement. Silas and his woman are ugly, profane, and sadistically abusive. The children are neglected, ill fed, beaten, and terrified. The elder child, a fair-haired boy of 10 with spiritual features, has clearly inherited the psychic powers his father lacks, for the boy sees visions of his deceased mother. As the two children cower in the attic after a particularly dreadful episode, the mother's ghost comes to lead the boy and his little sister out of the house, into the street, and to the doorstep of Tom Linden's wife, who takes them in. Meanwhile Silas, who has quarrelled and fought with his Jewish neighbour after she threatened to report him for neglecting the children, one night falls (or is pushed) to his death through an open cellar-flap, in an emphatic demonstration of poetic justice. His slatternly wife, now his widow, returns to the music-hall stage from which he had lured her, and descends, in the inexorable pattern of melodramatic female ruin, into "the awful silent quicksands of life which drew her down and down until that vacuous painted face and frowsy head were seen no more" (*LM*, 200). Most of *The Land of Mist*—apart, if you will, from the psychic phenomena—is couched in the language of novelistic realism, but in this episode Conan Doyle seems to have succumbed to the allure of a rich plangent melodrama, either remembered from the stage, or experienced afresh in the silent cinema.

Later Malone, Mailey, and Roxton travel to Paris to attend an experimental procedure undertaken by the psychical researcher Dr Maupuis (based on Gustav Geley, recently deceased) and the physiologist Professor Charles Richet (a real person, still alive and professionally active), at the Institut Métapsychique. Here they witness, in the austere secular atmosphere of French scientific investigation, the materialization of several entities including, apparently, a protohuman Pithecanthropus.[66] The next set-piece is a big public meeting, in the Queen's Hall, in which the irascible Challenger has been persuaded to debate with a Spiritualist unobtrusively named James Smith, an ex-printer's assistant and editor of a psychic newspaper. (Nobody remarks that Challenger has here returned to the scene of the great debate at the end of *The Lost World*, at which he released the pterodactyl.) Challenger is a celebrity scientist and a mighty orator, but he is bested by the insignificant-looking Smith, who shows that his opponent has not bothered to acquaint himself at all with the Spiritualist literature, and has not once attended a séance. Challenger, to his great rage, is accused of being unscientific: he has not done his elementary research. It was a dramatization of another of Conan Doyle's familiar arguments—his complaint that sceptics simply ignored all the published and attested evidence for psychic phenomena—and is also another triumph for the Spiritualist underdog, and for the humble man at the expense of the over-confident professional. And yet, as the narrative points out, in matters of the spirit it is the Spiritualists who are the specialists. Uncorrupted by useless education, Smith has been able to focus his intellect upon the one all-important field of knowledge. "Little as Challenger could appreciate it, the contest was really one between a brilliant discursive amateur and a concentrated highly-specialized professional" (*LM*, 221). It was an unexpected late victory for professionalism.

Now the main theme of the story becomes the campaign to recruit Challenger for the Spiritualist cause. The great man's favourite pupil is suffering from a painful and apparently terminal condition and Challenger, who is now for the first time revealed to have studied and practised medicine as a young man, is powerless to help. He learns, however, that the patient has responded miraculously to treatment by a mysterious Dr Felkin—and then learns that Felkin is a physician of the early nineteenth century, temporarily inhabiting (or being channelled by) the body of a young female nurse called Ursula. While the nurse is in a mediumistic trance, she has the medical expertise, and the

---

[66] In an appendix (*LM*, 293–945), Conan Doyle notes that the account of Pithecanthropus was taken from the *Bulletin de l'Institut Métapsychique*, and the account of the séance itself from Geley's *L'Ectoplasmie et la clairvoyance*.

masculine voice and gestures, of the ghostly consultant. This preposterous medico, while giving an impressive account of the case and a heartening prognosis, explains to an astonished Challenger that after his death he continued his medical studies, and has been permitted to return to earth to do something to help humanity. He works briskly, for, he says, he is due in Edinburgh in a few minutes. Challenger can hardly be expected to swallow this, and reacts as a professional, a male, and a materialist, turning his "paternal attentions" upon the nurse and advising her that she should "be content to be a bewitching nurse and resign all claim to the higher functions of doctor".

"Come now," said he, "who was the clever doctor with whom you acted as nurse—the man who taught you all these fine words? You must feel that it is hopeless to deceive me. You will be much happier, dear child, when you have made a clean breast of it all, and when we can laugh together over the lecture which you inflicted upon me." (LM, 246)

This monumentally patronizing speech earns Challenger a crushing rebuke from his former pupil. Indeed it would be hard to find a more compact expression of the depths of complacent prejudices—about gender, age, class, education, language, and profession, about authority and deference—upon which Challenger's ego floats. Yet every single aspect of what we may call the Challenger ideology, the knowledge about people and the world that seems to him natural and obvious and true, will be challenged in turn by his own encounter with the phenomena of the spirit world. The new revelation is a revolution, and requires of people like Challenger a radical overturning of everything they thought they knew. Here on the personal level is the pattern as before, and it recapitulates in miniature Conan Doyle's idea of human history: one form of knowledge must give way or adjust to another. Just as an orthodox Christian view of the world had to shift to accommodate the discoveries of Darwinian science (unless it chose to ignore them, thus condemning itself to irrelevance), so the whole worldview of people like Challenger must be revised in turn in the light of the new knowledge pouring into the world with the new revelation of the spirit—often through the agency of people they may have considered of little account, just as the great scientist here assumes that a person who is young, female, and only a nurse cannot possibly tell him anything actually worth knowing. Although Challenger does become uncharacteristically humble in the next chapter, there is not much evidence that he is capable of the wholesale makeover that the new knowledge demands of him; nonetheless, the challenge has been laid down.

A new alignment is in preparation, which will see Malone and Enid, Roxton and Challenger all enrolled in the Spiritualist counter-culture, all more or less disillusioned with the great institutions in which they once had a more or less comfortable place—the denying Church (for with the exception of Mason, churchmen fail to rise to the challenge of Spiritualism), the boneheaded scientific and medical establishment, the venal forces and organs of the law, even the hypocritical and cynical press—for Malone, too assiduous in his reporting of Spiritualist goings-on, is fired by his editor at the *Gazette* on the insistence of its proprietor, a millionaire playboy "living in a constant luxury which placed him always on the edge of vice and occasionally over the border" (*LM*, 260). Alienation from such discredited institutions is not to be lamented for long. It only remains, in the last séance which is the climax of the story, for Challenger himself to be confronted with such convincing knowledge from beyond—"evidential", as the Spiritualists called it—that he can no longer resist. He admits his error handsomely, and thereafter becomes a ferocious controversialist in the Spiritualist interest.

Malone and Enid are married, and the novel ends with the honeymoon couple contemplating the apocalypse. "Look at the solid old earth of England," Enid says (sounding like George Orwell contemplating "the deep, deep sleep of England" and the coming apocalypse of war).[67] "Look at our great hotel and the people on the Lees, and the stodgy morning papers and all the settled order of a civilized land. Do you really think that anything could come to destroy it all?" (*LM*, 284). But Malone is inclined to agree with the prophecy they heard from Miromar in the Spiritualist church, that a judgement is coming. Why? "It is the materialism, the wooden formalities of the churches, the alienation of all spiritual impulses, the denial of the Unseen, the ridicule of this new revelation—these are the causes according to [Miromar]" (*LM*, 284). Surely the world has been worse before now, says Enid. Malone replies:

[67] "Down here it was still the England I had known in my childhood...all sleeping the deep, deep sleep of England, from which I sometimes fear that we shall never wake till we are jerked out of it by the roar of bombs." Orwell, *Homage to Catalonia* (1938), in *Complete Works of George Orwell*, vi. 187.

But never with the same advantages—never with the education and knowledge and so-called civilization, which should have led it to higher things.
Look how everything has been turned to evil. We got the knowledge of air-
ships. We bomb cities with them. We learn how to steam under the sea. We
murder seamen with our new knowledge. We gain command over chemicals.
We turn them into explosives or poison gases. It goes from worse to worse. At
the present moment every nation upon earth is plotting how it can best poison the others. Did God create the planet for this end, and is it likely that he
will allow it to go on from bad to worse? (*LM*, 285)

The rhetoric is not especially striking—and after all, this is Edward
Malone—but what is confirmed here is the disenchantment and dis-
may with which Conan Doyle ended his history of the Great War, the
sense that he could no longer carry a banner for the "so-called civilization" which he had seemed to embody so stolidly. The difference is
that here, Spiritualism—its amazing revelations, and the indifference
and ridicule with which they were greeted—is now shown to have
made possible, even inevitable, that critique and rejection. If Conan
Doyle in his final years was in effect an apostate from the shared values
and collective business of the culture which had formed him, it is
because in the Spiritualist community and its practice he thought he
had found the ground for an alternative, revolutionary way of living
and knowing the truth about the world. This connects him, late in his
life and improbably, to a radical tradition that goes back to William
Blake, a man who also conversed with spirits and imagined a new-
built England.

Fairies

The Land of Mist provides, then, something of a synopsis of the beliefs,
activities, and struggles of the Spiritualist community, and these beliefs
are underwritten by the story of the conversion of Malone and Enid,
and finally the formidable Challenger himself. What Malone uncovers
in his researches is a community encompassing a wide variety of class
and education but united in a spiritual practice, not secret, but misun-
derstood, shown in the end to embody all that is best in the nation, and
to hold its future in trust. It was a remarkable discovery to be made by
way of that side street off the Edgware Road—a new spiritual nation,
waiting like the early Christians to come out and take its place in the

light. But Conan Doyle had already found a yet stranger version of England, on a riverbank by a village in Yorkshire, which has just as much to tell us about his vision of past and future.

Everyone knows Conan Doyle made a fool of himself over the case of the Cottingley fairies. Why and how he did so is the subject of this part of the chapter.

These are the facts. In the village of Cottingley in Yorkshire two young cousins, 10-year-old Frances Griffiths and 16-year-old Elsie Wright, borrowed Elsie's father's camera on an afternoon in July 1917, and produced a photograph showing Frances near the local beck or stream, surrounded by five fairies. In September they borrowed the camera again: this time, the result was a photograph of Elsie with a gnome. There the matter rested for a while, until the mothers of both girls took to attending meetings of the Bradford Theosophical Society. At one meeting in 1919 there was a lecture and discussion about "Fairy Life" and this is how the girls' photographs of two years before came to be shown at the Bradford Lodge, and later at the Theosophical Society's annual conference at Harrogate, where they were much admired. The glass negative plates and the original photographs came to the attention of Edward L. Gardner, a senior Theosophist and president of the Blavatsky (London) Lodge of the Society, and by May 1920 Gardner was using slides of the pictures in his lectures—he was already something of an authority on fairies. Arthur Conan Doyle, who had been commissioned by the *Strand* magazine to write an article about fairies for their Christmas 1920 number, came to hear of the photos and contacted Miss E. M. Blomfield, a cousin of Gardner's, who provided him with copies, which filled him with excitement.

The two men corresponded. After meeting Gardner in London, Conan Doyle subsequently wrote to Elsie Wright, the elder of the girls, and her father at the end of June 1920. He secured their agreement for the photographs to be used in his *Strand* article, though the family's name would not be given. The article finished, Conan Doyle departed on the first of his overseas Spiritualist speaking tours, to Australia and New Zealand. Meanwhile Gardner went to Cottingley to meet the girls (he met Elsie), verify their family credentials, and visit the locations of the photographs. He left them two cameras, and in due course, in August, a further three fairy photographs were produced. The issue of the *Strand* with Conan Doyle's article and the first two of the girls' photographs was published in December and rapidly sold out.

Conan Doyle's judgement was widely derided but the authenticity of the photographs was vigorously defended by Gardner. It was not long before the press had discovered the identity of the girls, and learned that there was a second batch of fairy photos. These were published by Conan Doyle in a second article in the *Strand*, "The Evidence for Fairies", in March 1921. No more photographs were forthcoming. Conan Doyle published the book called *The Coming of the Fairies* in 1922. It contained an account of the Cottingley affair, reports from some other observers, further evidence for the existence of fairies, elves, and so on, and some observations, mostly by Gardner, about the nature of the fairies. Decades later in old age, Frances and Elsie admitted that they had faked the fairy photographs, while Frances at least continued to maintain that they had seen the fairies.[68]

In the book Conan Doyle was not quite as absolute in his belief in the existence of the Cottingley fairies as he is usually remembered to be. The tone of *The Coming of the Fairies* is, for the most part, measured and judicious. This narrative is not a special plea for the authenticity of the photos, he says, but a review of facts the reader is invited to ponder. Once in possession of these facts, readers can make their own decisions, for they will be in as good a position as the writer to form a judgement on the authenticity of the girls' claims. In the original *Strand* article, reproduced in the book, he was ready to declare that "a strong *prima-facie* case has been built up" but "If I am myself asked whether I consider the case to be absolutely and finally proved, I should answer that in order to remove the last faint shadow of doubt I should wish to see the result repeated before a disinterested witness."[69] This is the fundamental scientific requirement that experimental results must be independently verified by repetition: as he does again and again in his Spiritualist writings, he is making the rhetorical point that he has not surrendered his scientific criteria and objectivity even while investigating occult phenomena. He is still thinking like a scientist.

Nonetheless, perhaps prompted by the misgivings of some of his Spiritualist allies, he is anxious to keep a distance between these fairy investigations and the more serious and profound Spiritualist

---

[68] Joe Cooper, *The Case of the Cottingley Fairies* (London: Simon and Schuster, 1990), 169–70.

[69] ACD, *The Coming of the Fairies* (1922) (Lincoln, Nebr.: University of Nebraska Press, 2006), 39–40. Hereafter *Coming*.

case with which he was by now strongly identified. He cannot have failed to anticipate a reaction of disbelief and mockery. "I would add that this whole subject of the objective existence of a subhuman form of life has nothing to do with the larger and far more vital question of spiritualism. I should be sorry if my arguments in favour of the latter should be in any way weakened by my exposition of this very strange episode, which really has no bearing on the continued existence of the individual" (*Coming*, xxiv). Evidence of "the continued existence of the individual"—that is, the afterlife—was the great victory of the Spiritualist revelation in its war against materialism, and in this matter the existence or non-existence of non-human elementals such as fairies was neither here nor there. And yet Conan Doyle could not help recruiting the Cottingley fairies, even so, as allies in that great struggle, as he wrote to Gardner from Australia.

The matter does not bear directly upon the more vital question of our fate and that of those we have lost, which has brought me out here. But anything which extends man's mental horizon, and proves to him that matter as we have known it is not really the limit of our universe, must have a good effect of breaking down materialism and leading human thought to a broader and more spiritual level. (*Coming*, 98)

Small, elusive, "subhuman", childish, even trivial and comic as the fairies might be (if they existed), Conan Doyle cannot resist making much of the Cottingley evidence, an "epoch-making" moment in the emancipation of mankind from materialism to which he had now dedicated his own life (*Coming*, 13). And often as he painstakingly enters the proper scientific cautions, postpones conclusions, and warns that the case is not fully proved, as often his narrative sweeps over these rhetorical defences as if they were already levelled. There were fairies in England. The photographs, and the testimony of Frances Griffiths and Elsie Wright, were evidence enough.

Since his belief in fairies is probably the most alienating aspect of Conan Doyle's intellectual character for most readers, it is important to show just what were the cultural conditions that made it possible. Then I shall want to argue that making the case for the Cottingley fairies was a consistent move in the practice of the latter part of his career, the representation and critique of the culture he inhabited and wanted to see transformed.

Fairies were, as it were, still in the air in the early 1920s, though their Victorian and Edwardian heyday was past.[70] "An explosion of interest in fairies had taken place during the first decades of the nineteenth century, and this was maintained in its various forms until well after the First World War."[71] They still featured in children's stories, their association with childhood having being established by the pretty and graceful illustrations made popular by Victorian artists like Richard Dadd, John Anster Fitzgerald, Conan Doyle's uncle Richard "Dicky" Doyle (it is often pointed out that fairies were also a favourite subject of Conan Doyle's father, Charles Altamont Doyle), and his younger contemporary Arthur Rackham. Shakespeare's fairy play *A Midsummer Night's Dream* was literally a stage where quite elaborate English fairy fantasies were frequently on display. Hans Christian Andersen's fairy tales were enormously popular, as were in turn Andrew Lang's "Fairy Books", of different colours and entrancingly illustrated, which appeared in a series of twelve volumes between 1889 and 1910. When the audience at J. M. Barrie's *Peter Pan* (1904) were asked "Do you believe in fairies?", everyone knew the right answer. Robert Louis Stevenson wrote about fairies, and so did W. B. Yeats and Robert Graves. In Rudyard Kipling's children's book *Puck of Pook's Hill* (1906), a fairy is the medium through whom the children are given visions of England's deep history, and there is a story, "Dymchurch Flit", about how the fairy folk evacuated England at a time of religious strife, demonstrating that the fairies or "Pharisees" were associated with the antiquity of rural England but vulnerable to upheavals in the human world, and could communicate, if they wished, with certain people and particularly with children.

None of this is proof that people believed in fairies, and yet the Kipling story gives a clue to the ubiquity of fairies in pictorial and narrative culture, especially that associated with childhood. A belief in fairies was a folk belief, and a widespread fascination with fairies is related to a renewed curiosity about folk beliefs and practices at a time when industry and cities and education were encroaching more and more on the rural grounds of folk culture. Fairyland prospered on a double nostalgia for childhood and for earlier and simpler ways of life,

[70] See Nicola Brown, *Fairies in Nineteenth-Century Art and Literature* (Cambridge: Cambridge University Press, 2001).

[71] Alex Owen, "'Borderland Forms': Arthur Conan Doyle, Albion's Daughters, and the Politics of the Cottingley Fairies", *History Workshop Journal*, 38 (1994), 48–85; at 50.

real or imaginary. Collectors of traditional fairy tales, from the Brothers Grimm to Yeats and Andrew Lang, were part of that ethnographic project, initiated by the romantic nationalism of Johann Gottfried Herder in the eighteenth century, that had researchers scouring the countryside of Europe for folk tales and songs, festivals, traditional remedies, arts and crafts, and dialectal idiosyncrasies. One reason for collecting such things was a concern to preserve them, before the juggernaut of modernity went over them for good. Another was the idea that such beliefs, practices, and texts (usually oral) issued directly out of the anonymous and collective folk—that they expressed some authentic and profound truth about a community, tribe, nation, people. At one end of this autoethnographic project lie the operas of Richard Wagner, in which a body of ancient legends is renewed in the name of an aggressive romantic nationalism. At another end of the project is *The Coming of the Fairies*.

An appetite for the subject seems confirmed by the fact that in 1920 the *Strand*, a commercial metropolitan publication with a circulation approaching half a million copies and not noted for eccentricity, commissioned its star writer to contribute an article on fairies.[72] Of course, Conan Doyle was well known to be interested in psychic and paranormal phenomena. His Spiritualist activities and reading provide another condition that made possible his belief in fairies; in investigating this topic, he was to some extent on home ground, and even the scepticism and mockery which greeted his reports on it were familiar to him. Though he wanted to keep fairies and communion with the dead separate in his mind and that of his readers, Spiritualism provided him with methodologies, explanations, and arguments that could be used to make the case for the fairies. As with spirit manifestations, he was careful to deal with the objection that these might be thought-forms, projected from the minds of observers, rather than actual phenomena. The reason the fairies were visible to some people but not to others could be explained by the familiar Spiritualist (and Theosophical) theory of vibrations, an adaptation of the wave theory of light and sound: just as we see objects and hear noise only within the limits that make up our colour spectrum and the compass of audible pitch, beings that send out shorter or longer vibrations may easily exist invisible to those

---

[72] It is no doubt also significant, though, that the article was commissioned for the *Strand*'s Christmas number.

of us who are not specially sensitive, "unless we could tune ourselves up or tone them down" (*Coming*, 14). As for these sensitives, writers on the subject had frequently noticed, since the Fox sisters on whose powers the modern Spiritualist movement had really been launched in the middle of the nineteenth century, that psychic abilities were often lodged in the young, female, and relatively uneducated. Such people, it was claimed, were inclined to be simple and lacking in guile. Conan Doyle and Gardner recognized that the Cottingley girls fell into a familiar pattern for clairvoyants, and they agreed that at least the younger, Frances, was mediumistic, and must, as Gardner put it, have harboured "loosely knit ectoplasmic material" in her body which the fairies could draw on to acquire a visible and photographable form of their own.[73] Such abilities seemed to be in some way dependent on sexual innocence, and were therefore liable to fade. Conan Doyle mentions as a fact that "the processes of puberty are often fatal to psychic power" (*Coming*, 93).

As for the inevitable charges of trickery, hard experience and particularly his ongoing dispute with Houdini meant that Conan Doyle was already primed with his defence against "the old discredited anti-spiritualist argument that because a trained conjurer can produce certain effects under his own conditions, therefore some woman or child who gets similar effects must get them by conjuring" (*Coming*, 33). His Spiritualist campaign undoubtedly prepared him both to believe in the Cottingley fairies and to make the case for this belief. His partnership with and trust in the Theosophist Edward Gardner, who was thoroughly convinced that fairies existed and who already seemed to know a lot about elemental fauna, no doubt was a factor too. Never before or after did Conan Doyle associate himself so closely with the Theosophists. Theosophy had a much more sophisticated taxonomy of ethereal, elemental, and spiritual life-forms than anything Spiritualists were accustomed to. Even before their first meeting, Gardner was lecturing Conan Doyle— as no doubt he lectured his Theosophical audiences—on the phenomena, assuring him that the elementals in the photographs were nature spirits of the non-individualized order, but he was hopeful that they might secure photos of some of the higher orders too (*Coming*, 24). Most of the more confident and loopy statements in *The Coming of the Fairies* about the nature of these apparitions derive from Gardner—for example,

---

[73] See Alex Owen, "Borderland Forms", 73.

that fairies are allied to the *Lepidoptera* or butterfly genus, and that their function is "to furnish the vital connecting link between the stimulating energy of the sun and the raw material of form" (*Coming*, 174, 175). Conan Doyle rather unwisely entered into the spirit of Gardner's specialist knowledgeability when after studying the photos long and earnestly with a high-powered lens he gave his opinion that the fairies might be a compound of the human and the butterfly, "while the gnome has more of the moth" (*Coming*, 55). This knowledge is offered in the language of expertise, coming from the metropolitan consultant to whom the case has been referred, and is quite different from the knowledge of fairies offered, rather reluctantly it must be said, by the girls who claimed actually to have seen them. Further accreditation was provided by Geoffrey Hodson ("Mr Sergeant" in the book), a friend of Gardner's and a fellow Theosophist. Hodson, a clairvoyant, was invited to join the girls for a week in August 1921 and reported, happily, that the whole Cottingley glen "was swarming with many forms of elemental life, and he saw not only wood-elves, gnomes, and goblins, but the rarer undines, floating over the stream" (*Coming*, 107).

But the testimony of Frances Griffiths and Elsie Wright was supported by photographic evidence, and it is clear that this was crucial for Conan Doyle's belief. Photography had been one of the passions of his youth. We have seen before what importance he attached to photos, especially to those that made visible the hitherto invisible, like the photomicrographs of bacilli made by Robert Koch. It was in the power of the photograph to constitute emphatic proof. Naturally Spiritualists were keen to record psychic phenomena—ectoplasm, materializations, and so on—and an extensive body of such photographic work was produced, which in turn generated accusations of fraud from the sceptics. Conan Doyle had a considerable library of his own and he used slides of spirit photographs to illustrate the lectures on which he spent so much of the time of his last decade or so. The same year as *The Coming of the Fairies*, 1922, he published *The Case for Spirit Photography*, which is largely a defence of the most famous of such photographers, William Hope of the Crewe Circle of Spiritualists, who had been accused of fraud by Harry Price in the *Proceedings of the Society for Psychical Research*.[74] Conan Doyle had had personal sessions with Hope

---

[74] ACD and others, *The Case for Spirit Photography*. Some chapters are by Miss F. R. Scatcherd and Fred Barlow.

which produced spirit photographs, one featuring a human face which might have been that of his dead sister. He could attest personally that these images were authentic: how could such results be produced, he challenged, "under the mediumship of an unlearned carpenter at Crewe"?[75] There were fraudulent photographs and photographers, he conceded, but if fraud could be ruled out, if only in a single instance, then a spirit photograph was incontrovertible proof of spirit phenomena. A studio chief and photographers from Kodak Ltd. were consulted, and could find no evidence of fakery in the Cottingley photos though they were not prepared to give a written guarantee of authenticity. But another professional studio photographer, a Mr Snelling, endorsed the genuineness of the original negatives.[76] Much is made in the book about this professional endorsement, which enabled the photographs to be presented as a faithful record of real fairies. Not for the first time, an attack was to be launched against materialism by appealing to the most material form of evidence. If Spiritualism predisposed Conan Doyle to believe in the fairies, photography convinced him that that belief was verified.

But if there was one thing stronger than his belief in photography, it was his belief in his knowledge of people, his reading of character, and in some ways this is the most remarkable as well as the simplest aspect of the case, the apparently unruffled confidence of a gentleman and man of the world in his ability to take the measure of the integrity of others.[77] This has to do with his kindness and his disposition to think well of people, but it rests also on the solidity of his worldview, inflected by a moderate, liberal, and generally optimistic outlook, underwritten by his personal success but more importantly by the prestige and authority vested in his class, gender, and nation, and practised in the reading of "character" as it was represented, in all its transparency, in his

---

[75] ACD and others, *The Case for Spirit Photography*, 23. It is an interesting coincidence that Carpenter is the pseudonym under which Conan Doyle sought to disguise the identity of the two Cottingley girls. *The Case for Spirit Photography* also defends another working-class photographic medium, Mrs Deane, from accusations of fraud. Mrs Deane was a charwoman.

[76] Indeed the photographs themselves were not fakes. Elsie Wright had drawn and cut out the fairy figures, pinned them to the ground with hatpins, and photographed them.

[77] "It was clear that at the last it was the character and surroundings of the children upon which the enquiry must turn, rather than upon the photos themselves" (*Coming*, 33). To this end, he felt it necessary to "open up human relations" with the girls, and he initiated this by sending Elsie one of his books.

favourite novels. The human world was a knowable place. Conan Doyle's own life was lived in the open, and while it certainly had its unhappiness, he met each crisis swiftly, with a courageous decisiveness he almost never came to regret. Doubt is not a significant theme in his adult life, and is a state of mind rare in his fictional characters, who do not have the dark troubled and recessive psychic depths that both psychology and fiction had started to explore in his lifetime.[78] (Stark Munro could be described as intellectually unformed, but his ramblings are enthusiastic and speculative rather than anxious.) The world, like Conan Doyle's prose, could be exciting but was always plain. It was a visible place. And so with people. Most of them were what they seemed, and what his education and cultural prejudices had taught him to expect. Germans usually blustered. Women were inspiring. Boys loved adventure. Men were patriotic. Poets were dreamy. Sportsmen were sporting. And children were innocent. If there were exceptions to these rules, they were easily discovered. People could be known.

The innocence of children was a particularly cherished belief of a pre-Freudian public, and a theme repeated endlessly across the culture in which Conan Doyle grew up, from portraiture to melodrama. Once he and Gardner had established, much to their relief, that the girls' families' were not interested in profiting from the fairies (the "money consideration", as Gardner termed it in a letter (*Coming*, 24), was a familiar embarrassment for the apologists for Spiritualist mediums, many of whom charged fees for their services), there was no reason not to believe their sincerity. Children, and especially girls, were known to be psychically sensitive, a quality that seemed to depend on their innocence and simplicity. Conan Doyle mentions in *The Coming of the Fairies* that the two sons and daughter of his own second marriage, "very truthful children", had each independently seen and described a fairy: his enquiries suggested that many children had had the same experience, but kept it to themselves when met by ridicule and incredulity (*Coming*, 128). It has been noted that Conan Doyle and Gardner consistently exaggerated the girls' youth, making it seem that they were both children when in fact in 1920 Elsie was 19 and Frances 13,

---

[78] From, for example, the practice of "character" in Dickens's *A Tale of Two Cities* (1859) and Reade's *The Cloister and the Hearth* (1861) to that in Lawrence's *Women in Love* (1920) and Freud's *Beyond the Pleasure Principle* (1920).

and both were at work.[79] They believed in the girls as pure and natural, almost as organic emanations from the natural scene just as the fairies were—and as Frances appears in the superbly composed first photograph, "Frances and the Fairies".[80] Gardner wrote to Conan Doyle that all too soon, their vision would become obscured by the experience of falling in love, and indeed both men were disappointed in the failure of the girls to produce any more photographs after 1920, a failure attributed by Conan Doyle to "the change in the girls, the one through womanhood and the other through board-school education" (*Coming*, 105).

The vision their photographs had vouchsafed, before they were overtaken by sexual maturity and modern education, was of an England similarly unsullied by passion and history—pure, authentic, and unspoilt. Or so it became, once Gardner and Doyle had, by publishing and discussing them, "turned the photographs from images the girls made for themselves into documents in the public domain".[81] In doing so, they transformed the photographic texts from one order of knowledge into another.[82] "The fairies depicted in the Cottingley photographs were...interpreted by Conan Doyle, Gardner, and Hodson in the light of all they knew of esoteric lore, and in turn slipped easily into an already developed naturalistic theosophical paradigm of elemental fauna."[83] At the same time they became for Conan Doyle a vehicle for something he wanted to say about England.

For though *The Coming of the Fairies* is framed as a "case"—with its air of scientific procedure, its credentialling of the enquirers and careful chronological exposition of the enquiry, and its inclusion of supporting documents, material evidence (the photographs), independent

[79] See Diane Purkiss, *Troublesome Things: A History of Fairies and Fairy Stories* (London: Allen Lane, Penguin Press, 2000), 288–9. *The Coming of the Fairies* does not mention that Elsie had worked for some time in a portrait photographer's studio in Bradford.

[80] Originally titled by Conan Doyle "Alice and the Fairies"—again significantly, Alice was the pseudonym he chose to protect Frances's real identity. In the first photograph, only the girl's face and upper body are visible, as if she were a part of the flowery bank on which she leans; her elbow rests on the turf, where four fairies are sporting in the shade. She ignores them. With a little waterfall behind her, she belongs completely to the natural scene. Her pose is that of a studio portrait, as she stares winsomely towards the viewer.

[81] Brown, *Fairies in Nineteenth-Century Art and Literature*, 191.

[82] It seems the girls took the original photographs to substantiate Frances's story to her aunt that she had come home with a wet dress because she had been playing with fairies by the brook.

[83] Alex Owen, "'Borderland Forms'", 69.

testimony, expert opinion, and dissenting views—at its centre is pure idyll. If the Spiritualist community in *The Land of Mist* was Conan Doyle's novelistic vision of a new England, *The Coming of the Fairies* discloses a lyrical vision of the country as it might long ago have been, as it might be in a future redeemed by the new revelation.

Cottingley, like paradise, existed in both past and future. Yorkshire had been the great workshop of the industrial revolution, with Leeds and Bradford (where Elsie Wright worked) the centre of the textile industry and, at the time of the First World War, of armaments production. This was not the Yorkshire in which the fairies were photographed in 1917. That country was one in which it might be possible, at least in the eyes of an outsider, to imagine that things were as they had always been. After the lengthy journey up from London, Gardner found Cottingley "a quaint, old-world village" (*Coming*, 48–9); to enter it was like stepping back into the past. Most obviously, it was the war itself that the enchanted dell teeming with fairies seemed to deny, or defy—the grossest form of destructive materialism, with its insane competition between nations, its infernal machines, and dehumanizing organization.[84] The fairies, so childlike, frail, and whimsical, were the opposite of this, as they are in Robert Graves's wartime collection of poems, *Fairies and Fusiliers* (1918). They, and the girls who were pure enough to see and play with them, were a covenant, an assurance that the true spirit of England survived, indigenous and innocent. It could be argued that Conan Doyle believed in the fairies in the same way that he believed in Elsie and Frances. For him they embodied a possibility, a kind of England that, however naively, he was determined to assert.

Far from the metropolis, from the world made and spoiled by men, here was a form of life that was feminine, young, playful, and neighbourly. Its appearance, in these unpropitious times, seemed to herald a change.

Other well-authenticated cases will come along. These little folk who appear to be our neighbours, with only some small difference of vibration to separate us, will become familiar. The thought of them even when unseen, will add a charm to every brook and valley and give romantic interest to every country

---

[84] Children too felt the need to escape from the ordeal of war. Frances Griffiths was from a regular army background. Her father was away at the war, and she had had to come back from South Africa to Yorkshire with her mother. Late in life she told Joe Cooper that "it was horrible coming to Cottingley and wartime and black bread and sleeping all crammed up with Elsie in the attic". Cooper, *The Case of the Cottingley Fairies*, 171.

walk. The recognition of their existence will jolt the material twentieth-century mind out of its heavy ruts in the mud, and will make it admit that there is a glamour and a mystery to life. Having discovered this, the world will not find it so difficult to accept that spiritual message supported by physical facts which has already been so convincingly put before it. (*Coming*, 58)

This is a curious passage. Those "ruts in the mud" come from the familiar iconography of the Western Front, and of the Great War that was the most fatal consequence of the false turn taken by the "material twentieth-century mind". The fairies are considered at first as just another rural amenity, lending extra charm to the enjoyment of the countryside. But a sentence later, inevitably they have been recruited in the great struggle against materialism, preparing the way for the spiritual revolution to come, and the great change of heart which would accompany general acceptance of the spiritual message, "supported by physical facts", which Conan Doyle had now begun to preach all over the world. And it might be no coincidence that the fairies had come to light at the same time as the worldwide Spiritualist mission was afoot. Proof of one kind of psychic phenomenon would hasten acceptance of another kind, and this no doubt was all part of the plan of "our friends beyond", "those wise entities who are conducting this campaign from the other side" (*Coming*, 99, 98). Cottingley was the second front in the spirit wars.

While the fairies seemed then to have a part to play in spiritual geopolitics—and almost everything in Conan Doyle's late practice, his writings and his activism, has to be seen in the context of that urgent and overarching theme—they are also always for him an English phenomenon and a manifestation of a kind of Englishness. The fairies "appear to be our neighbours". They share the land; they were there before us. Fairies were local. This was part of the Theosophical orthodoxy about them. Gardner in the book adduces the authority of no less than the heavyweight Theosophical Bishop Leadbeater, for the knowledge that fairies in different parts of the world are distinguished not only by different colours but by different national characteristics. Leadbeater reported "with all the assurance of an actual observer" that Sicilian fairies, for example, are orange-and-purple or scarlet-and-gold, and are vivacious and rollicking, as you would expect of Mediterranean folk, while the wistful grey-and-green creatures of Brittany are much more sedate (*Coming*, 189).[85]

---

[85] Leadbeater reports sighting fairies as far afield as Java, the plains of the Dakotas, and Scotland. It may be guessed that he visited all these locations on his travels in the astral body.

But for Conan Doyle there was a deep reassurance in the fact that his country was revealed as the dwelling-place of these charming and innocent indigenes, his invisible neighbours. Cottingley was not just an old-world country landscape, but something like a counter-culture, in which a harmless, delicate, costumed life was pursued, entirely at odds with the England that was coming into being elsewhere, in industrial towns, on European battlefields, and in the greedy and heartless metropolis. This alternative life had become knowable in an England that had little stake in the rush of modernity, and was in most ways the opposite of the metropolitan busyness and the specialized knowledges of professional society. Its location was provincial rural England, in a northern village, a pocket that seemed still relatively untouched by the headlong changes of modernity, and among people of a respectable artisanal class, a family uninterested in personal enrichment or celebrity; in a conjunction between those thoroughly disadvantaged in social capital—females, children, amateurs (what could be more amateur than a girl?)—and a miraculous population of shy, childlike, picturesque, but puny creatures coming out to play. This weightless and innocent world seemed to carry the chance of redemption for that heavy, sluggish, demoralized post-war England, its unknowing neighbour. It had an almost ineffable value, but its images were not for sale.

If this seems too portentous a significance to lay on something as slight and silly as the affair of the fairy photographs, it is useful to put the case in the context of the larger discourse of the study of folklore and autoethnography which is generally agreed to form a part of a broad reconsideration of questions of national identity, and of what was authentically indigenous, forced upon the English late in the nineteenth century. And to be sure, the moment we recall Conan Doyle's Irish heritage, a yet more startling context becomes visible. Writers of the Irish Literary Revival, under the leadership of W. B. Yeats and Lady Gregory, had been assiduously collecting and adding to Irish fairy lore since the 1880s, and doing so in the belief, as Diane Purkiss has it, that it was "a distinctive, special feature of Irish culture that could be used to give Ireland a separate and meaningful national identity, at a time when Ireland was struggling to free itself from British rule".[86] Yeats's fairies (and his giants and heroes of Hibernian legend) are, or become, a

---

[86] Purkiss, *Troublesome Things*, 293–4. The whole discussion of "Fairies of the Celtic Twilight" (293–303) is of interest.

weapon in his campaign to distinguish and then emancipate Celtic Ireland from the imperial culture of Great Britain; he brings them back, represents them, from an indigenous past that owes nothing to the centuries of British domination.[87] We can recognize this as an example, often repeated in postcolonial contexts, of cultural retrieval and what has been called structural nostalgia: inherited (to some extent invented) cultural capital is deployed as a way of resisting a hegemonic occupying power and building an independent national identity.[88] In Yeats's case, the Celtic supernatural—and, of course, his spiritualist and psychic practice, the Rosicrucianism and the Golden Dawn and the symbolic scheme of *A Vision* and all the rest—is deployed against another, related enemy: the materialistic, calculating, urban, philistine, priest-ridden, bourgeois culture which he had always loathed and which, as he saw it, kept Ireland firmly in its deadly clutches even after the British had gone. This is where we can make the strongest link with Conan Doyle, who identified and championed Cottingley as a version of England—simple, natural, authentic—to set against and perhaps redeem the spiritual death of modern England. In this way Cottingley came to perform the double critical and redemptive functions that belong to pastoral.

Finally, invoking the postcolonial can give us a further perspective on Conan Doyle and the fairies. It did not escape his notice that the world that made the fairies possible, or at least visible, was one quite different from his own. Elsie Wright and Frances Griffiths were northern, provincial, board-school-educated, teenage females. Their fairies were indigenous to a very small locality, diaphanous, childlike, unworldly. Conan Doyle and Gardner were none of these things. Gardner the expert on elementals, and Sir Arthur the celebrity writer, both well-travelled lecturers, coming north from London to inspect the phenomenon and publish their report on it, must have seemed to the locals, as they were, beings of a different order. No fairies ever appeared to them. Sympathetic, kindly, and eager though he was,

---

[87] There were fairies in the English tradition, Yeats conceded, but they were probably appropriated from elsewhere: "Shakespeare found his Mab, and probably his Puck, and one knows not how much else of his faery kingdom, in Celtic legend." W. B. Yeats, "The Celtic Element in Literature" (1902), in *Essays and Introductions* (London: Macmillan, 1961), 173–88; at 185–6. But Yeats, like Conan Doyle, derived many of his ideas about the Celtic imagination from Matthew Arnold's *The Study of Celtic Literature* (1867).

[88] For "structural nostalgia", see Michael Herzfeld, *Cultural Intimacy: Social Poetics in the Nation-State*, 2nd edn. (New York: Routledge, 2005), 147–82.

Conan Doyle belonged to that modern world of scientific knowledge, technical materialism, and brisk masculine affairs far more closely than he ever could to the sensitive, feminine, lyrical, simple domain captured in the photographs. There is a particular poignancy—with an edge of the grotesque, to be sure—about the intrusion of this big powerful gentleman from London into the Wright household at Cottingley, and the charming little valley (as Gardner called it) behind the house. To the student of colonial literature—or indeed of anthropological writing—the situation has its analogues. For the recorder and celebrant of a traditional local culture may at the same time be the unwitting bearer of that culture's destruction, the harbinger of the whole panoply of modernity whose absence gave the local culture its character and charm.

Conan Doyle felt that, like Columbus, he was involved in a discovery of momentous proportions. "When Columbus knelt in prayer upon the edge of America, what prophetic eye saw all that a new continent might do to affect the destinies of the world?" (*Coming*, 58). Conan Doyle was certain that the European settlement of the Americas would have, in the long term, a beneficent effect on the destinies of the world. But no one could deny that, from the point of view of the indigenous people of the "new" continents, the arrival of Columbus was a catastrophe. Conan Doyle himself had come from the modern world with the best of intentions, to learn, praise, and report. But could the phenomenon that so beguiled him survive his attentions?

We also seem to be on the edge of a new continent, separated not by oceans but by subtle and surmountable psychic conditions. I look at the prospect with awe. May those little creatures suffer from the contact and some Las Casas bewail their ruin! If so, it would be an evil day when the world defined their existence. (*Coming*, 58)[89]

The Challenger expedition to the Lost World, also undertaken to verify some disputed photographic evidence, and which led to the extermination of the indigenous creatures of the plateau, was another precedent. The fairies might offer a reproach to the grossness of modernity, but what if their alternative culture was too frail to withstand contact with the materialistic twentieth century? After the publication

---

[89] Bartolomé de Las Casas was the sixteenth-century Spanish priest who campaigned against the mistreatment of the natives of the New World at the hands of Spanish settlers. I assume the Conan Doyle text ought to read "May those little creatures not suffer, etc."

of Conan Doyle's first article about them in the *Strand*, fairies were never again photographed at Cottingley. The spiritual change Conan Doyle hoped they might help to hasten did not seem likely to happen. The nation did not recover its innocence. How could it? The ecological lesson, "that there were other orders of being which used the same earth and shared its blessings" (*Coming*, 150–1), was not learned.

At the age of 66, Conan Doyle moved his family for the last time, to Bignell Wood in the New Forest, a location which his spirit advisors had told him was favourable to psychic activity, but which was also deepest England, redolent of the national past. There, as Andrew Lycett reports, he was sometimes to be seen in the nearby woods, waiting for the fairies he was sure inhabited the place.[90] He carried a music box and a camera. But the New Forest fairies too were gone.

The new life

Concluding his history of the British campaign in France and Flanders, Conan Doyle had contemplated a scene of exhaustion and ruin.

He [the historian] lays down his pen at last with the deep conviction that the final results of this great convulsion are meant to be spiritual rather than material, and that upon an enlightened recognition of this depends the future history of mankind. Not to change rival frontiers, but to mould the hearts and spirits of men—there lies the explanation and the justification of all that we have endured.[91]

The system that left seven million dead on the battlefields must be "rotten to the core", he went on, but if the true message of the war were mastered, then 1914 might be regarded as "the end of the dark ages and the start of that upward path which leads away from personal or national selfishness towards the City Beautiful upon the distant hills".[92] I have argued that it was the failure symbolized by the war, and his belief in the need for a new spiritual life, that licensed the radicalism of his later years. But as the post-war decade drew on, there was little objective evidence of that hoped-for change of heart. If the Jazz Age did usher in

---

[90] Lycett, *Conan Doyle*, 424.
[91] ACD, *The British Campaign in France and Flanders*, vi: *July to November 1918*, 169.
[92] ACD, *The British Campaign in France and Flanders*, vi. 169.

a new morality, it was one that was profoundly uncongenial to Conan Doyle—"contrary to the very core of his character", as Martin Booth puts it.[93] As for spiritual beliefs, Conan Doyle might have anticipated the question put by T. S. Eliot on the threshold of a second war: "Was our society, which had always been so assured of its superiority and rectitude, so confident of its unexamined premises, assembled round anything more permanent than a congeries of banks, insurance companies, and industries, and had it any beliefs more essential than a belief in compound interest and the maintenance of dividends?"[94]

As old age approached, Conan Doyle's world became at once wider and narrower. These were the years of his tireless travels around the world—or, strictly speaking, around Greater Britain, the English-speaking world—to lecture on Spiritualism and rally the faithful. But while he remained to the end a vigorous and aggressive promoter of his beliefs, he was disappointed that truths which, to him, were not only obvious but had been manifestly and repeatedly demonstrated, should still fail to convince the majority of mankind. He increasingly sought the company of spiritually like-minded friends, and began to lose patience with what he called "controversy with bumptious and ignorant people" (M&A, 405). In 1925 he founded the Psychic Book-shop and Library in Victoria Street in London, which maintained a library, and a Press, which published in March 1927 the volume called *Pheneas Speaks*. This is a record of "home-circle communications" (*Pheneas*, 5). Like many Spiritualists, Conan Doyle with his second wife Jean and their three children held séances at home without a professional medium, and (like W. B. Yeats) he had been delighted to discover that his wife had the gift of automatic writing. In this way they were able to communicate with friends and relations who had passed away, and at the end of 1922 Pheneas, Conan Doyle's spirit guide, came through. In 1924 the writing mediumship changed to semi-trance inspirational talking. *Pheneas Speaks* records some of these messages from beyond, from the spirits of the departed, and increasingly from Pheneas himself, who described himself as "the vibrant link between you and God" (*Pheneas*, 167).

It would have been pleasing to finish this study with a more enjoy-able text. But *Pheneas Speaks* does give a remarkable and unique picture

---

[93] Booth, *The Doctor, the Detective, and Arthur Conan Doyle*, 334.
[94] T. S. Eliot, *The Idea of a Christian Society* (London: Faber and Faber, 1939), 64.

of Conan Doyle's world, as it was and as he would have wished it, in the last years of his life. It continues that practice of representation and transformation that began with his earliest stories.

First, in its practice and in the spirit texts that it produced, the circle was a reconfiguration of the family. Of the children of Conan Doyle's first marriage, Kingsley was dead and Marie found her father's Spiritualist activities an embarrassment.[95] His second family was more amenable to his shaping hand. In the circle, his wife Jean is elevated from household and child-rearing duties to a position of great importance: traffic with the other world literally flows through her (Conan Doyle had no psychic powers of his own).[96] As we have seen, mediumship often empowered women and the young, if temporarily; but while mediumship could be subversive of patriarchal divisions and norms, as Jenny Hazelgrove has argued, Spiritualist discourse also frequently contained the female medium within traditional images of femininity.[97] So while Jean was the focus of the home circle (as of the home), the greater part of her function was to enable masculine business and conversation, the spirits communicating with her husband through her. The three children, aged 13, 11, and 9 when the sessions began, are adjunct to this adult activity. Occasionally the Control sends them messages appropriate to their age, but their place within the family circle, as illustrated by the photograph in the book's frontispiece, is subordinate and bound in, as catechumens or novices.

Beyond this, one of the functions of the spirit messages is to make over the whole family, and household, in a general reconciliation.[98] The spirits of Conan Doyle's mother and his brother-in-law E.W. Hornung are heard from, both of them now naturally apologetic about their scepticism, while alive, on the question of spirit communication.

[95] See Lycett, *Conan Doyle*, 381.

[96] There is a case to be made for the Pheneas communications actually conveying Jean Conan Doyle's own wishes on certain domestic and travel questions. "After years in her husband's shadow, spiritualism had given Jean a role apart from mere housekeeping. Once she had hoped to sing for a living; now, through Pheneas, she could articulate whatever she desired." Lycett, *Conan Doyle*, 409.

[97] See Hazelgrove, *Spiritualism and British Society Between the Wars*, 6. For women and mediumship, see also Marlene Trump, *Altered States: Sex, Nation, Drugs, and Self-Transformation in Victorian Spiritualism* (New York: SUNY Press, 2006), and Alex Owen, *The Darkened Room*.

[98] Like the portrait of Thomas More and his family by Holbein which hangs in the National Portrait Gallery in London, *Pheneas Speaks* contrives to bring together relatives both living and dead into a single harmonious scene.

Kingsley Conan Doyle, who died of pneumonia in 1918, makes contact to say, "We are a great party, all one and so happy" (*Pheneas*, 23). Earlier divisions and dissensions are dissolved; the great Conan Doyle theme of reconciliation is extended beyond the grave to announce the healing of both family and religious differences. "All the uncles and all the other Catholic relatives are very much in sympathy with you now in your work," Conan Doyle is assured (*Pheneas*, 33). The family is a spirit community and the spirit world is like a family. "I love being with you," Pheneas tells them. "I am one of the family in the home circle" (*Pheneas*, 87). A very conspicuous absentee is Conan Doyle's first wife Touie who had died in 1906: as *The Land of Mist* explained, each soul has only one spiritual mate. Pheneas and the spirits had advised the family to move to Bignell Wood on the edge of the New Forest because of the benign spiritual vibrations of the place, but they are promised that there is a reproduction of the New Forest on the other side too, but "without any ugly elements" (*Pheneas*, 84–5)—it has more flowers, no ugly buildings, and no motor cars to disturb the peace, and much is made of the beautiful home that the spirits are preparing there for the family. In quite simple and transparent ways, Spiritualism goes about its work of envisaging and guaranteeing a utopian culture at the level of family and domestic life. It is a task that frequently and cruelly exposes the limits of the imagination and language of the ageing Conan Doyle (or Jean, or Pheneas and the spirits): but this is, after all, another instance of the way Spiritualist language and practice is always haunted by the banal. "Your eyes have never seen any form or colour so lovely as your home [being prepared in the afterlife]—beauty, peace, sweetness, flowers, nature, sunshine, all vibrating with golden light" (*Pheneas*, 121).

If this reconfiguration of domestic life reflects the shrinking of Conan Doyle's world in his final years, Pheneas has another set of subjects that connects him to the wider sphere of world—indeed universal—affairs. Pheneas introduces himself as an Arabian who lived thousands of years ago near the Abrahamic city of Ur in Mesopotamia (Jean's own spirit guide was called Julius). He has a busy life on the other side. From time to time he mentions current affairs—natural disasters, the League of Nations, the General Strike of 1926. Pheneas seems to be some kind of spiritual diplomat; he travels to trouble spots: Australia, Persia, the South Seas, Kamchatka, Dalmatia. "I have been in the East all day. We had some evil vibrations to dissipate, and we have done it"

(*Pheneas*, 125). In the other world, he reveals, there exist tasks, hierarchies, organization, research, a reporting system, even a Central Committee (*Pheneas*, 132). It sounds a little like the projects for world government which were born out of the internecine folly of the Great War, championed by the likes of H. G. Wells. At one point Pheneas confides that there was an evil strong material influence in Central Africa, but they had built a wall round it to contain it. Soon they were going to have a conference on the condition of Italy. "Who?" asks Conan Doyle, and is told: "Those who have been deputed to organize, control, guide, and prepare the world" (*Pheneas*, 152). On the other side, many people are working for "human change and upliftment" (*Pheneas*, 126). Pheneas says that England is important in the spiritual scheme of things. "England is to be the centre to which all humanity will turn. She is to be the beacon of light in this dark, dark world.... England leads the world, and if England quickly accepts this then it paves the way for every other country" (*Pheneas*, 79, 80).

And so on. It is clear that the main function of this spirit communication is to provide support and encouragement and hope to Conan Doyle in the many issues—domestic, political, missionary—that preoccupied him, and in so doing to enable him, and perhaps his readers, to envisage their lives and creation itself under the benign protection of an army, an organization, and a government of spirits. England might have failed to heed his warnings and reform itself as a spiritual nation. But the smaller society of the family, and the greater one of humankind, past and present and future, were firmly on the right path. And if people did prove incapable of making the changes required, the spirits would see to it that they happened nonetheless. Defending Pheneas from reproach by the orthodox, Conan Doyle spelled out his message.

He proclaims that the world must prepare itself for great changes, physical and spiritual, all leading to a higher level of human existence, which would seem, so far as we can trace it, to imply a more equal distribution of wealth, greater simplicity of life, far greater humanity both to fellow creatures and to animals, abstinence from flesh diet, and the end of all dogmatic religions, forms, and rituals, coming direct from constant contact with the spirit world, so that the two spheres will act in close harmony and co-operation. Such is the future as Pheneas foresees it. (*Pheneas*, 214–15)

Even Conan Doyle's own preference for a plain and serviceable style was vindicated. "Long words don't matter," Pheneas tells him. "We use short ones over here, which are better" (*Pheneas*, 113). Since all these were messages from beyond the human world, Conan Doyle could claim to be dispensing knowledge of a supremely authoritative kind. But for just the same reason, it was teaching that almost nobody was able to take seriously.

In his last years Conan Doyle understood that there was a limit to what he could do, for all his great energy and efforts, to accomplish the changes foreseen by his spirit guide. But they had been prophesied by a great soul as a matter of knowledge, and were sure to come to pass; they could be left in the hands of the spirits. Still, he continued to struggle manfully both to interpret and to change the more and more bewildering world around him. And if this changing world frustrated and disappointed and perhaps confused him in his later years, his practice became increasingly focused on the world beyond. As for what awaited him and those he loved there, he had Pheneas's word for this also. The future too was knowable. "There is no death. There is a lovely portal with 'Welcome' written over it" (*Pheneas*, 177).

Bibliography

WORKS BY ARTHUR CONAN DOYLE

The Adventures of Sherlock Holmes (1892), ed. Richard Lancelyn Green (Oxford: Oxford University Press, 1993).

The Annotated Lost World, ed. Roy Pilot and Alvin Rodin (Indianapolis: Wessex Press, 1996).

Arthur Conan Doyle: A Life in Letters, ed. John Lellenberg, Daniel Stashower, and Charles Foley (London: Harper, 2007).

Beyond the City: The Idyll of a Suburb (1892) (Bloomington, Ind.: Gaslight Publications, 1982).

The British Campaign in France and Flanders, 6 vols. (1916–20) (Newcastle upon Tyne: Cambridge Scholars, 2009).

The Case for Spirit Photography [with others] (London: Hutchinson, 1922).

The Case of Oscar Slater (London: Hodder and Stoughton, 1912).

The Case-Book of Sherlock Holmes (1927), ed. W. W. Robson (Oxford: Oxford University Press, 1993).

The Coming of the Fairies (1922) (Lincoln, Nebr.: University of Nebraska Press, 2006).

The Complete Brigadier Gerard, ed. Owen Dudley Edwards (Edinburgh: Canongate Classics, 1995).

The Crime of the Congo (London: Hutchinson, 1909).

Dangerous Work: Diary of an Arctic Adventure, ed. Jon Lellenberg and Daniel Stashower (London: The British Library, 2012).

The Doings of Raffles Haw (London: Cassell, 1892).

"Dr. Koch and his Cure", *Review of Reviews*, 2 (1890), 552–6.

A Duet with an Occasional Chorus (London: Grant Richards, 1899).

The Edge of the Unknown (London: John Murray, 1930).

"An essay upon the vasomotor changes in tabes dorsalis and on the influence which is exerted by the sympathetic nervous system in that disease", Edinburgh University MD thesis, 1885 (Edinburgh Research Archive, <http://hdl.handle.net/1842/418>).

The Firm of Girdlestone (London: Chatto & Windus, 1890).

The Great Boer War (1900), 2nd edn. (London: Thomas Nelson, 1908).

The Great Shadow and Beyond the City (Bristol: J. W. Arrowsmith, 1893).

The Green Flag and Other Stories of War and Sport (London: Smith, Elder, 1900).

His Last Bow (1917), ed. Owen Dudley Edwards (Oxford: Oxford University Press, 1993).

The History of Spiritualism, 2 vols. (London: Cassell, 1926).

The Hound of the Baskervilles (1902), ed. W. W. Robson (Oxford: Oxford University Press, 1993).

The Land of Mist (London: Hutchinson, 1926).

Lecture on Spiritualism (Worthing: *The Worthing Gazette*, 1919).

Letters to the Press, ed. John Michael Gibson and Richard Lancelyn Green (Iowa City: University of Iowa Press, 1986).

"Life and Death in the Blood", *Good Words* (March 1883), 178–81.

"Life on a Greenland Whaler", *Strand Magazine*, 13 (January 1897), 16–25.

"The Lord of Falconbridge", *Strand Magazine*, 38 (August 1909), 139–51.

The Lost World (1912), ed. Ian Duncan (Oxford: Oxford University Press, 1998).

The Maracot Deep and Other Stories (London: John Murray, 1929).

The Memoirs of Sherlock Holmes (1893), ed. Christopher Roden (Oxford: Oxford University Press, 1993).

Memories and Adventures (1924, repr. with additions and deletions 1930) (Oxford: Oxford University Press, 1989).

Micah Clarke (London: Longmans, Green, 1889).

The Mystery of Cloomber (London: Ward and Downey, 1889).

The Narrative of John Smith, ed. John Lellenberg, Daniel Stashower, and Rachel Foss (London: The British Library, 2011).

The New Revelation (Toronto: Hodder and Stoughton, 1918).

Our African Winter (London: John Murray, 1929).

The Parasite (1894) (New York: Harper & Brothers, 1895).

A Petition to the Prime Minister on behalf of Roger Casement, by Sir Arthur Conan Doyle and Others, privately printed, n.d. (1916).

Pheneas Speaks (London: Psychic Review and Bookshop, 1927).

"Preface" to Christina Sinclair Bremner, *Divorce and Morality* (London: Frank Palmer, 1912), 7–15.

The Return of Sherlock Holmes (1905), ed. Richard Lancelyn Green (Oxford: Oxford University Press, 1993).

Rodney Stone (London: Smith, Elder, 1896).

Round the Red Lamp: Being Facts and Fancies of Medical Life, 2nd edn. (London: Methuen, 1894).

The Sign of the Four (1890), ed. Christopher Roden (Oxford: Oxford University Press, 1993).

The Stark Munro Letters (London: Longmans, Green, 1895).

The Story of Mr. George Edalji (1907), ed. Richard and Molly Whittington-Egan (London: Grey House Books, 1985).

A Study in Scarlet (1888), ed. Owen Dudley Edwards (Oxford: Oxford University Press, 1993).

Through the Magic Door (London: Smith, Elder, 1907).

The Tragedy of the Korosko (London: Smith, Elder, 1898).

The Valley of Fear (1915), ed. Owen Dudley Edwards (Oxford: Oxford University Press, 1993).

The Vital Message (London: Hodder and Stoughton, 1919).

"The Voice of Science", *Strand Magazine*, 1 (March 1891), 312–17.

The Wanderings of a Spiritualist (London: Collins, 1922).

The War in South Africa: Its Causes and Conduct (1902) (Toronto: George N. Morang, 1902).

The White Company, 3 vols. (London: Smith, Elder, 1891).

OTHER WORKS CITED

Accardo, Pasquale. *Diagnosis and Detection: The Medical Iconography of Sherlock Holmes* (London: Associated University Press, 1987).

Adams, James Eli. *Dandies and Desert Saints: Styles of Victorian Manhood* (Ithaca, NY: Cornell University Press, 1995).

Arata, Stephen. *Fictions of Loss in the Victorian Fin de Siècle* (Cambridge: Cambridge University Press, 1996).

Armstrong, David. "Bodies of Knowledge/Knowledge of Bodies", in Colin Jones and Roy Porter (eds.), *Reassessing Foucault: Power, Medicine, and the Body* (London: Routledge, 1994), 17–27.

Armstrong, Tim. *Modernism: A Cultural History* (Cambridge: Polity, 2005).

Aronson, Theo. *The Kaisers* (London: Cassell, 1971).

Bailey, Victor. "The Metropolitan Police, the Home Office and the Threat of Outcast London", in Victor Bailey (ed.), *Policing and Punishment in Nineteenth Century Britain* (London: Croom Helm, 1981), 94–125.

Barnes, Julian. *Arthur and George* (London: Jonathan Cape, 2005).

Barsham, Diana. *Arthur Conan Doyle and the Meaning of Masculinity* (Aldershot: Ashgate, 2000).

Belloc, Hilaire. *The Modern Traveller* (London: Edward Arnold, 1898).

Belsey, Catherine. "Sherlock Holmes", in *Critical Practice* (London: Methuen, 1980), 109–17.

Besant, Walter. "Literature as a Career", *Forum*, 13 (March–August 1892), 693–708.

Birley, Derek. *Sport and the Making of Britain* (Manchester: Manchester University Press, 1993).

Blathwayt, Raymond. "A Talk with Dr Conan Doyle", *The Bookman*, 2/8 (May 1892), 50–1, in Harold Orel (ed.), *Sir Arthur Conan Doyle: Interviews and Recollections* (Basingstoke: Macmillan, 1991), 51–76.

Bloor, D. U. "The Rise of the General Practitioner in the Nineteenth Century", *Journal of the Royal College of General Practitioners*, 28 (May 1978), 288–91.

Boddy, Kasia. "'A Straight Left against a Slogging Ruffian': National Boxing Styles in the Years Preceding the First World War", *Journal of Historical Sociology*,

24/4, Special Issue on Sports and History, ed. Alan Tomlinson and Christopher Young (December 2011), 428–50.

Booth, Martin. *The Doctor, the Detective and Arthur Conan Doyle: A Biography of Arthur Conan Doyle* (London: Hodder and Stoughton, 1997).

Brailsford, Dennis. *British Sport: A Social History* (Cambridge: Lutterworth Press, 1992).

Bramwell, J. Milne. *Hypnotism* (London: Grant Richards, 1903).

Brantlinger, Patrick. *Rule of Darkness: British Literature and Imperialism 1830–1914* (Ithaca, NY: Cornell University Press, 1988).

Brock, William H. *Science for All: Studies in the History of Victorian Science and Education* (Aldershot: Variorum, 1996).

Brown, Nicola. *Fairies in Nineteenth-Century Art and Literature* (Cambridge: Cambridge University Press, 2001).

Carlyle, Thomas. *A Carlyle Reader*, ed. G. B. Tennyson (Cambridge: Cambridge University Press, 1969).

Carter, Henry (ed.). *The Church and the Drink Evil* (London: Epworth Press, 1922).

"Character Sketch: Dr. Robert Koch", *Review of Reviews*, 2 (1890), 547–51.

Collingwood, R. G. *The Idea of History* (Oxford: Clarendon Press, 1946).

Collini, Stefan. *Public Moralists: Political Thought and Intellectual Life in Britain 1850–1930* (Oxford: Clarendon, 1991).

Colls, Robert, and Dodd, Philip (eds.). *Englishness: Politics and Culture 1880–1920* (London: Croom Helm, 1986).

Conrad, Joseph. *The Collected Letters of Joseph Conrad*, i: *1861–1897*, ed. Frederick R. Karl and Laurence Davies (Cambridge: Cambridge University Press, 1983).

—— *Heart of Darkness* (1902), Norton Critical Edition, ed. Robert Kimbrough, 3rd edn. (New York: Norton, 1988).

Cooper, Joe. *The Case of the Cottingley Fairies* (London: Simon and Schuster, 1990).

Costello, Peter. *Conan Doyle Detective* (London: Constable and Robinson, 2006).

Crawford, Dorothy H. *Deadly Companions: How Microbes Shaped our History* (Oxford: Oxford University Press, 2007).

Dalby, J. Thomas. "Sherlock Holmes's Cocaine Habit", *ACD: Journal of the Arthur Conan Doyle Society*, 4 (1993), 12–15.

Daly, Nicholas. *Modernism, Romance and the Fin de Siècle* (Cambridge: Cambridge University Press, 1999).

Daniel, Thomas M. *Captain of Death: The Story of Tuberculosis* (Rochester, NY: University of Rochester Press, 1997).

Darwin, Charles. *On the Origin of Species* (1859) (Harmondsworth: Penguin, 1968).

Digby, Anne. *The Evolution of British General Practice 1850–1948* (Oxford: Oxford University Press, 1999).

——— *Making a Medical Living: Doctors and Patients in the English Market for Medicine 1720–1911* (Cambridge: Cambridge University Press, 1994).

Dirda, Michael. *On Conan Doyle* (Princeton: Princeton University Press, 2012).

Dodd, Philip. "Englishness and the National Culture", in Robert Colls and Philip Dodd (eds.), *Englishness: Politics and Culture 1880–1920* (London: Croom Helm, 1986), 1–28.

Dolin, Kieran. *Fiction and the Law: Legal Discourse in Victorian and Modernist Literature* (Cambridge: Cambridge University Press, 1999).

Dowling, Andrew. *Manliness and the Male Novelist in Victorian Literature* (Aldershot: Ashgate, 2001).

Early, Gerald. *The Culture of Bruising: Essays on Prizefighting, Literature and Modern American Culture* (Hopewell, NJ: Ecco Press. 1994).

Edwards, Owen Dudley. "Conan Doyle as Historian: A Starting Point", *ACD: Journal of the Arthur Conan Doyle Society*, 1/2 (March 1990), 95–111.

——— "The Mystery of the Mystery of Cloomber", *ACD: Journal of the Arthur Conan Doyle Society*, 2/2 (Autumn 1991), 101–33.

——— *The Quest for Sherlock Holmes: A Biographical Study of Arthur Conan Doyle* (Harmondsworth: Penguin, 1984).

Eliot, George. *The George Eliot Letters*, vi: *1874–1877*, ed. Gordon S. Haight (New Haven: Yale University Press, 1955).

Eliot, T. S. *The Idea of a Christian Society* (London: Faber and Faber, 1939).

Empson, William. *Some Versions of Pastoral* (London: Chatto, 1950).

Emsley, Clive. *The English Police: A Political and Social History* (London: Longman, 1996).

Engelhardt, Carol Marie. "Victorian Masculinity and the Virgin Mary", in Andrew Bradstock, Sean Gill, Anne Hogan, and Sue Morgan (eds.), *Masculinity and Spirituality in Victorian Culture* (Basingstoke: Macmillan, 2000), 44–57.

Farmer, Lindsay. "Arthur and Oscar (and Sherlock): The Reconstructive Trial and the 'Hermeneutics of Suspicion'", *International Commentary on Evidence*, 5/1, article 4 (<http://www.bepress.com/ice/vol5/iss1/art4>: accessed 25 May 2011).

"The First English Case of Lupus Treated by Koch's Method", *BMJ* (22 November 1890), 1197.

Fistiana; or, The Oracle of the Ring. Comprising a Defence of British Boxing; a Brief History of Pugilism, from the Earliest Ages to the Present Period; Practical Instructions for Training; Together with Chronological Tables of Prize Battles, from 1780 to 1840 Inclusive, Alphabetically Arranged with the Issue of Each Event. Scientific Hints on Sparring &c. &c. &c. By the Editor of Bell's Life in London (London: Wm. Clement, 1841).

Fitzwilliam, Mary. " 'Mr Harrison's Confessions': A Study of the General Practitioner's Social and Professional Dis-ease in Mid-Nineteenth Century England", *Gaskell Society Journal*, 12 (1998), 28–36.

Flint, Kate. *The Woman Reader 1837–1914* (Oxford: Clarendon Press, 1993).

Frank, Lawrence. *Victorian Detective Fiction and the Nature of Evidence: The Scientific Investigations of Poe, Dickens, and Doyle* (Basingstoke: Palgrave, 2003).

Frazer, Sir James George. *The Golden Bough: A Study in Magic and Religion* (London: Macmillan, 1922).

Freud, Sigmund. *The Complete Letters of Sigmund Freud to Wilhelm Fliess, 1887–1904*, ed. Geoffrey Moussaieff Masson (Cambridge, Mass.: Belknap Press of Harvard University Press, 1985).

——"Fragments of an Analysis of a Case of Hysteria ('Dora')", in *Case Histories 1* (Harmondsworth: Penguin, 1977), 29–164.

Furse, Ralph. *Aucuparius: Recollections of a Recruiting Officer* (London: Oxford University Press, 1962).

Furst, Lilian R. (ed.). *Medical Progress and Social Reality: A Reader in Nineteenth-Century Medicine and Literature* (Albany, NY: State University of New York Press, 2000).

Galton, Francis. *English Men of Science: Their Nature and Nurture* (1874), 2nd edn. (London: Frank Cass, 1970).

Gibson, Andrew. *Joyce's Revenge: History, Politics and Aesthetics in* Ulysses (Oxford: Oxford University Press, 2002).

Ginzburg, Carlo. *Clues, Myths and the Historical Method*, trans. John and Anne C. Tedeschi (Baltimore: Johns Hopkins University Press, 1989).

Gissing, George. *New Grub Street* (London: Smith, Elder, 1891).

Gosse, Philip Henry. *The Romance of Natural History* (London: James Nisbet, 1861).

Green, Martin. *Dreams of Adventure, Deeds of Empire* (London: Routledge and Kegan Paul, 1980).

Green, Richard Lancelyn, and Gibson, John Michael (eds.). *A Bibliography of A. Conan Doyle* (Oxford: Clarendon Press, 1984).

Gross, John. *The Rise and Fall of the Man of Letters* (London: Weidenfeld and Nicolson, 1969).

Haley, Bruce. *The Healthy Body and Victorian Culture* (Cambridge, Mass.: Harvard University Press, 1978).

Harris, José. *Private Lives, Public Spirit: Britain 1870–1914* (Harmondsworth: Penguin, 1994).

Hart, Ernest. *Hypnotism, Mesmerism and the New Witchcraft* (London: Smith, Elder, 1896).

Haynes, Renée. *The Society for Psychical Research 1882–1982: A History* (London: Macdonald, 1982).

Hazelgrove, Jenny. *Spiritualism and British Society Between the Wars* (Manchester: Manchester University Press, 2000).

Hazlitt, William. *Selected Writings*, ed. Ronald Blythe (Harmondsworth: Penguin, 1985).

Herzfeld, Michael. *Cultural Intimacy: Social Poetics in the Nation-State*, 2nd edn. (New York: Routledge, 2005).

Hobson, J. A. *The War in South Africa: Its Causes and Effects* (London: James Nisbet, 1900).

Hochschild, Adam. *King Leopold's Ghost: A Story of Greed, Terror and Heroism in Colonial Africa* (London: Macmillan, 1999).

Hodge, Harry, and Hodge, James H. (eds.). *Famous Trials*, introd. John Mortimer (Harmondsworth: Penguin, 1984).

Hodgson, Richard, et al. "Report of the Committee Appointed to Investigate Phenomena Connected with the Theosophical Society", *Proceedings of the Society for Psychical Research*, 3 (December 1885), 201–400.

Holt, Richard. *Sport and the British: A Modern History* (Oxford: Clarendon, 1989).

How, Harry. "A Day with Dr Conan Doyle", *Strand Magazine*, 4 (August 1892), 182–8, in Harold Orel (ed.), *Sir Arthur Conan Doyle: Interviews and Recollections* (Basingstoke: Macmillan, 1991), 62–8.

Hurwitz, Brian. "Form and Representation in Clinical Case Reports", *Literature and Medicine*, 25/2 (Fall 2006), 216–40.

Huxley, T. H. "On the Method of Zadig", in *Collected Essays*, vol. iv (London: Macmillan, 1911), 1–23.

Huyssen, Andreas. *After the Great Divide: Modernism, Mass Culture, Postmodernism* (Bloomington, Ind.: Indiana University Press, 1986).

James, Henry. "The Art of Fiction", in *Partial Portraits* (London: Macmillan, 1884), 375–408.

Jones, Kelvin I. *Conan Doyle and the Spirits: The Spiritualist World of Sir Arthur Conan Doyle* (Wellingborough: Aquarian Press, 1989).

Joyce, Simon. *Capital Offences: Geographies of Class and Crime in Victorian London* (Charlottesville, Va.: University of Virginia Press, 2003).

Keating, Peter. *The Haunted Study: A Social History of the English Novel 1875–1914* (Athens, Oh.: Ohio University Press, 1986).

Keats, John. *The Letters of John Keats*, ed. Maurice Buxton Forman, 3rd edn. (London: Oxford University Press, 1948), 72.

Kerr, Douglas. *Eastern Figures: Orient and Empire in British Writing* (Hong Kong: Hong Kong University Press, 2008).

Kipling, Rudyard. *The Definitive Edition of Rudyard Kipling's Verse* (London: Hodder and Stoughton, 1940).

Knightley, Philip. *The First Casualty: From the Crimea to Vietnam: The War Correspondent as Hero, Propagandist, and Myth Maker* (London: Quartet, 1978).

Koch, Robert. "A Further Communication on a Remedy for Tuberculosis", *BMJ* (22 November 1890), 1193.

Kuhn, Thomas S. *The Structure of Scientific Revolutions* (Chicago: University of Chicago Press, 1962).

Kumar, Krishan. *The Making of English National Identity* (Cambridge: Cambridge University Press, 2003).

Kynaston, David. *WG's Birthday Party* (London: Bloomsbury, 2010).

Lang, Andrew. "Realism and Romance", *Contemporary Review*, 52 (July–December 1887), 683–93.

Lankester, E. Ray. *Extinct Animals* (London: Archibald Constable, 1909).

Lombroso-Ferrero, Gina. *Criminal Man According to the Classification of Cesare Lombroso* (1911) (Montclair, NJ: Patterson Smith, 1972).

Loudon, Irvine. *Medical Care and the General Practitioner 1750–1850* (Oxford: Clarendon Press, 1986).

Luckhurst, Roger. *The Invention of Telepathy 1870–1901* (Oxford: Oxford University Press, 2002).

Lukács, Georg. *The Historical Novel* (1937), trans. Hannah and Stanley Mitchell (Harmondsworth: Penguin, 1976).

Lycett, Andrew. *Arthur Conan Doyle: The Man Who Created Sherlock Holmes* (London: Weidenfeld and Nicholson, 2007).

McDonald, Peter D. "The Adventures of the Literary Agent: Conan Doyle, A. P. Watt, Holmes and *The Strand* in 1891", *ACD: Journal of the Arthur Conan Doyle Society*, 8 (1998), 17–27.

Maitland, F. W. *Justice and Police* (London: Macmillan, 1885).

Mangan, J. A. *Athleticism in the Victorian and Edwardian Public School* (Cambridge: Cambridge University Press, 1981).

—— *The Games Ethic and Imperialism: Aspects of the Diffusion of an Ideal* (Harmondsworth: Viking, 1986).

Maxwell, Richard. *The Historical Novel in Europe 1650–1950* (Cambridge: Cambridge University Press, 2009).

Mill, Robert Hugh. *The Record of the Royal Geographical Society 1830–1930* (London: Royal Geographical Society, 1930).

Miller, D. A. *The Novel and the Police* (Berkeley and Los Angeles: University of California Press, 1988).

Miller, Russell. *The Adventures of Arthur Conan Doyle* (London: Harvill Secker, 2008).

Moretti, Franco. *Atlas of the European Novel 1800–1900* (London: Verso, 1998).

—— *Signs Taken for Wonders* (London: NLB, 1983).

Morris, James. *Heaven's Command: An Imperial Progress* (Harmondsworth: Penguin, 1979).

Murtagh, Joseph. "George Eliot and the Rise of the Language of Expertise", *Novel: A Forum on Fiction*, 44/1 (2011), 88–105.

Myers, Frederic. *Human Personality and its Survival of Bodily Death* (London: Longmans, Green, 1903).

"Obituary, Sir Malcolm Morris, K.C.V.O., F.R.C.S.Ed", *BMJ* (1 March 1924), 407–9.

Oppenheim, Janet. *The Other World: Spiritualism and Psychical Research in England, 1850–1914* (Cambridge: Cambridge University Press, 1985).

Orel, Harold. "Conan Doyle's Sense of Justice", *ACD: Journal of the Arthur Conan Doyle Society*, 4 (1993), 128–33.

—— *The Historical Novel from Scott to Sabatini* (New York: St Martin's Press, 1995).

——(ed.). *Sir Arthur Conan Doyle: Interviews and Recollections* (Basingstoke: Macmillan, 1991).

Orwell, George. *Homage to Catalonia* (1938), in *The Complete Works of George Orwell*, ed. Peter Davison, 20 vols. (London: Secker and Warburg, 1998), vol. vi.

——"Marrakech" (1939), in *The Complete Works of George Orwell*, ed. Peter Davison, 20 vols. (London: Secker and Warburg, 1998), xi. 416–21.

Otis, Laura. *Membranes: Metaphors of Invasion in Nineteenth-Century Literature, Science and Politics* (Baltimore: Johns Hopkins University Press, 1999).

Owen, Alex. " 'Borderland Forms': Arthur Conan Doyle, Albion's Daughters, and the Politics of the Cottingley Fairies", *History Workshop Journal*, 38 (1994), 48–85.

——*The Darkened Room: Women, Power and Spiritualism in Late Victorian England* (London: Virago, 1989).

Owen, Wilfred. *Collected Letters*, ed. Harold Owen and John Bell (London: Oxford University Press, 1967).

Pancratia, or a History of Pugilism. Containing a full account of every battle of note from the time of Broughton and Slack, down to the present day. Interspersed with anecdotes of all the celebrated pugilists of this country; With an argumentative Proof, that Pugilism, considered as a Gymnic Exercise, demands the Admiration, and Patronage of every free State, being calculated to inspire manly Courage, and a Spirit of Independence—enabling us to resist Slavery at Home and Enemies from Abroad (London: W. Oxberry, 1812).

Perkin, Harold. *The Rise of Professional Society: England since 1880* (London: Routledge, 1990).

Poovey, Mary. "Forgotten Writers, Neglected Histories: Charles Reade and the Nineteenth-Century Transformation of the British Literary Field", *ELH* 72/2 (2004), 433–53.

Porter, Roy. *Disease, Medicine and Society in England 1550–1860*, 2nd edn. (Basingstoke: Macmillan, 1993).

Purkiss, Diane. *Troublesome Things: A History of Fairies and Fairy Stories* (London: Allen Lane, Penguin Press, 2000).

Rauch, Alan. *Useful Knowledge: The Victorians, Morality, and the March of Intellect* (Durham, NC: Duke University Press, 2001).

Rawlings, Philip. *Policing: A Short History* (Cullompton: Willan Publishing, 2002).

Robbins, Bruce. *Secular Vocations: Intellectuals, Professionalism, Culture* (London: Verso, 1993).

Roden, Christopher. "Conan Doyle and *The Strand Magazine*", *ACD: Journal of the Arthur Conan Doyle Society*, 2/2 (1991), 135–40.

Rodin, Alvin E., and Key, Jack D. (eds.). *Medical Casebook of Doctor Arthur Conan Doyle: From Practitioner to Sherlock Holmes and Beyond* (Malabar, Fla.: Robert E. Krieger, 1984).

Rose, Jonathan. *The Edwardian Temperament 1895–1919* (Athens, Oh.: Ohio University Press, 1986).

——and Anderson, Patricia J. (eds.). *British Literary Publishing House 1881–1965* (Detroit: Gale Research, 1991).

Rose, Nikolas. "Medicine, History and the Present", in Colin Jones and Roy Porter (eds.), *Reassessing Foucault: Power, Medicine and the Body* (London: Routledge, 1994), 48–72.

Santayana, George. *Soliloquies in England and Later Soliloquies* (London: Constable, 1922).

Sargent, Neil C. "Mys-Reading the Past in Detective Fiction and Law", *Law and Literature*, 22/2 (Summer 2010), 288–306.

Saunders, Frances Stonor. *Hawkwood: Diabolical Englishman* (London: Faber, 2004).

Sebeok, Thomas A., and Umiker-Sebeok, Jean. "You Know my Method: A Juxtaposition of Charles S. Pierce and Sherlock Holmes", in Umberto Eco and Thomas A. Sebeok (eds.), *The Sign of Three: Holmes, Dupin, Peirce* (Bloomington, Ind.: Indiana University Press, 1983), 11–54.

Seeley, John R. *The Expansion of England* (1883), ed. John Gross (Chicago: University of Chicago Press, 1971).

Senn, Alfred E. *Power, Politics and the Olympic Games* (Champaign, Ill.: Human Kinetics, 1999).

Sewell, J. S. N. *The Straight Left: being nine talks to boys who are about to leave their preparatory schools* (London: SPCK, 1928).

Shermer, Michael. *In Darwin's Shadow: The Life and Science of Alfred Russel Wallace* (Oxford: Oxford University Press, 2002).

Smith, Edgar W. "Up from the Needle", in Philip A. Shreffler (ed.), *Sherlock Holmes by Gas-Lamp: Highlights from the First Four Decades of the Baker Street Journal* (New York: Fordham University Press, 1989), 67–70.

Smith, R. Dixon. "Feminism and the Role of Women in Conan Doyle's Domestic Fiction", *ACD: Journal of the Arthur Conan Doyle Society*, 5 (1994), 50–60.

Snyder, Laura J. "Sherlock Holmes: Scientific Detective", *Endeavour*, 28/3 (September 2004), 104–8.

Spencer, Herbert. "The Factors of Social Evolution", in *On Social Evolution: Selected Writings*, ed. J. D. Y. Peel (Chicago: Chicago University Press, 1972), 121–33.

——"Re-barbarization", in *Facts and Comments* (London: Williams and Norgate, 1902), 122–33.

Spiers, Edward M. *The Army and Society 1815–1914* (London: Longman, 1980).

Spurgeon, C. H. *Fifty Most Remarkable Sermons* (London: Passmore and Alabaster, 1908).

Stashower, Daniel. *Teller of Tales: The Life of Arthur Conan Doyle* (London: Allen Lane, 1999).

Stavert, Geoffrey. *A Study in Southsea: The Unrevealed Life of Doctor Arthur Conan Doyle* (Portsmouth: Milestone, 1987).

Stead, W. T. *Methods of Barbarism* (London: Mowbray House, 1901).

Stevenson, Robert Louis. "A Gossip on Romance" (1882), in *R. L. Stevenson on Fiction*, ed. Glenda Norquay (Edinburgh: Edinburgh University Press, 1999), 51–64.

——"A Humble Remonstrance" (1884), in *R. L. Stevenson on Fiction*, ed. Glenda Norquay (Edinburgh: Edinburgh University Press, 1999), 80–91.

——"A Note on Realism" (1883), in *R. L. Stevenson on Fiction*, ed. Glenda Norquay (Edinburgh: Edinburgh University Press, 1999), 65–71.

Stoker, Bram. *Dracula* (1897) (Harmondsworth: Penguin, 1979).

Sussman, Herbert. *Victorian Masculinities: Manhood and Masculine Poetics in Early Victorian Literature and Art* (Cambridge: Cambridge University Press, 1995).

Taylor, David. *Crime, Policing and Punishment in England 1750–1914* (Basingstoke: Macmillan, 1998).

Telfer, Kevin. *Peter Pan's First Eleven: The Extraordinary Story of J. M. Barrie's Cricket Team* (London: Sceptre, 2010).

Tennyson, Alfred. *Tennyson: A Selected Edition*, ed. Christopher Ricks (London: Longman, 1969).

Thomas, Ronald R. *Detective Fiction and the Rise of Forensic Science* (Cambridge: Cambridge University Press, 1999).

——*Dreams of Authority: Freud and the Fictions of the Unconscious* (Ithaca, NY: Cornell University Press, 1990).

——"Specters of the Novel: *Dracula* and the Cinematic Afterlife of the Victorian Novel", *Nineteenth-Century Contexts*, 22 (2000), 77–102.

Thompson, Jon. *Fiction, Crime and Empire: Clues to Modernity and Postmodernism* (Urbana. Ill.: University of Illinois Press, 1993).

Todorov, Tzvetan. *The Poetics of Prose*, trans. Richard Howard (Oxford: Blackwell, 1977).

Toohey, Kristine, and Veal, A. J. *The Olympic Games: A Social Science Perspective* (Wallingford: CABI Publishing, 2000).

Trump, Marlene. *Altered States: Sex, Nation, Drugs, and Self-Transformation in Victorian Spiritualism* (New York: SUNY Press, 2006).

Tucker, Jennifer. "Photography as Witness, Detective, and Impostor: Visual Representation in Victorian Science", in Bernard Lightman (ed.), *Victorian Science in Context* (Chicago: University of Chicago Press, 1997), 378–408.

Tyndall, John. *Scientific Addresses* (1870) (Ann Arbor: University of Michigan Press, 1995).

Waller, Philip. *Writers, Readers, and Reputations: Literary Life in Britain 1870–1918* (Oxford: Oxford University Press, 2006).

Washington, Peter. *Madame Blavatsky's Baboon: Theosophy and the Emergence of the Western Guru* (London: Secker & Warburg, 1993).

Watson, J. R. "Soldiers and Saints: The Fighting Man and the Christian Life", in Andrew Bradstock, Sean Gill, Anne Hogan, and Sue Morgan (eds.), *Masculinity and Spirituality in Victorian Culture* (Basingstoke: Macmillan, 2000), 10–26.

Weber, Max. *Economy and Society* (1920), 2 vols, ed. Guenther Roth and Claus Wittich (Berkeley and Los Angeles: University of California Press, 1978).

Whitehead, John. "Gasconade: Conan Doyle's Brigadier Gerard", *ACD: Journal of the Arthur Conan Doyle Society*, 6 (1995), 103–11.

Williams, Raymond. *The Country and the City* (1973) (London: Hogarth Press, 1993).

Woolf, Virginia. "Modern Fiction" (1919), in *The Common Reader: First Series*, ed. Andrew McNeillie (London: Hogarth Press, 1984).

Wynne, Catherine. "Arthur Conan Doyle's Domestic Desires: Mesmerism, Mediumship and *Femmes Fatales*", in Martin Willis and Catherine Wynne (eds.), *Victorian Literary Mesmerism* (Amsterdam: Rodopi, 2006), 227–44.

—— *The Colonial Conan Doyle: British Imperialism, Irish Nationalism, and the Gothic* (Westport, Conn.: Greenwood Press, 2002).

Yeats, W. B. "The Celtic Element in Literature" (1902), in *Essays and Introductions* (London: Macmillan, 1961), 173–88.

Young, Robert J. C. *The Idea of English Ethnicity* (Oxford: Blackwell, 2008).

Younghusband, Francis. "Natural Beauty and Geographical Science", *Geographical Journal*, 56/1 (July 1920), 1–13.

Index

Printed and bound by CPI Group (UK) Ltd, Croydon, CR0 4YY